FUN IS BACK

MG TF LE500

A mid-engined, rear wheel drive two seater. Pure in design and intent. Special. Very Special. Limited to only 500 cars in the UK, each individually numbered. Leather seats, air conditioning and body colour hardtop are standard. And that's just for starters.

Get ready to immerse yourself totally in the pleasure of the MG experience. Check out the new LE500 at your local MG dealer and book your test drive.†

Call 0845 303 6464

Kent
SMC MG
Prospect House, 4 Canterbury Road
Sittingbourne
ME10 4SD
01795 592 100

Leicestershire
Luffield Cars
Belton Road
Loughborough
LE11 1LR
01509 216 100

Lincs
Victor Wood
Spittlegate Level
Grantham
NG31 7UH
01476 566 110

Middlesex
SMC MG*
139 Cowley Road
Uxbridge
UB8 2AG
0844 576 2487

Norfolk
Holden MG
21 Heigham Street
Norwich
NR2 4TF
01603 628911

Northern Ireland
Howard Abraham
65-93 Avenue Road, Lurgan
Co. Armagh
BT66 7BG
02838 323 275

North Shields
Silverlink MG
Vroom Retail Park, Unit 7, Orion
Business Park
Tyne Tunnel Trading Estate
NE29 7SN
0191 2961162

North Yorkshire
Drivestyle Horseless
Carriages
Lime Street, Skipton Road
Harrogate
HG1 4BG
01423 561 666

Oxon
JayBee Motors
Oxford Road
Bodicote, Banbury
OX15 4AB
01295 227 100

Perthshire
Dreadnought Garage*
Stirling Road
Callander
FK17 8LE
01878 331 099

Scotland
Morrisons Garages
Whins of Milton
Stirling
FK7 8HQ
01786 811411

South Glamorgan
MG Cardiff
281 Penarth Road
Cardiff
CF11 8YZ
02920 223 100

South Glamorgan
Panda Motors
Cwm Level Road
Landore, Swansea
SA1 2PG
01792 - 648946

Staffordshire
Hopton Garage
Sandon Road
Stafford
ST18 9TH
01785 251641

Surrey
Spur Garage
Unit 1
Molesey Business Centre
31 Central Avenue
West Molesey
KT8 2QZ
020 89419848

West Midlands
Summit Garage
413-415 Himley Road, Lower Gornal
Dudley
DY3 2RA
01384 259555

West Sussex
Crawley Down Garage
Snow Hill Copthorne
Crawley
RH10 3EQ
01342 859 200

Wigan
Michael Edwards
208 Wigan Rd
Hindley
WN23 BU
01942 246 688

Worcester
Startin of Worcester
Bowling Green Garage
Powick
WR2 4SF
01905 830 361

A NEW JOURNEY

www.mgmotor.co.uk

Suggested Retail Price £16,055.00 OTR. OTR price includes 12 month road fund licence and first registration fee.

Please contact your dealer for further information. †Test drives are subject to individual dealer terms and conditions. *Authorised repairer only

Come Up

Trumps

With A

Quote

- ✳ **Multi-car** discounts

- ✳ **Limited & Unlimited** mileage options

- ✳ **Europewide Breakdown & Recovery**

- ✳ **NCB** not normally needed

- ✳ **Agreed values**

- ✳ Household Scheme available
  with car parts/accessories cover
  with a 10% discount for existing
  policyholders

01621 840400

From

⚓ 19|85 PBIS

PETER BEST INSURANCE

Authorised & Regulated by the Financial Services Authority

Contents

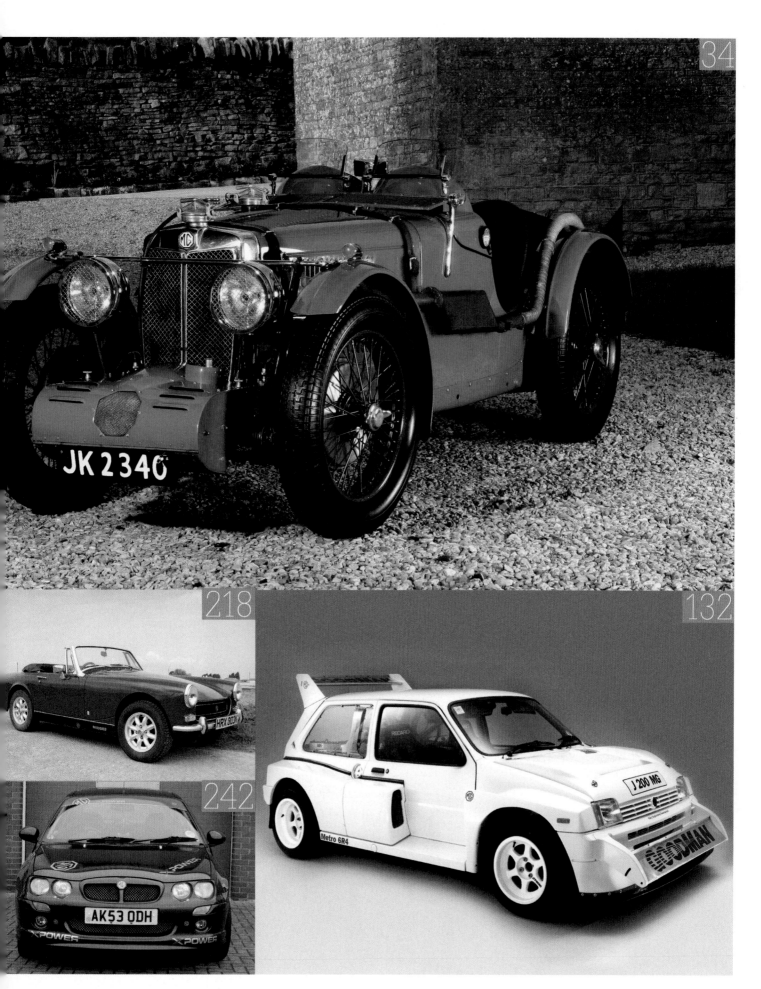

34

218

132

242

Welcome

The world loves MG. Sure, we all know that the marque has its flaws, but we also know that when an MG is good, it's really really good. And this publication is all about celebrating the MG marque, regardless of the age of the car.

So, we have MGs of every era, from Old Number One, the first MG built specifically for motor sport events, to the current TF LE 500 sports car from the rejuvenated, Chinese-owned MG company. In between are all the greats.

Read the inspirational tales of the brave MG racers at the bumpy, dangerous Brooklands circuit in the late 1920s and early '30s; or the contrasting but curiously similar stories of running a 580bhp ZS drag car or a 200mph ZT-T at Bonneville.

Compare the competition cars of the various eras: the wonderful 1930s C-type Le Mans; the gorgeous 1950s MGA Mille Miglia entries; the brutish MG GTS, a wide-arched cross between MGB and C; and the crazy Metro 6R4 rally weapon.

But most of all, wallow in the wonder of the road cars, because there are some greats in here. The T-series, the Midgets, the Magnettes, Bs and Cs, the Metros, Maestros and Montegos, the RV8s, the Fs and TFs, the Z-cars... they're all here. Sure, some were more successful than others but all provide a way into a world of shows, racing, rallying or just the simple pleasure of cleaning, maintaining, tweaking and even restoring.

That's the great thing about MG. We love them because they're so varied and the things you can do with them are so varied. If you'll forgive the cliché, with MG there really is a model for every pocket and interest. And with that, I'm off to check on my MGB GT track car... Enjoy your reading!

David Lillywhite, managing editor

THE COMPLETE STORY

Editorial office
Octane, 1 Tower Court, Irchester Road,
Wollaston, Northants NN29 7PJ, UK
Tel: +44 (0)207 907 6585. Fax: +44 (0)1933 663367
Email: info@octane-magazine.com
Website: www.octane-magazine.com

Advertising office
Octane Media Advertising Dept, 19 Highfield Lane,
Maidenhead, Berkshire SL6 3AN, UK
Tel: +44 (0)1628 510080. Fax: +44 (0)1628 510090
Email: ads@octane-magazine.com

Managing editor: David Lillywhite
Art editor: Phil Long
Designer: Dean Lettice
Production: Sarah Bradley

Advertising director: Sanjay Seetanah
Advertising sales: Madeleine Lillywhite
Advertising production: Anisha Mogra

Publisher: Geoff Love
Newstrade director: Martin Belson
Marketing manager: Juliette Cooper
Subscriptions manager: Shelley Kernaghan
Managing director: Ian Westwood
Group finance director: Ian Leggett
COO: Brett Reynolds
CEO: James Tye
Chairman: Felix Dennis

MG: The Complete Story is published under licence from Octane Media Ltd, a subsidiary company of Dennis Publishing Limited, United Kingdom. All rights in the licensed material belong to Felix Dennis, Octane Media or Dennis Publishing and may not be reproduced, whether in whole or in part, without their prior written consent. Octane is a registered trademark.

Printed by BGP, Bicester
Distribution: Seymour. Tel: +44 (0)20 7429 4000

Periodicals Postage paid @ Emigsville, PA.
Postmaster: send address corrections to Octane Media c/o 3330 Pacific Ave, Suite 404, Virginia Beach, VA 23451

MG: The Complete Story is available for international licensing. For information, please contact Winnie Liesenfeld, winnie_liesenfeld@dennis.co.uk, +44 (0) 20 7907 6134

The publisher makes every effort to ensure the magazine's contents are correct. All material published in MG: The Complete Story is copyright and unauthorised reproduction is forbidden. The editors and publishers of this magazine give no warranties, guarantees or assurances and make no representations regarding any goods or services advertised in this edition.

The text paper used within this magazine is produced from sustainable forestation, from a chain of custody manufacturer

recycle
When you have finished with this magazine please recycle it.

In association with **and**  PBIS www.ClassicInsurance.co.uk

Contributors

Simon Goldsworthy
A great MG fan, who drives an impact bumper MGB GT as his everyday transport and edits *MG Enthusiast* magazine.

Peter Browning
Former team manager in the days of the MGB, with so many tales of the good and bad days of motor sport with BMC and British Leyland.

Andrew Roberts
The UK's foremost MG authority, with a long history of competing in MGs. He's never without an MG in his car collection.

Martyn Wise
The founder of *MG Enthusiast* magazine, Martyn is now enjoying an easier life fettling his numerous classic and modern MGs.

Keith Adams
More than 'just' an MG fan, Keith Adams is an Austin Rover obsessive and keeps up to date with all that's happening at the revived Longbridge site.

MG Today

It's been a tough few years for MG, but the
marque's Chinese owner is determined
to bring success back to the fold with
an exciting line-up of new models...

Words: Keith Adams

Left: **MG TF LE500 was launched in a blaze of glory at Longbridge in 2007**

MG TF

Mention the 'R' word to any MG enthusiast, and the chances are that you'll be greeted by a wry smile. You see, as the global recession of 2009 casts a chill wind in the direction of the more vulnerable car makers, the famous Octagon looks set to ride out the storm with the benefit of a seasoned pro.

The past 30 years have seen MG disappear from the new car price lists on several occasions – only to make, what seems, a miraculous recovery. When Abingdon closed in 1980, killing off the MGB, many thought it was the end for the Octagon – only for a resurrection the following year on the snout of the surprisingly good Metro. Then, in 1991, when the last Montego rolled off the line, it looked like the end – until the RV8 heralded the re-emergence of the MG roadster a couple of years later. Next, in 2000, BMW decided to offload MG and Rover, and it seemed a certain death would ensue. And indeed it did – after five years under Phoenix.

The Chinese stake a claim

In 2005, it appeared MG had finally used up all of its nine lives. The Phoenix-run MG Rover had spent its dowry from BMW, had sold off anything worth selling (including the rights to the K-series engine, Rover 75 and 25 to the Chinese car company Shanghai Automotive), run out of credit with its suppliers – and finally came to a grinding halt. Administration followed, and anything left that was worthwhile was offered in a fire sale to end all others. And what was actually left to sell? The MG marque, some assembly equipment and the lease on Longbridge – not an enticing prospect for anyone.

However, one company saw the potential – and after putting a bid of £53million with MG Rover's administrator, Nanjing Automobile Corporation (NAC), a minnow in the Chinese car industry, became the new custodian of the MG marque. Initially, it looked like an uphill struggle – certainly for Longbridge. By late 2005, NAC sent in the disassembly engineers to lift and shift great swathes of production-line tooling from the Birmingham factory, leaving it looking something like a ghost town – and enthusiasts wondering if MG would ever roll again in the UK.

Meanwhile, in an interesting twist in the MG story, Shanghai Automotive (SAIC) with a little help from Ricardo in the UK had began producing its own facelifted version of the Rover 75, powered by a K-series engine in V6 form. SAIC's venture into 'British' car production had serious financial backing befitting a company involved in joint ventures with General Motors and Volkswagen, and the British engineering input was mainly ex-MG Rover – but unfortunately, it didn't have the badge that mattered...

Shanghai vs Nanjing

In a cruel twist of fate – for SAIC – MG Rover never actually owned the Rover marque name; it was merely licenced for use by BMW. So, when MGR went into administration, the Rover title was retained by the Germans. SAIC put in a bid for the brand name, but Ford offered a little more, paying out £10m to buy it (to protect Land Rover from the threat of similarly badged rivals from China). What that all meant was that SAIC then needed to invent a marque name for its new-generation 75, launched in 2006 – and it came up with the clumsy and contrived Roewe nameplate.

Right: The European-spec TF LE500, exclusively snapped at Millbrook, Bedfordshire in 2007.

Above: Photograph shows Chinese market TF, which retains 'Peter Stevens' nose.

Above: MG's SW sporting its new livery, with glamour models in matching outfits.

Above: MG badge and aggressive styling will feature on UK versions of Roewe 550.

Above: SAIC's new-generation 75, named Roewe 750, went on sale in China in 2006. ❯

Above: **With quality control sorted, the dustsheets at Longbridge are about to be removed.**

'Although limited to 500, it was good to see vehicles coming out of the factory once again'

NAC had the all-important MG badge, though, and within the year it was producing the cars in China, too – against all odds. The company's start-up factory in Pukou may have used a production line transported halfway across the globe, but the factory that housed it was all-new and state-of-the-art, and a perfect launch pad for MG in China.

When the production cars were wheeled out for the press, they were met with a little disappointment: the Chinese MG ZT, now known as the MG7, was cosmetically identical to the car MGR launched in 2001. The power unit may have been badged as the N-series, but underneath the new engine covers nestled a K-series. However, first drives were positive, proving the effectiveness of the ZT as a package, and initial reactions from buyers were very positive indeed.

Longbridge reopens

Although Longbridge was quiet by the time the MG7 had strutted its stuff, NAC's management continued to make encouraging noises. It asserted that the factory would produce cars again, and although not at volume levels initially, that situation was likely to change once further new MGs came on stream.

However, the situation the Anglo-Chinese industry now found itself in was little short of ludicrous: two competing firms were producing almost identical cars (MG7 vs Roewe 750) and it was clear that a degree of rationalisation was going to happen if the two were serious about exporting their products. And so, on December 27, 2007, after long Government-sponsored talks, NAC and SAIC merged – although, in truth, it was the latter that wielded all of the influence in the partnership (read takeover), given the two companies' relatives sizes.

Back at Longbridge, and with that much-needed additional finance from SAIC, the modest refit of the MG TF line at the factory gained momentum. Although

NAC had announced the re-opening of the Birmingham facility and briefly shown the TF LE500 it intended to build there, no start dates had been mentioned, and the impression on the ground at the launch was that NAC simply didn't have the money to make a serious go of Longbridge.

But with that situation changed, it was full steam ahead. In August 2008 the MG TF LE500 was formally announced, and the lines were finally rolling at Longbridge. Although the production run of this model was limited to a mere 500, and the cars were being virtually hand-built on the line, assembled using a high proportion of Chinese parts (including the body-in-white), it was good to see vehicles coming out of the factory once again.

The range today

The MG range today is a tale of two factories. In the UK, Longbridge currently produces only one car, the TF LE500. Although very similar to its 2002 namesake, the LE500 has received a number of improvements over the Phoenix-era models, most of which are aimed at improving quality and durability while making the car easier to live with. For one, the troubled K-series engine has been fettled to finally rid it of its fearsome reputation for eating head gaskets.

The chassis settings have been revised to take some of the edge off the original TF's skateboard-like ride quality, while retaining its roll-free cornering and high levels of lateral grip. In that, the adjustments have been successful – and the TF remains more fun to drive than any of its rivals. All the better that its £16,399 OTR price undercuts a similarly equipped Mazda MX-5 by over £3000...

In China, the MG range looks rather different. The MG7 (nee MG ZT) and MG3 (nee MG ZR) form the cornerstone of the range, with limited production of the TF adding glamour to the line-up. However, MG has confirmed that neither of these models will be making it to the UK market, despite there being some demand for what were very popular sporting saloons when they last bowed out in 2005. The surprise hit of the reborn MGs in China has been the MG3 SW – although you might know it as a Rover Streetwise. Yes, the original 'urban on-roader' has gone down a storm in its home market, where the concept of a jacked-up hatchback with funky detailing remains an original one. Right now the MG range is far from complete, but the future plans – with an integrated SAIC-inspired model programme – look set to deliver some exciting new machines.

Future models

As appealing as it is, the MG TF LE500 is merely an entrée. With its fully specced equipment list, it's a glamorous limited-run special edition designed to entice dubious customers back to their dealers. The series production model is due to appear later in 2009, and is expected wear an attractive £14,999 price sticker, countered by a longer options list. The main difference will be the loss of the LE's standard hardtop.

Beyond that, model plans begin to look murkier. We hear a facelifted TF could appear within few years, where it will feature much-modified front and rear styling, as well as a new dash – needed ever since it first saw the light of day back in 1995 in the original MGF. It's also likely that the chassis will be further modified, as engineers are keen to improve the adjustability of the platform near its limit. Eliminating snap oversteer is the prime consideration.

On the saloon front, Sales and Marketing Director Gary Hagen confirmed that production in Longbridge rested on the underlying economic climate in the run-up to launch. 'We're planning a four-car range: first to arrive will be a mid-sized saloon sharing its platform with the Roewe 550, planned for late 2010.

'After that, there will be a C-segment compact and a B-segment supermini – and, no, that won't be the MG3 SW, which has been a major success in China. Clearly we have the capacity to build these cars in Longbridge, and the Chinese are keen for this to happen.'

The most important MG will be one based on SAIC's impressive Roewe 550 mid-liner. That car was on the still-capable Rover 75 platform but clothed in a Ford Focus-sized package, and early impressions in China are that it is very good. Given an N-series turbo engine and a much more driver-focused package, the sophisticated MG ZS replacement should do well.

Hagen wasn't prepared to give anything else away regarding the fourth model – but the current favourite is a SsangYong-based MPV, which in SAIC form has been spied cold-weather testing in the Far East. If that comes to pass, it's a great indicator of the confidence SAIC has in the MG marque – enough to see it enter market sectors in which the company has never been represented before.

Whether or not that confidence pays off, one thing is sure – MG looks set to ride out the recession in style. How much of that renaissance takes place in Longbridge remains to be seen, but MG's new Chinese custodians will give the task their best shot. MG

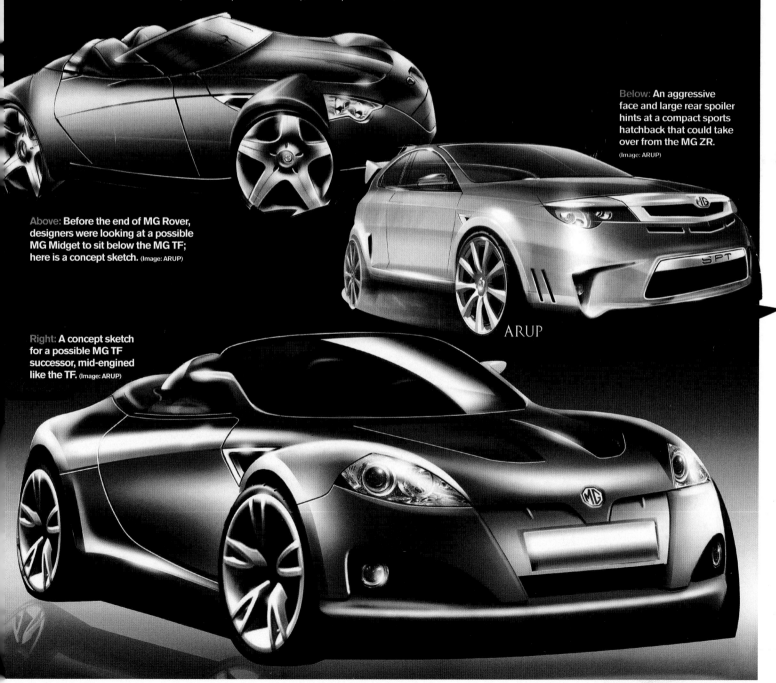

Below: An aggressive face and large rear spoiler hints at a compact sports hatchback that could take over from the MG ZR. (Image: ARUP)

Above: Before the end of MG Rover, designers were looking at a possible MG Midget to sit below the MG TF; here is a concept sketch. (Image: ARUP)

Right: A concept sketch for a possible MG TF successor, mid-engined like the TF. (Image: ARUP)

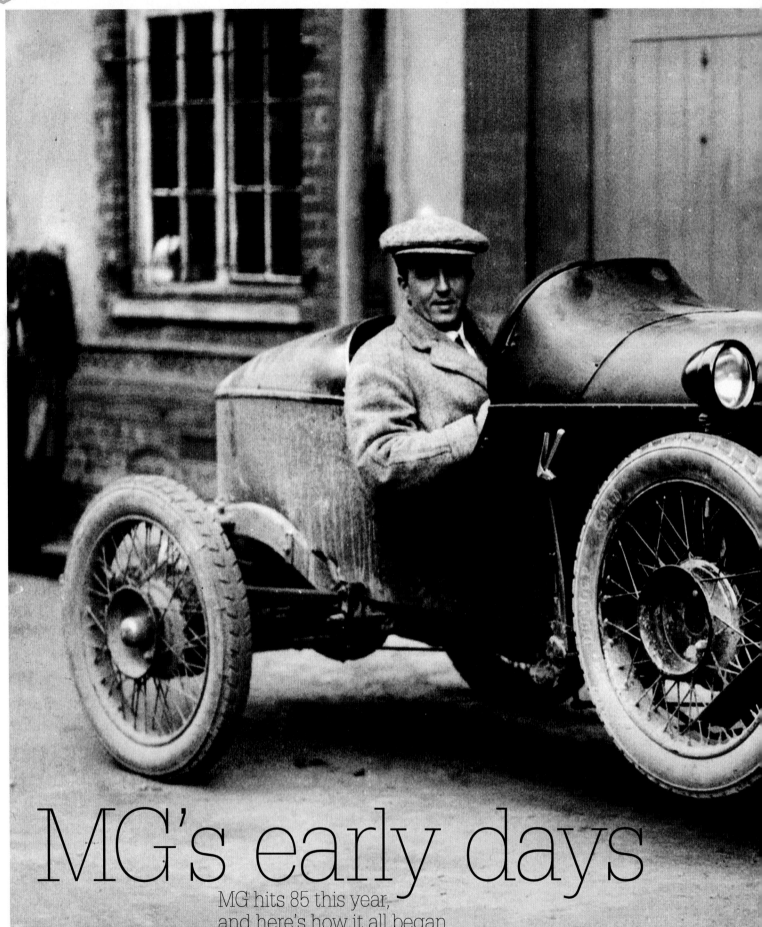

MG's early days

MG hits 85 this year,
and here's how it all began...
Words: Keith Adams

Left: MG
founder
Cecil Kimber
in Old No 1,
the first MG
that he
built for
competition.

FC 7900

L ike all of the greatest car companies, MG was created as a result of the vision of one man – Cecil Kimber. Given that he grew up surrounded by engineers, it was almost pre-ordained that he would end up easing into the fledgling car industry, although his path in was far from conventional.

To find out where it all began, we must rewind to the late 19th century, an exciting time for anyone with a keen interest in engineering. Cecil was born in London on April 12, 1888 to his father, Henry Kimber, a printing engineer and wife Fanny – and from the youngest of ages, Cecil took a keen interest in his father's company. Although he enjoyed his time at the Stockport Grammar School, Cecil was keen to join his father and take an active role in running it. But despite that, Cecil's head was turned by motorcycles, and as soon as he could, he bought a Rex.

But that changed following an accident when riding a friend's motorcycle left Cecil with a damaged right leg and a loss of appetite for two-wheeled motoring. That inevitably led him towards cars – and soon after, he picked up his first, a 1913 Singer 10HP.

Cecil soon found he loved cars even more than motorbikes, and that passion would eventually lead him to leave the family firm. In 1914, he picked up a job with Sheffield-Simplex as an assistant to the chief designer – standing him in good stead for a life in the motor industry. Due to his injuries and his training in engineering, he didn't fight in World War One, instead moving to AC Cars before going on to component supplier EG Wrigley.

This would be the move that would end up with the formation of MG. Following the war, Cecil invested heavily in the company he'd joined. Sadly, Wrigley suffered in a deal with which ended up being a takeover – but thanks to styling the company's radiator design, and picking up some useful contacts in the process, Cecil was retained as an employee despite his personal loss.

EG Wrigley was a major supplier to the Morris Motor Company at the time, and in 1923 it swallowed up by William Morris' fast-growing organisation. Thanks to that close association, Cecil had already joined Morris a couple of years' previously, taking on the role of general manager with Morris Garages, the company's flagship agency in Oxford.

As part of this role, he commissioned six Raworth bodied, two-seater convertibles based on the Morris Cowley chassis to be built – a move that proved highly successful. The £300 convertibles flew out of the Oxford showroom, encouraging Cecil that this was the right direction to take his career. Were these the first MGs? Yes, and no.

It is unclear as to what would constitute the first MG car proper, but it certainly was not the FC-7900, or MG Old Number One as it is universally known. This was special, though, as it was Cecil Kimber's first attempt at building a car exclusively for competition use, in 1924.

Now Cecil was in a role where he could satisfy his desire to create sporting

Right: The Midget was highly successful and helped set the style for the many two-seater sports cars that followed.

Right: K3 racers are among the most valuable of MGs, some worth £250,000.

'William Morris made sure he was a major shareholder in Cecil's start-up company'

Left: the awkward-looking 14/28 was MG's first truly successful model.

cars based on humble underpinnings, he went on to develop a range of special bodies that transformed the cars they were based on. They were so successful that in 1928 he founded MG as a separate marque.

However, the real beginning for MG proved to be when Cecil moved his company from the protective bosom of Oxford down the road to Abingdon during 1929 – before installing himself as the company's managing director the following summer. But William Morris was a wily operator, and once it was clear that MG was a success, he made sure that he was a major shareholder in Cecil's start-up company – controlling it from within as a result.

MG went from strength to strength. The first MGs to be produced in any serious numbers was the 14/28 Super Sport, based on the Morris-Oxford chassis, of which approximately 400 were built. From there, the 14/28 Super Sport was introduced, with either two or four seats and open or closed Salonette coachwork – and proved to be another success.

That developed into the 14/40, then the 18/80 – a move upmarket that benefited from Morris' decision not to take the six-cylinder 2.5-litre OHC car which it was based on into production. But Cecil's true passion lay with lightweight two-seater roadsters – and perhaps his most lasting contribution to MG history came into being as a result.

The 1929 MG Midget, was Cecil's masterpiece. Based around the 847cc Morris Minor, it was introduced as the move to a much larger

W. L. Handley. M.G.R. Maximum Bo

Above: single-seater R-type, with all-round independent suspension had great motorsport potential.

factory in the former Pavlova Leather Works in Abingdon was competed – no coincidence. Cecil had big plans to expand the MG range, and the Midget was the centrepiece of his grand plan. Sales soon bloomed, and Cecil's place in history was now assured.

The first M-Type Midget was soon developed into the 746cc C-Type Racing Midget, capable of 90mph in supercharged form. At the same time as the C-Type was coming into its own, MG entered into a very fertile period of its history.

However, despite the success, Cecil was beginning to lose heart – his grip on the company was never that strong thanks to the ever brooding presence of its owner, William Morris, and his continuous interventions in the product plan.

But the new MGs continued to come thick and fast. In late 1931, the F-Type Magna, powered by a six-cylinder 1271cc Wolseley Hornet engine, was launched. In usual MG style, it was available with a variety of bodywork options, ranging from the standard two-seat sports through four-seat open or closed versions, plus a variety of special coachbuilt bodies.

But it was the Midgets that everyone wanted – and in 1932 when the J-Type Midget was launched, the orders continued to flood in. It was this car that set the trend with the classic MG shape of double humped scuttle, cutaway doors, 'slab' tank hung on the back. It came in open two-seat (J2) or four-seat (J1), along with a closed Salonette version. This model also came with a variety of engine specifications as the supercharged racing J3 and later J4 models.

That was followed in quick succession by the K-Type Magnette, the shorter K2-Type, as well as the L-Type Magna, and subsequently – in 1933 – the K3 Magnette. MG was now a force in competition, too – when the K3 made its competition debut, it was powered by a supercharged 1100cc engine that delivered anything up to 124bhp. In real terms, that equated to a 125mph top speed and a 0-60mph time of less than 10 seconds.

The racing cars continued to shine: the Q-Type replaced the J4 and was boosted by an even bigger supercharger, giving up to 146bhp at 7500rpm from 750cc. This gave way to the single seater R-Type with all independent suspension system, to cope with the increasing performance available. However, it was never fully developed because, in 1935, William Morris sold his personal stake, thereby handing over ownership of MG to Morris Motors Ltd.

As a result of the Morris takeover of MG in 1935, all Works competition activity was ceased so that the company could concentrate on development and sales of the road-going MG range, which now was comprised of the 1935 MG TA Midget, the two-litre MG SA, its 2.6-litre derivative the MG WA and the 1.5-litre MG VA.

Cecil ended up being asked to resign from MG in 1941 after taking contract work on aircraft building, without seeking approval from the management first. He then worked for coachbuilder Charlesworth and then piston maker Specialloid before dying in a freak railway accident in 1945.

After the war, the MG TC (a wider cockpit version of the pre-war MG TA and TB models) brought the company international success. The Y-Type also came with the advancement of independent front suspension, which found its way on to the 1949 MG TD – another of the successful line of T-Types.

As part of the Nuffield Group (the group of companies that were owned by Morris), MG became part of the British Motor Corporation in 1952 and it was after the merger that MG found its greatest sales success with the MGA, the Austin-Healey based Midget and the MGB models. Few would have known that the MGB would be the final all-new sports car produced by MG until the arrival of the MGF in 1995.

Under BMC, and latterly British Leyland, MG was often reduced to mere badge engineering. So, when BL's chairman and chief executive, Michael Edwardes, closed down the Abingdon plant in 1980, it looked as if the marque would only carry on as an octagonal badge on the snouts of very humble cars.

Motors such as the MG1100, Farina Magnette and latterly Metro, Maestro and Montego were all worthy, but lacked the magic of the pre-war Kimber designed cars. But they did allow the MG name to live on – something that could not be said for its contemporaries, Triumph, Wolseley, Rover, Austin, Riley and so many more. The ultimate irony is that while MG lives on today, it's progenitor, Morris, has long since slipped into oblivion. And that's one of Cecil's legacies that would no doubt make him smile if he were around today to see it...

1935

Right: the four-door K3 Magnette made for a fine sporting saloon that's now highly soughtafter.

Old No.1 is a winner!

Peter Taylor was the lucky man who won a day with Old No.1 at the Heritage Motor Centre in Gaydon. It couldn't have happened to a bigger MG enthusiast, and he never stopped smiling

Words and photography by
Simon Goldsworthy

You could argue that every MG is special, and I wouldn't disagree with you. But there are some cars that stand out as particularly special and Old No.1 has to be near the top of anybody's list.

Despite the name, it is not the first MG ever built, although it has to be said there is no universal consensus as to what can claim to be the original. On the face of it this appears to be a curious state of affairs, although many of you will be well aware of the reasons behind the uncertainty. But not everyone is familiar with the roots of the MG Car Company, so forgive me for briefly explaining the background.

Morris Garages Ltd was owned by William Morris, and was the Oxford-based distributor for Morris Motors Ltd. In 1921, Cecil Kimber was appointed Sales Manager, quickly rising to become General Manager the following year. He felt strongly that Morris lacked a sporting variant in its extensive model range and set about designing a sporty body that would fit easily onto the bullnose Cowley chassis. Over 200 of these were then sold as The Chummy in 1922 and 1923.

In 1923, Kimber commissioned a new and sporty body from the Oxford-based coachbuilder Raworth. This was moving further away from its Morris roots and developing more of its own identity – the chassis was modified from the Morris 14/28 frame and the car was advertised as the MG Super Sports Morris. It still carried the trademark bullnose Morris radiator, though,

a feature finally dropped by the parent company in favour of a new flat-rad design for the 1927 model year 14/40.

By this time, demand for the sporting MG variants was great enough to justify a move to independent facilities in Edmund Road in Oxford, thus putting further distance between MG and Morris. In 1928 the 18/80 cemented this move away from standard mechanical components, even enjoying its own non-Morris chassis. The MG Car Company was officially established that same year.

So where does Old No.1 fit into all this? Well, in 1923 Kimber had won a Gold Medal in a modified Chummy at the Land's End Trial. This had a modest effect on sales, and late in 1924 he commissioned a car specifically for the same

event in 1925. While this utilised many Morris components, the standard Morris Cowley chassis was modified at the back to curve over the rear axle and mate with half-elliptic rear springs instead of the standard model's three-quarter items. With a lightweight body designed and built by Carbodies of Coventry, the car was registered on 27th March, 1925 and carried Kimber to a Gold Medal in the Light Car Class.

It was sold soon afterwards and started along an inevitable path of decline. It could have disappeared entirely, but an MG employee discovered it in a Manchester scrapyard in 1932. The company bought it back for £15 to restore, used it for promotional work and gave it the Old No.1 name tag in the process.

Now a prized exhibit in the Heritage Motor Centre museum at Gaydon, Warks, Old No.1 may not have been the first MG, but it was certainly the first one to be designed and built specifically for competition and is now perhaps the marque's most famous ambassador. Which is why, when we offered a ride in this historic vehicle as a competition prize for sister magazine *MG Enthusiast* readers, Peter Taylor from Saltash in Cornwall was inspired to give it a go.

An MG fan through and through, Peter started off with a brand new Midget in 1971, progressed through a BGT and MG Metro (he bought that one new as well and kept it for 16 years) to the 1.4ZR and MGF he owns today. He has pictures of Old No.1 at home, not to mention an engraving of the car on a plaque he won at a local driving test and concours competition. So it was entirely fitting that Peter's name was the first to be drawn out of the competition hat at MGE HQ, the final icing on the cake being to arrange the victory ride in time to celebrate Peter's retirement after 30 years in the ambulance service.

We arrive at Gaydon early on a Monday morning and, while the workshop staff are busy getting a fresh MoT on Old No.1, Peter and his wife Molly are given a tour of the museum's other MG exhibits. I am worried that keeping Peter in suspense like this for just a little bit longer could be construed as cruel and unusual punishment, but fortunately he is soon engrossed in the displays. After walking through the centre of the dissected MGB GT and examining the very first bullnose Morris that spawned the ❯

Great British Marques: MG **23**

'The glorious bark from the exhaust grabs everyone's attention as we pass through the village of Gaydon'

The Bullnose Morris that inspired MG.

MG styling concepts that were not pursued.

fledgling MGs, we wander past the empty space that normally houses Old No.1 to the banked display of MG record breakers. Appropriately enough it is in the midst of this sporting excellence that a discreet cough from Workshop Assistant Brian Norwood turns our attention back to the main purpose of our visit. It seems that Old No.1 is now awaiting our pleasure outside the workshop.

Trying hard to contain the excitement, we make our way through and there she is, looking surprisingly small and delicate parked between rows of assorted Land Rovers and the occasional

P5. Originally raced in grey primer, the MG Car Company sprayed the old girl bright red during the 1930s restoration and that is the colour she still wears today. We admire her from all angles (there isn't a bad one on the car!) as Brian runs through the starting procedure.

This is not entirely original as one or two changes have been made to reflect the fact that Old No.1 is still regularly called upon to perform in public, although nothing has been altered that can't be easily put back should the need arise. So there is still a switch for the magneto, but instead of using the hand-operated air-pressure pump

for the fuel, an extra panel has been added to the dash to house one switch for an electric fuel pump and another for an electric fan.

With everything primed and activated, Brian moves round to the front of the car to swing the starting handle. The engine is between cold and warm so it takes a little tickle of the carburettor's float, but then the Hotchkiss motor springs into life. Peter grins like a loon as the exhaust note bounces off the workshop wall before settling down to a smooth and inoffensive idle, and the two of them clamber aboard.

The seats are staggered, but Brian and Peter

Left: Peter's wife Molly is given the unexpected treat of being taken for a ride in Old No.1.
Right: Brian Norwood introduces Peter to Old No.1 and points out some of the finer details and the starting procedure.
Below: It's a snug fit in the staggered seats, but Peter gets ready for the adventure to begin.

Slow-speed thrill ride on the Land Rover experience.

Cutaway MGB GT never fails to impress.

are still packed tightly shoulder-to-shoulder in the narrow body as they set off down the road. There is some transmission whine evident from the gearing, but it's the glorious exhaust bark that grabs everybody's attention as we pass through Gaydon village and the noise echoes off the buildings on one side of the street and across to the other. At this point I am following in my MGB and it is remarkable how everybody turns and smiles as Old No.1 passes. There is even the obligatory small boy who turns and points in a time-honoured ritual that must have been enacted countless times over the years since 1925.

From my position in Old No.1's wake, it is apparent just how narrow the body tub is with the skinniest of wheels sticking well out on their spindly axles. Brian and Peter look as though they've been shoe-horned into their seats, although from the front the high scuttle only just leaves their heads poking up into the air stream. There are no indicators on the car, in fact there are barely any lights at all, just a pair of forward-facing sidelamps and one tiny rear light next to the numberplate. I am reminded of this as I follow Brian's signals and rack my brains trying to recall whether a rotating right hand means he's slowing

down or turning left. (Turns out to be left.)

Old No.1 is a popular car among the Gaydon staff, being both easy and fun to drive. The clutch is heavier than we are used to today, but certainly not extreme despite its competition origins. The gearstick is cranked so far back that it is almost horizontal and the action is more up-and-down than forward-and-back as you go through the gears. These are arranged in a conventional H pattern, with reverse to the left and up and straight back into first. The gate is quite wide so the stick comes across behind your left knee before you can shift it awkwardly up ›

Vehicle Technician Steve Kite and apprentice Martin Brown soon have us rolling again.

Numberplate light is only lamp at the rear.

Dash is both functional and stylish.

1548cc Hotchkiss motor is topped with OHV head.

into second, then it is back and down into top. On the way up, a simple pause in neutral is sufficient, but double-declutching is the order of the day when going back down before you can feel the cogs ease into position.

The Morris steering column was considerably raked for Old No.1, and there is only a modest inch and a quarter of free play at the wheel's rim. The narrow 710x90 tyres do tend to skip around minor bumps rather than go over them, and you can feel a jiffle through the seats as they're pulled across by imperfections. It's not a harsh ride though, despite the minimal body weight and leaf spring suspension, and Peter reports afterwards that as a passenger he felt entirely safe. That is

'It is this kind of beautiful detail that is everywhere you look on cars of this era'

even more impressive when I ask why he kept peering down at the rear wheel, only to discover that Brian had asked him to keep an eye on it as the inner tubes do have a propensity to blow!

That information must have been imparted when Brian had lifted off the throttle because under load, the noise from the exhaust makes conversation all but impossible. Not that Peter is complaining, because for him the exhaust note was one of the most enjoyable aspects of the trip. The 1548cc engine puts out around 25bhp thanks in part to its overhead-valve head, enough to propel the car to a top speed of 80mph and a 0-60mph sprint of just 20 seconds. It is not only a respect for age that encourages Brian to keep well below these limits on the day of our visit, though – with neither screen nor goggles to deflect it, the rush of wind provides more than enough incentive not to stray beyond 50mph.

On many cars of this era, the brakes can be a trifle underwhelming and the handbrake is called in to help for more than just parking. But as Peter and Brian pull back into the car park at Gaydon, Old No.1's drums are plenty strong enough despite being standard Morris fayre. This shouldn't be surprising given how much lighter Old No.1 is than a Morris Cowley, but it is just one more reason why, among the Gaydon staff and the fortunate few who get the opportunity

to drive her, she is still such a popular car.

Mind you, it still pays to keep on your toes. As I prepare to take a few more photos, that nearside rear tyre which Peter had been watching so closely suddenly decides it has had enough and goes pop. Fortunately Old No.1 carries a couple of spares, and the museum's Vehicle Technician, Steve Kite, quickly joins us with a trolley jack to change a wheel.

Meanwhile, Peter and I take the chance to examine some of the car's finer points such as the temperature gauge atop the radiator, and the rotating bezel on the ammeter that doubles as a light switch. It may be the exhaust roar that stays in Peter's mind the longest, but as Brian says, it's this kind of beautiful detail that is everywhere you look on cars of this era and which makes driving each of them such a unique experience. We are just delighted that we were able to share it with such a genuine MG enthusiast. MG

Our thanks to all at the Heritage Motor Centre in Gaydon, Warwickshire, for arranging this unforgettable experience. The Centre is open daily from 10am-5pm, but closed December 24–January 1 inclusive). Free guided tours of the exhibitions operate at 11.15am and 2.15pm daily. Telephone 01926 641188 or visit www.heritage-motor-centre.co.uk for more details.

n 1906, work began on a 300-acre woodland site in the Surrey countryside that was destined to become the world's first purpose-built motor-racing circuit and the spiritual home of British motor sport. The first official event took place a year later in July 1907 and Brooklands quickly established itself as a motoring version of Ascot races, where the good and the great of high society pleasured themselves in a glamorous world pitching man and machine in automotive combat.

Over the next 30 years Brooklands became the centre of motor sport in the country and the likes of Malcolm Campbell became recognised household names, while powerful race cars from Bentley, Delage, Napier and Bugatti dominated the frighteningly banked circuit. But the big boys did not have things all their own way thanks to a clever handicapping system, introduced to encourage other manufacturers to enter their motoring minnows.

Faced with a 100-yard-wide track and two huge banked sections, the likes of the tiny Austins and Rileys that competed in the early races looked at odds with their surroundings. But their decent performances were not lost on MG founder Cecil Kimber, who was keen to establish a competition background for his fledgling sports car company.

The earliest MGs to compete at Brooklands were the company's 14/28 MG Super Sports models, which earned first-class awards in the MCC High Speed Trials at the Weybridge circuit. Recorded as the first track success for the ❯

Above: **Double twelve M-types climb Brooklands banking in the 1930 Double Twelve Race, in which three cars – 'The Tomato Growers' – claimed the Team Prize.**

BROOKLANDS

the spiritual home of motor racing in Britain

The first purpose-built motor-racing circuit was also the scene of a remarkable string of triumphs by the fledgeling MG marque, cementing Cecil Kimber's small-engine, high-output maxim **Words: Martyn Wise**

'It was the new, diminutive M-types introduced in late 1928 that were to form the cornerstone of MG's success at Brooklands'

marque was the MG Super Sports Morris Oxford driven by Billy Cooper to medal victory in the 1924 event, with further awards being achieved over the next two years by others driving MG 'Bullnose' models.

But it was the new, diminutive M-types introduced in late 1928 that were to form the cornerstone of MG's success at Brooklands and lay the foundations for Kimber's small-engine, high-output maxim that was to dominate the circuit's handicap results for a decade. Fortune played into the hands of MG thanks to the British Racing Drivers Club, which pushed for a true long-distance event to be staged on the Outer Circuit. The first Brooklands 500-mile race held in October 1929 was won at an average of over 107mph, pipping the Indianapolis 500 to become the fastest long-distance event in the world.

That year, several new M-type Midgets competed in minor Brooklands events, taking five first-class awards in the JCC and MCC High Speed Trials. And, although there was no Abingdon entry in the inaugural Brooklands 500, it was noted that a supercharged Austin finished sixth overall at a respectable average speed of just over 80mph. The following year also saw MG absent from the prestigious 500-mile race, but 1930 was a busy year at the factory with designers and engineers working long and hard on several fronts.

Work was progressing on preparing MG's first record-breaker, EX-120, which in February 1931 became the first 750cc car to break the magic 100mph barrier. Plans were also well ahead on Kimber's pet project to emulate the likes of Bentley with the MG 18/100, or Tigress, model which he hoped may challenge for honours at Le Mans.

For 1930, though, as the new Racing Workshop readied the monstrous 18/100 MkIII Tigress MG intended for that year's Double Twelve Race, Kimber was approached by friends

Edmondson and Randall who wanted to try for the Team Prize with a three-car MG Midget entry. In the end Kimber sanctioned that five cars be prepared, which took advantage of recent engineering developments to increase power from 20bhp to 27bhp. With modified engines, longer-range fuel tanks, stronger wheels and the distinguished Brooklands exhaust system, they were finished in MG's brown and cream colour scheme which mirrored that of the Tigress. Two of the five Double Twelve Midgets were prepared for private owners, with the three-car Abingdon team entered by Randall becoming known as 'The Tomato Growers' in recognition of Edmondson and Randall's business interests in market gardening!

Little period documentary evidence exists on the race itself, but there can have been little doubt that the well turned-out cars would have been the talk of the paddock. More so once the race started, as just two hours into the first day's 12 hours the Tigress ran its bearings and was out of the race, whilst the Midgets ran almost faultlessly throughout the day. As no night-time driving was allowed, the Double Twelve was named after the 12 hours spent racing on a Saturday, after which the event would be stopped and time and positions noted, with crews returning to Brooklands for a further 12 hours' racing the following day. With the Midgets well placed at the overnight halt, Sunday's restart saw the tiny MGs continue to battle with two works Austin Sevens. Although these finished ahead of the Midgets, their third car lay well down the running order so the Team Prize was claimed by Randall's Tomato Growers.

Despite the setback with the 18/100 MG Kimber pushed ahead with his project, intending to produce 25 cars. But a doubt over its sustained high-speed ability coupled with a massive price tag meant that production ceased after only five models were completed, the remaining 20 engines being sold off and unused

Below: Band leader Billy Cotton seen here enjoying the champagne lifestyle after a successful day at the races.

Above: **A 1934 MG K3 does battle with a Bugatti on banked circuit at Brooklands.**

bodies fitted to the 18/18 Mark I chassis. By now, though, even Kimber could see MG's future competition success lay in developing smaller sports cars with a good power-to-weight ratio and supercharging to make the most of the handicap system.

The success of EX-120 at the banked circuit of Montlhery on the outskirts of Paris led to the development of the 750cc-engined C-type on a chassis modelled on that of the record-breaker. Known as the Montlhery Midget, 44 examples were produced and made available in both supercharged and un-supercharged tune for privateer racers. With Kimber convinced of the new car's potential and having assured MG's owner Sir William Morris that he could follow up on the record-breaking success, he instructed the works to have 14 cars made ready in time for the 1931 Double Twelve race in two months' time.

To an outsider the task looked impossible, as new bodies were required to fit the new longer and lower chassis, while the actual engines were not even designed yet. Almost all of the Abingdon factory, which had itself been reduced by a third in a cost-cutting exercise in response to depression-hit times, was roped in to work on the project. The aptly named 'Insomnia Crew' of elite staff put in through-the-night stints to ready the race cars, and a Herculean effort saw MG produce 14 C-type Midgets in just 14 days. All were delivered to Brooklands in time to qualify for the first practice period and, as the weekend approached, it seemed the entire Abingdon workforce had made their way down to Weybridge by train, charabanc and bicycle to cheer 'their' cars on.

Three four-car C-type teams were entered for the 1931 event, which was so heavily handicapped in the favour of smaller-engined motors that only two examples of more than three litres bothered entering. The MG teams were drilled to make the most of pit stops with the combination of car, drivers and team work paying handsome dividends as the Earl of March/Staniland outfit won the event outright at an average speed of over 65mph, faster even than the 1100cc Brooklands Riley, while further C-types occupied the next four places. In all, seven Montlhery Midgets were amongst the 24 finishers and MG was awarded the coveted Team Prize.

The C-type was nothing short of a racing phenomenon, and in the same 1931 season in the hands of Norman Black a C-type won the Irish Grand Prix and Ulster TT. Back at Brooklands later in the year for the BRDC 500 the nine-car C-type entry, with all but one model supercharged, found themselves victims of their own success as, in a bid to avoid a repetition of the Double Twelve dominance in the spring, the handicap set for the blown 750cc models had been raised by over 10mph to 93.79mph. Eddie Hall almost achieved the impossible, bringing his C-type home third overall at an average of 92.17mph. There was consolation for MG, though, as yet again it claimed the Team Prize thanks to Crabtree's fifth place in what became a race of attrition – only seven classified finishers out of a starting field of 40.

Undoubtedly 1931 had proved a watershed year for MG, and the significant record-breaking success of EX-120, coupled with a stunning debut season for the Montlhery C-type Midgets, demonstrated the company's arrival as a serious contender in British motor sport.

The following year MG was to find the Brooklands 500 handicap system working against it once more as speeds for supercharged cars were raised yet again. However, realising set speeds remained unchanged for the unblown 750cc models; four of the MG entries decided to run in standard mode, while

Above: **C-type at speed in 1931**

five others kept their blowers in place. Amongst these, record-breakers Eyston and Horton soon took an early lead in their single-seat C-types, lapping the banked circuit at over 100mph. The big Bentley thundered by at more than 126mph before disaster struck: climbing high to pass another car, one wheel slipped over the edge and the Bentley crashed into trees, instantly killing the driver Dunfee. The debris affected Bert Denly in the Magic Midget record-breaker, who fell back with a broken piston – a similar fate being suffered by both Evans and Letts – while Hall's car had a broken rear axle. Of the blown C-types Horton vied with both a Riley and Talbot for the lead and, following a quick pit stop for new plugs, he came out of the pits lapping faster than ever to win the 1932 Brooklands 500 outright. With three of the other unblown C-types also amongst the six finishers in yet another demanding race, MG retained the Team Prize.

If this race had proved hard, then the 1933 event was to be even tougher. MG entries consisted of the C-types, which were now running in their third Brooklands 500, as well as the out-and-out racing J4 Midget and two examples of the new K3 Magnette, which had won the Team Prize on that year's Mille Miglia. For Brooklands, though, top driver Eddie Hall specified a long-tailed body similar to the one fitted to his old C-type.

The 1933 race once again proved unforgiving, with only eight cars completing the designated 500 miles. Of the finishers though, half were MGs, with outright victory going to Hall, who averaged more than 106mph and came home first almost 30 minutes ahead of Martin and Welch in an L-type Magna. A further K3 driven by Yallop and Fronteras was fifth and MG just missed out on the Team Prize when the sixth-placed L-type of the Earl of March and Wright missed being classified as a finisher by only 35 seconds.

With the remarkable C-type's mantle now passing to the equally impressive K3 Magnettes, Eyston turned his attention to making the most of his new record-breaker EX-135. With the choice of two single-seater bodies – the track version being striped in brown and cream and becoming known as the 'Humbug' – he was confident that 1934 would see him break his MG Brooklands duck. He circulated in torrential rain at speeds around 115mph and, together with co-driver Handley, appeared to have the race in the bag when a hub tightened up, locking a back wheel and spinning the K3 out of the running. The chasing Riley of Dixon took the race, having driven single-handed. Of the seven finishers out of 32 starters, most were MG again – all K3 Magnettes with the third-placed finisher also claiming a class win.

The introduction of the Q-type Midget in 1934 and the single-seat R-type racer the following year both failed to have the impact that had been hoped for. For the 1935 International Trophy Race held at Brooklands, Kimber coaxed Malcolm Campbell out of retirement in what he hoped would prove a PR success. But it was evident that Campbell did not expect to have to put any money up for the privilege and so was provided with only a development car for the race. The official team entry was headed by Eyston, along with Handley and Black. The race was best forgotten by MG as all the Eyston cars retired, as did

> 'Following a pit stop for plugs, Horton came out of the pits lapping faster than ever to win the 1932 Brooklands 500 outright'

Evans, while Campbell and co-driver Everitt managed to bring the development car home sixth. MG's face was saved with Hall's third place in his K3.

In the mid-season of 1935, Kimber announced to a stunned racing department that the recently formed Nuffield Group had issued a statement that all motor sport would cease, and that the successful team which had taken MG from unknown to one of the most successful British marques in the past ten years would be broken up. As outright speeds increased, MG found itself more and more off the pace on a track which was, by now, beginning to show its age. Following the acquisition by Morris Motors, MG was also attracting reduced interest and private entries were getting less support from Abingdon. With little chance of outright success the leading drivers of the day were moving on, and it was left to celebrities such as band leader Billy Cotton and privateer dealers like Bellevue Garage to fly the Octagon flag at Brooklands.

The last BRDC 500 ran in 1936 with an entry of only 18 cars. MG formed the largest single marque with three Magnettes and a Midget. While the ex-Hamilton single-seater K3 lasted just four laps and the ex-Eyston Magic Magnette 'Humbug' cracked its head after 100 laps, Cotton's K3 driven by the experienced Norman Black won the 1100cc class and the single-seat J3 Midget of Humphreys/Denly claimed the 750cc class, despite neither being classified as finishers.

Although there was still some success to come in the form of 750cc Outer Circuit records achieved by Harvey-Noble in an ageing and cobbled-together Q-type that also featured K3 and J4 Midget parts, MG's association with Brooklands was drawing to a close. As storm clouds gathered over the continent it was becoming obvious that the final curtain was also falling on the Surrey circuit. When peacetime racing resumed it would be with technological advances that brought about a brand new breed of racing car – and with it, a need for fresh, challenging circuits, committing Brooklands and the cars that so valiantly raced there to the role of museum pieces. Ⓜ

FACT FILE

Brooklands opened its doors to racing in June 1907 on the estate of entrepreneur Hugh Fortescue Locke-King as the world's first purpose-built motor sport track. Designed by Colonel Holden of the Royal Artillery, the three-and-a-quarter-mile track took advantage of the natural lie of the land to include a brace of banked sections rising 30 feet, joined together by two long straights. With little guidance as to what to expect or provide, the circuit drew heavily on the world of horse racing for ideas. As such, the course included a clubhouse, changing rooms and even a weighbridge.

Initially concerned that the ground-breaking exercise could become nothing more than a white elephant, Locke-King was delighted when crowds flocked to the Surrey circuit, which lay some 20 miles to the south-west of London. Brooklands soon became a regular stomping ground for the likes of Malcolm Campbell and John Cobb, who gained movie star status thanks to their exploits on the track which were captured on newsreel footage and shown at cinemas throughout the country.

Aside from cars, the track was also used by motorcycles and racing cyclists. It also went on to become home to the pioneers of aviation: the first British-built plane flew from here in 1908 and in addition Brooklands became home to Thomas Sopwith's fledgling Sopwith Aviation Company; he developed and flew his Pup and Camel planes from the facility. During the dark years of World War Two, Hurricane fighters and Wellington bombers were both built on the site.

But it was in the 1920s and 1930s that the Brooklands track really came into its own as a venue for high-speed racing and record breaking. The prestigious Outer Circuit Record was set in 1935 by John Cobb driving a Napier Railton at over 143mph. Fittingly, this car can be still viewed in the Brooklands Museum, which is open to the public every day from 10.00am.

The circuit fell into disrepair and general decline in post-war years, before the Brooklands Museum Trust acquired the old clubhouse and part of the former track and gradually transformed this important part of Britain's motoring heritage. Today the site boasts an excellent museum with numerous exhibits that once raced at the track, as well as a number of aircraft including a Concorde and the Wellington bomber recovered from Loch Ness.

Regular events are held at the circuit throughout the summer months and many clubs now make use of the facilities such as Test Hill, which has become a favourite of those drivers of older cars which may have tackled the steep gradient in their heyday.

• For further details, contact Brooklands Museum on 01932 857381 or visit the dedicated website at www.brooklandsmuseum.co.uk.

LE MANS GIANT KILLER

As a private entry with factory backing, this C-type
Midget built on the model's outstanding success at Brooklands
to record one of MG's greatest-ever performances at the Le Mans
24 Hours, leaving a host of bigger-engined cars trailing in its wake

Words: Andrew Roberts Photography: Richard Meadows

W hile the MG marque has never been an outright winner of the Le Mans 24 Hours, the class performances have invariably been strong right up to the present day with the dual success of the MG Lola EX264. But the fact that many of MG's triumphs came not from factory entries – the 1955 EX182 and the 1964/1965 MGBs were the only cars officially entered under the Works banner – but from private entries makes these achievements even more significant. One of the most notable is that of a C-type Montlhèry Midget, which not only completed the 1933 24 Hours, but finished in an astonishing sixth place, winning its class and being placed second in the Index of Performance. It remains the second highest placing of any MG at Le Mans.

With the C-type racing performances being headlined by the model's success in the 1931 Brooklands Double 12, when MG not only won the event outright but also took the top five places and won the Team Prize, it was clear that Abingdon had again produced an outstanding new model. It was the most auspicious of starts and there was more to follow. The C-types took the first three places in the Saorstat Cup Race and outright victory in the Irish Grand Prix, together with the Team Prize, outright victory in the Ulster TT and third overall in the Brooklands 500 Miles, where the cars were effectively handicapped out of the top placing. For a first year of racing, this was a phenomenal set of results.

But while the C-type was an undoubted racing success, the same could unfortunately not be said for the British and world economies. The 1929 Wall Street Crash had seen economic depression setting in and MG was not the only motor manufacturer feeling the pinch. Although production of C-type C0291 with its pointed-tail body had commenced on 21st August 1931 – the car being dispatched to H Leeson of University Motors Ltd, London – it was not until early 1933 that it found a buyer. The purchaser was Cowden Services Ltd of Dove Mews, Old Brompton Road, London, the proprietors of which were Maurice Baumer and John Ludovic Ford.

Indications are that the C-type had previously run in a handicap race at Brooklands but, unlike many of its brothers, it was not fatigued from competition. Ford had run at Le Mans in 1932 with an Alta, co-driven by Baumer, but their entry lasted only a few laps. However, nothing daunted, Ford had made an entry for the 1933 race. Being well proven in long-distance racing,

the C-type would seemingly be the ideal choice – the other MG entry for 1933 was the new J3 Midget of Gordon Hendy and H Dines Parker.

While the glory days of Bentley victories were now long gone, British interest in the race was still high. It was to be the sheer professionalism, albeit in an amateur age, of both Baumer and Ford which would be the decisive factor in the C-type's ultimate success. Nothing was left to chance and the MG Car Company was involved from the start. Factory records show that the car was being prepared and serviced at Abingdon, in accordance with Cecil Kimber's established practice of supporting selected private owners, a policy that avoided the cost and responsibility of a full Works programme. A surviving example of this in the factory service records is an invoice dated 28th March 1933 covering the cost of fitting the newly introduced 12-inch brake drums and the latest crossflow cylinder head. The invoice was subject to a 15 per cent discount, with a further 10 per cent off promised if the car ran in the German Grand Prix and at the Mannin Beg race in the Isle of Man.

As part of this factory support, the car was returned to Abingdon to be inspected and overhauled under the supervision of Reg 'Jacko' Jackson. The Ford/Baumer pairing also exhaustively checked the car over on its return from Abingdon, after which it was driven to Le Mans in the company of a Mercedes-Benz tender car.

The Le Mans circuit comprised an 8.4-mile lap of what were all public roads, and there is little or no comparison with the billiard-smooth surfaces of today's track. The one factor that has not changed, though, is the need for reliability – an objective that obsesses today's team managers with their multi-million budgets as much as it did Ford and Baumer back in 1933. Practice demonstrated the value of the C-type's painstaking preparation with only a rocker-gear problem, quickly solved by Reg Jackson who was on hand to assist the MG entries. Scrutineering, a perennial worry at Le Mans, saw a dispute over the car's exhaust. This was quickly solved when Ford produced a Brooklands fishtail, which he forced on to the Midget's exhaust pipe to the reluctant satisfaction of the officials.

The MG pairing knew that there was no chance of an outright victory but a strong finish was within their reach, provided reliability issues did not intervene. Discussing the matter at length they concluded that they should endeavour to average 100kph for the entire 24 hours. This would give them an average speed of some 62.5mph and they arrived at this figure by looking at the previous ❯

year's results in which an Alfa Romeo took fourth place at a speed of 62.6mph. They concluded that such a target would not stress the C-type mechanicals unduly and decided to make a final reconnaissance of the circuit the day before initial practice. Their novel method was to carry this out from the trackside Café de l'Hippodrome where they were dining. Barré Lyndon records that while Baumer was toying with hors d'oeuvres, Ford completed two laps. He then returned to begin his dinner while Baumer took the wheel of the Mercedes. Between courses they each completed eight laps – what today's Health & Safety mafia would make of it is best not considered.

Twenty-nine cars were to start the 1933 24 Heures du Mans from an original entry of 41. Eleven were French, ten British, seven Italian and one American. Five Alfa Romeo 2.3s, two of which were the short-chassis Mille Miglia models for the pairings of Raymond Sommer/Tazio Nuvolari and Louis Chiron/Cortese, were the pre-race favourites. The traditional sprint across the track to the waiting protagonists saw the faster cars off at flat-out speeds as though this was a grand prix rather than a 24-hour enduro. Wisely, Baumer, who had taken the first stint, refused to be drawn into the battle, but he was held up in slow traffic and the MG oiled a plug. This necessitated a pit stop and the J3 displaced the C-type, but soon both Abingdon cars were circulating steadily, the earlier Midget lapping at its predetermined speed.

The pit stop had seen Ford at the wheel since his driving in darkening conditions was excellent. As the French dusk fell he was piloting the C-type without lights, much to the consternation of the officials. He was warned that he must use them after 9.30pm and he complied with the directive, only to switch them off out of view of the stands. When it was completely dark, he ran with them on but his earlier decision must have helped conserve his battery and relieve the pressure on the dynamo.

The discipline of the two C-type drivers was exemplary. Tempted as they undoubtedly were to take a tow from a faster car down the Mulsanne Straight, they resisted, limiting their gearchanges to two per lap. Not so the J3, which ultimately ran a big end in lapping 10mph faster than the C-type in its efforts to regain lost time.

With the first streaks of dawn lighting the French sky, the C-type was continuing to run like the proverbial sewing machine as its rivals fell out. By

> ## 'Discussing it at length, they concluded they should endeavour to average 100kph for the entire 24 hours'

breakfast time the Midget was up to ninth place and further retirements saw the car further rise to sixth position. Experienced Le Mans watchers then and now know that the final hours of the race, from noon until 4pm, can be the most challenging and frequently result in retirement and unpredictability. Such was the case in 1933.

The drama among the leading cars, so much a feature of the 24 Hours, now entered its final act. The Sommer/Nuvolari Alfa, which had been plagued with a leaking fuel tank and surviving only through the use of copious quantities of soap and chewing gum as a sealant, lost its lead to the Chinetti/Varent Alfa. With just 45 minutes to go, Varent led. Four laps later Nuvolari took the lead again. Then with just eight minutes to go it was Chinetti cutting ahead in front of the stands. On the last lap Nuvolari demonstrated why he is still regarded by many as the greatest driver ever. He passed Chinetti at the Hippodrome, but was then repassed. The flying Mantuan was not to be denied however, and in a last desperate effort retook the lead to win by under 10 seconds in what was his only appearance at Le Mans.

This titanic duel had inevitably overshadowed the performance of the C-type, which took the flag with Ford at the wheel. Ahead of him the Alfa Romeos had recorded their predictable 1-2-3, with a Riley and Aston Martin in fourth and fifth places. The MG was a triumphant sixth, testament to the controlled lapping of its drivers. A slower final lap because of a misfire meant the average speed for the 24 Hours was 99.5kph, fractionally under the target.

Putting the C-type's performance into perspective, seven cars finished behind

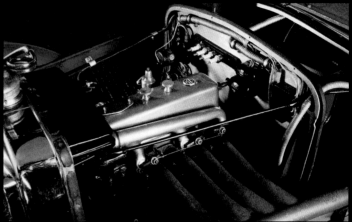

the MG, all of greater engine capacity. The Index of Performance was won by the 1100cc Riley of Von der Becke/Peacock, with the 746cc MG second. It was MG's best finish to date at Le Mans (the fourth-placed MG K3 of Charlie Martin/Roy Eccles would better this the following year) and no car with so small an engine capacity has ever placed higher.

Following the Le Mans success, Ford/Baumer took the car to the Isle of Man for the Mannin Beg. Here, in a race of enormous attrition, they were the third and final car home. Next, the C-type ran in the RAC TT where it was well placed until a broken crankshaft forced it into retirement.

With Ford and Baumer setting their sights on a K3 for the 1934 Le Mans, the C-type was now sold by the famous London dealer Jack Bartlett. Like one of the factory Mille Miglia K3s, the Midget was to head to Australia in the hands of John Dutton, a member of the well known South Australia racing family. The car's competition days were not yet done; it was used in various events including the South Australia Centenary Grand Prix on Boxing Day 1936.

It changed hands again, being sold to Bill Howard who in turn passed it to

the O'Leary family. In 1947 it was sold again and purchased by Gavin Sandford-Morgan. He was to use it in many events as well as for general road use, and it was back on track for the support race for the 1990 Australian Grand Prix.

After 55 years of ownership the car was sold to a UK buyer who commenced a sympathetic restoration to the highest standards. The engine was fully rebuilt by Tom Dark Engineering with a new steel crank, rods and camshaft. The original registration number has been reunited with the car by the DVLA and this truly famous C-type made its return to the track at a recent VSCC Silverstone race meeting. Like the Mille Miglia K3, which has also returned from Australia, this Montlhèry Midget is regarded as one of the most original competition cars to have survived from MG's 1930s' heyday. ⑯

■ Thanks to: Full acknowledgement is made to Barré Lyndon's book, Circuit Dust, David Hodge's The Le Mans 24 Hour Race, the Triple M Register Yearbook 2001 for Graham Arrondelle's treatise on MGs at Le Mans and to Malcolm Green and Martin Chisholm in the preparation of this article.

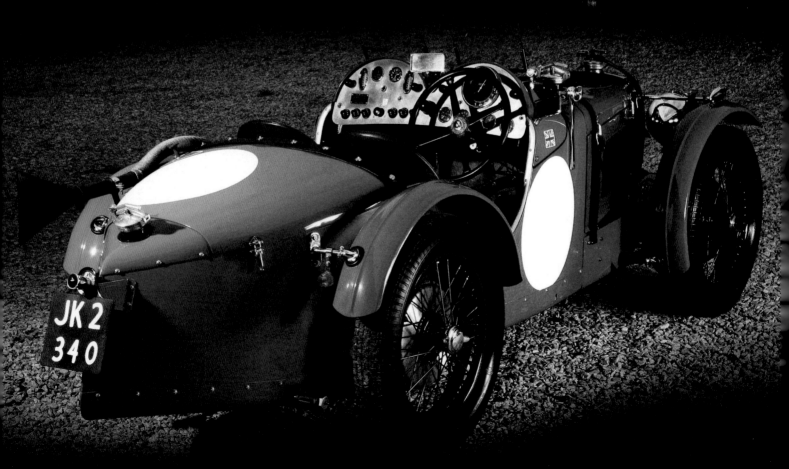

TC0721 on blocks for engine repairs in the farm shed near Sydney that was its home for many years in late '60s.

Above: Screen-mounted wiper motor could be operated manually – a useful feature.
Centre: Not a reproduction, but lovingly restored, the ubiquitous Lucas D Lamp.
Right: NOL quart oil cannister and holder was original equipment on all early TCs.

THE 1940s
WRX

Malcolm Robertson has a close look at one of Australia's finest MG TCs, a car that enjoyed a long and varied life before being rescued from the brink

Words and photographs: Malcolm Robertson

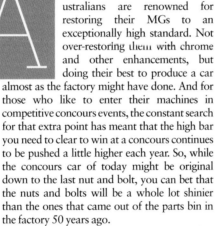

Australians are renowned for restoring their MGs to an exceptionally high standard. Not over-restoring them with chrome and other enhancements, but doing their best to produce a car almost as the factory might have done. And for those who like to enter their machines in competitive concours events, the constant search for that extra point has meant that the high bar you need to clear to win at a concours continues to be pushed a little higher each year. So, while the concours car of today might be original down to the last nut and bolt, you can bet that the nuts and bolts will be a whole lot shinier than the ones that came out of the parts bin in the factory 50 years ago.

One such beautiful car made its first appearance at the Australian National MG Meeting in Tasmania in April 2006, where it won not only its class, but also the outright trophy at the concours. The car, a very early MG TC (TC0721), has been the result of a ten-year rebuild to bring it back to its as-new state after a long, slow and painful slide into derelict condition that probably began when it first took to the roads in Sydney in 1946. Now that the scars on his hands have healed, Julian Beville-Anderson from the Sydney MG Car Club, who masterminded the restoration including doing as much of the work as he could, can look back on the agonising process philosophically.

'The car was rolled in an earlier life and fought all the way through the restoration,' says Julian. 'At times I thought it didn't want to go back together, but in the end good sense prevailed and we got there. My ethic was to try and do a little each night and one day of the weekend.'

Those of us who have restored a car from the ground up know just what an understatement that is. 'A little each night' usually means several hours on most evenings culminating with all-night episodes as concours deadlines approach. And even 'one day of the weekend' sounds a bit conservative, too. We all know that once you've

got all the tools out, you might as well keep going for as long as you can.

The history of Julian's car is fairly well documented. Unlike many TCs, which changed hands often during the first ten years of their lives, TC0721 seemed to have had only a few owners. The earliest of these who Julian has been able to trace is Max Hazelton, better known to Australians for his company's commuter airline in regional New South Wales. Max bought the car from his then boss, Clem Wenbourne, although he recalls that he thought Clem was perhaps the car's second owner.

Max had bought the MG because he was commuting quite long distances between his home in Wahroonga, on Sydney's outer northern fringe, and the Technical College in Sydney itself where he was studying. After one accident on his motorbike late one night riding home after Tech, he decided that he'd be safer in a TC.

'The police used to give me a hard time, though,' recalls Max. 'They drove Hudsons in those days and used to follow me for miles along the highway, waiting for me to do something, anything, so they could stop me.

'So one night I decided to give them something to stop me for, if they could catch me,' he continues with a chuckle. 'The roads used to be really clear in those days, and the highway winds around a fair bit, so I took the TC up as fast as it would go and they had no end of trouble keeping up in their great yank tank!'

Max terminated the run by switching off his lights and turning off the highway down a side street while he was far enough ahead of the Hudson for the police to lose sight of him momentarily. However, the downside of there being relatively few cars on the road was that the police knew exactly who was driving the TC – and the next day they were waiting for him when he turned up for work!

Max owned TC0721 for only a year or two before trading it in on a Hillman saloon. The next owner was Malcolm Russ, who again owned the car for only a short time before selling ❯

MG TC

MG TC

'Early TCs are different from cars manufactured later in several aspects'

it to Chris Terry. Chris kept it for 20 years, using it as his only car for the first few years, and for weekend motorsport, before retiring it in the late 1960s with the intention of rebuilding it.

It was before Chris's ownership that the TC was rolled, and the scars remained with the car until Julian started the restoration in the 1990s. According to the vehicle's next owner, Brian Langlands, Chris used to reminisce about being told of the sparks streaming past the driver's face as the scuttle scraped along the road!

Brian Langlands is well known in the Sydney MG movement. His first car when he was just a 17-year-old youth was a TC, so in the 1970s when he was looking to get back into a sports car, it had to be a TC. Life is full of strange coincidences, and in Brian's case it turned out that the model he spotted advertised in the *Sydney Morning Herald* one Saturday morning belonged to his friend, Chris Terry. A deal was done, and TC0721 became Brian's.

By this stage in its life the TC was in dire need of some TLC, so Brian began to dismantle the car to fix it up a bit. However, about then he found another TC that he thought would be easier to restore, and so TC0721 was pushed to the back of the shed. Now, Brian is not known for selling his MGs, but like many young men who grew up in the era of the T-type MG, the approach of the new Millennium seems to have softened their life-long plans to own a fleet of fully restored models. And perhaps if the right person came along, one or two of the treasured

possessions might be let go. In Brian's case, two things persuaded him to sell TC0721. Firstly, he also owned a very nice TB which he was restoring slowly, and selling the TC would not only inject some cash into that project, it would also free up some space in the garage. Secondly, the person who was pestering him to sell TC0721 was his friend Julian Beville-Anderson, who seemed to be serious enough about the restoration to perhaps be classed as 'the right sort of person'. An added bonus was that Julian had a rather nice rubber-nose MGB to throw into the negotiations, and Brian's wife Bev thought that this sounded pretty good – a modern and comfortable MG that actually ran, in exchange for that old pile of bits.

Agreement was reached and, in 1996, TC0721 found not only a new owner, but also someone who was committed to bringing the old car back from the brink to its original state.

TC owners will know this, but many other MG enthusiasts might not be aware that the very early TCs are different from the cars manufactured later in the production run in several important aspects. They are almost TBs, the very last MGs manufactured (along with the magnificent six-cylinder WA saloons, tourers and drophead coupés) before World War Two curtailed production and Abingdon was given over to the war effort. The TB had heralded the introduction of the worthy XP-series engine, used in most MGs right up to 1955, and this was carried over into the TC along with other components probably manufactured before the war and kept in storage waiting for sports car production to recommence.

TC0721 was built in May 1946, the 470th car built, and it still has the cutouts in the timber coachwork in the rear of the car to leave room for the two six-volt batteries that the TB would have had mounted on either side of the tailshaft, even though the TC was produced with one 12-volt battery mounted on the firewall. The early TCs also had grey/green firewalls and green engines along with a brass

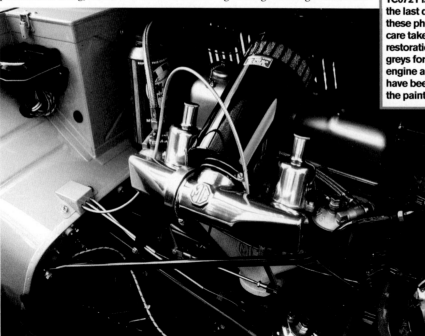

Above right: The Nepean River, in Sydney's west, makes an idyllic setting for the perfect TC.
Below left to right: The engine bay of TC0721 is original to the last detail, and these photos show the care taken in the car's restoration. The correct greys for an early TC engine and firewall have been used for the paint colour.

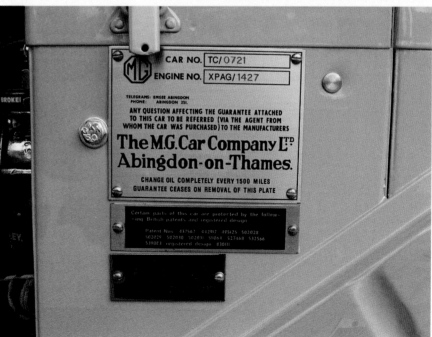

Hardly ergonomic, but the only word to describe a TC dashboard is 'gorgeous'.

body SU fuel pump and an early voltage regulator. The hood bows are different in their shape where they mount on the windscreen and they have the early foglight. They came in black body colour with either red, green or beige interior and matching grille slats.

The story of Julian's restoration of TC0721 is probably very similar to others, a tale of skinned knuckles, long hours swearing at the construction methods of Abingdon's engineers, much searching the world over for elusive parts and finally the care and attention to detail in the assembly and presentation of the finished car.

Julian has a couple of anecdotes to share. The radiator shell, for instance, came out of a wrecking yard in Miami, Florida, and cost him about $200. At the time he was working in the United States, so he put the shell in his suitcase for the plane trip home and surrounded it with all his clothes for protection.

'My bag did not make the connection to Australia,' says Julian, 'so eventually when I got the call from Qantas to come and collect the bag I wasn't concerned about the clothes, but I can tell you I was very relieved to find the shell in one piece and with no damage.'

As with all restorations, Julian also has a long list of people he'd like to acknowledge for their help and support over the long process of bringing TC0721 back from the brink. First on the list, he says, is his wife Di.

'Di's been very supportive,' he explains. 'She did a lot chasing down and picking up of parts from all the exciting places every girl loves to go to, like the sandblasters, nut and bolt shops and

aluminium sprayers.' All that to-ing and fro-ing seems to have planted a seed, though. Now that the TC's finally on the road, Julian says there is always a race to see who's going to drive.

'Di drives the TC very well. She has an understanding of mechanical sympathy which is important with these old cars,' says Julian generously. 'She says it must come from growing up with Austin A40s and Morris 1000s. I guess she's showing her age?'

Now that the restoration is over and the car has achieved the highest accolades from the Australian MG community, Julian is not averse to also taking it out for a hard drive along the mountain roads around his Blue Mountain home town to the west of Sydney.

'It often attracts the young blokes when I park it at the shops,' says Julian. 'When they ask me what on earth it is, I tell them it's a 1940s Impreza WRX – they seem to understand!' MG

Julian Beville-Anderson enjoying the car into which he invested so much time and effort.

TECH SPEC

1946 MG TC

Engine

Nuffield Type XPAG in-line four-cylinder, pushrod with overhead valves, 65.5 x 90mm, 1250cc, 7.25:1, Max power: 54.4bhp at 5200rpm, Max torque: 63.7lb.ft at 2600rpm. Fuel system: Twin 1.25in SU

Transmission

Clutch: Single 7¼in dry clutch Four-speed manual gearbox, synchro on top three gears Final drive: 5.125:1 (8/41)

Suspension

Semi-elliptic leaf front and rear, lever arm hydraulic shock absorbers Steering: Bishop cam 11:1

Brakes

Front: Lockheed hydraulic drums 9in dia Rear: Lockheed hydraulic drums 9in dia

Wheels and tyres

Spoked wheels 2.25x19in with 4.50x19in tyres Wheelbase: 7ft 10in Track: 3ft 9in front and rear

Dimensions

Length: 11ft 7½in Width: 4ft 8in Height: 4ft 5in Weight overall: 770kg (approx.)

Production

Late 1945-late 1949 Number built: 10,000

TWO OF A Kind

The K-type family tree contains some of the most famous racing MGs ever, along with some other distinguished branches of which you may be significantly less aware...

Words by Dale Drinnon. Pictures by Simon Goldsworthy

'Well, I suppose at heart, I'm just a tin-top man,' Peter Prosser says, gazing contentedly across the pair of KN saloons resting in his driveway. At considerably over six feet in height, he gazes across them with notable ease, too, which may provide an alternative explanation for his attraction to MG's taller, boxier models; it's hard to picture him folding comfortably into anything called a Midget.

Then again, he was very happy with his MGA Twin Cam Coupé, so elbow room clearly isn't his foremost consideration, and he once owned a cosy little F-Type Magna – which later wound up hanging on an office wall in Japan, proving that you can never truly know what fate awaits a car after you sell it.

But returning to the point, the truth is Peter simply likes closed cars. His first serious restoration was an SA he found in the Middle East while working there in the '60s as a civil engineer, and when he saw a slightly scruffy 1935 KN pillarless saloon advertised in 1988, he basically thought: 'Hmmm, what a lovely thing that could be' and bought it.

Which historically speaking makes him a

Two sporting saloons with a similar style but very different characters.

quite unusual MG fancier; for some others over the years, the early enclosed MGs (being essentially the same under the skin as their open brethren) were seen primarily as a good source of spares for the sports cars. Many of the K-type saloons in fact became sports models, or possibly four-seat open tourers. Of the roughly 200 built, Peter reckons 14 are left, and many otherwise savvy enthusiasts are only vaguely aware the cars were ever produced.

It's a sad story, but not really a surprising one. MG's strength for years was plainly in bare-bones sportsters, and different people measure the utility of a vehicle in vastly differing ways (see previously mentioned MG wall-hanging). Thusly, like Rembrandts, there are far more racing K3s around than were created by the original artist. Closed cars were a constant fixture in the MG line-up, however, with varying numbers of doors and seats, from the very start; Cecil Kimber was never one to let a potential market segment go untapped for want of a model permutation.

The K saloons are a case in point. At the turn of the 1930s, MG basically had two models to sell: the big car, the 18/80 and siblings, somewhat Bentley-esque but still plainly related to the

modified Morris Oxfords and Cowleys that spawned the brand, and the small cars, the Midgets, that spun off from the Morris Minor.

These came in a mind-numbing alphabet soup proliferation of model/chassis/engine designations, but at the bottom line, there was a big car and a little car. The former made a dandy four-door saloon, but it was getting a bit past its prime, and the Great Depression was seriously depressing demand for Bentley-esque (even from Bentley); the small cars barely had room for doors of any kind, let alone four of them, and any rear passengers had to hang off behind the back axle like a steamer trunk. What would clearly be handy was what's known these days as a C-segment platform.

The answer came in October 1932 with the K-type Magnette. Abingdon had already taken a step towards bigging-up its small car by endowing it with a Wolseley-derived sohc six as an alternative to the Wolseley-derived sohc four (on the six, Kimber actually tried to hide the parentage at first behind bogus sheet metal side covers); the K-type carried the process onward with an extra half-foot of track, and more significantly, the offer of a long-chassis option. MG now had what it needed to produce a

mid-sized, four-seat family sports saloon with an entrance for each occupant, and to prove it, the very first K-type built was exactly that.

This original long-chassis model, also available as an open tourer, was appropriately enough called the K1. The quasi-Wolseley six was given triple SUs and a new MG cross-flow head; it was de-stroked from the 1271cc of the F-type down to 1087cc to fit the K-cars into the then-popular 1100cc racing formulae, and labelled the KA engine. The standard gearbox for the K1 Saloon was a Wilson-patent ENV pre-selector with a spiffy new floor-mounted shift lever (most everyone else's was boringly stuck up on the dashboard) and the brakes were healthy 13-inch drums of the exotic magnesium alloy Elektron.

Most impressive to the critics, however, was the bold and stylish pillarless four-door bodywork: the front doors hinged at the leading edge, the rear doors hinged at the trailing edge, and where they overlapped in the middle there was – nothing. An artfully blended shut-line and a lack of outside rear handles meant the design could easily be mistaken for a two-door, and rear passenger access was unparalleled. Add in tasteful amounts of interior leather and wood ❯

Small body, six-cylinder engine –a winning formula.

Well stocked dash and floor-mounted shifter for a sporting saloon.

and exterior chrome, a sliding sunroof and a clever and spacious luggage arrangement, and the car was a sure-fire winner.

At least, it was on paper. Unfortunately, the works had miscalculated in some areas of the actual execution, the biggest of which was probably the decision, in addition to short-stroking the engine, to short-tune it as well. The intention was to present the pre-selector box with a lower tickover and therefore allow a smoother power take-up from rest during its centrifugally controlled engagement sequence; the reality was a 39bhp output that made road performance a touch less than sparkling.

There were also issues with the pillarless bodywork. Most designs in this particular styling mode have featured rigid steel monocoque construction: pillarless Lancias of the period, for example, are solid as steam locomotives. In contrast, MG body panels were still draped over a wooden frame and mounted atop a separate chassis. It was elegant, but not particularly stiff, and K1s suffered from stress cracks, water leaks and wonky panel alignment from the very beginning.

Thankfully, help was soon at hand for the horsepower woes; in 1933, the works went back

to the 1271cc engine, lopped off one SU, tuned it for 48bhp, and called it the KD. They also slipped a standard clutch in between that and the pre-selector box, and the saloon's driveability was greatly improved by the new combination. By the way, you should probably disregard factory quotes of 1286cc for the KD engine: the lads reportedly pencilled an imaginary extra millimetre of stroke onto the spec sheets purely as physiological warfare.

The following year, the K saloon reached its highest evolution with the engine and four-speed manual transmission from the new N-type; the 1271 was now up to 56 horses and both the engine and the model it went into were known as type KN. MG had finally got the driveline right, and the car so thrilled one motoring journalist that he proclaimed it, in the popular vernacular, hot stuff. How frightfully common.

As for the overly flexible superstructure, however, Abingdon apparently decided to leave that fix up to future generations. 'We added a discreet bit of metal bracing to the wood frames when we restored these cars,' Peter says, running a hand along the roofline of the blue example, 'but I still keep watching the C-pillars on the Green One for cracks…'

The Green One was the first, the car from that 1988 advert, and therefore the older of the two restorations. 'And someone had obviously been in there before,' says Peter. 'When we opened it up, one of the A-posts still had bark on it.'

Initially, Peter had every good intention of tackling the complete restoration himself; an untimely illness, however, led him to enlist the help of Adrian Priestley at Chisbon Restorations, 'and I'm glad I did, it turned out to be much more complicated than I imagined, and he did a fantastic job.'

Peter Green, Chairman of the Triple-M Register, provided invaluable help with the engine rebuild, and although a far larger portion of owner labour went into the second resto, Chisbon and Peter Green were still heavily involved, and Peter Prosser gives them full credit

Below right: Overhead cam and dynamo are both driven by vertical shaft at front of engine.
Below centre: The KN's many octagons include a unique winged example on the optional trunk.
Below left: Excellent access thanks to pillarless four-door construction.

for the beautiful final results on both machines.

Peter's game plan for the first car was strictly orthodox. He wanted it exactly as MG prepared a standard KN saloon for a 'family man' customer, someone who drove the car to work during the week, and on the weekends would set the family under a shady tree with a picnic lunch, empty the boot, remove the back seat and go hill climbing. As the first post-war owner, a Mr. W.E.V. Kethro, had indeed done. The only variations from original factory spec are a well camouflaged electric fan and a Bosch distributor, and the same updates are on the other car as well – some modern concessions just make sense if you want to drive briskly and often, and Peter certainly does that.

After a few years with the finished car, though, Peter was starting to think about finding another

K saloon, maybe something a little more adventurous, when an acquaintance mentioned she knew of a KN coming on the market in Perth. 'I said: "You know, I'm going up to Scotland next week, maybe I could go by and take a look." And the lady kind of laughed and said: "No, Peter, not that Perth..." '

The vehicle that would become the Blue One arrived from Perth, Western Australia, in the summer of 1998, and this time Peter had decided on what he calls 'sort of an RAF-man type of car,' something a dashing young hot-shoe of the '30s might have ordered with all the factory special goodies as semi-racing road transportation. He restored it to the same high standards as the Green One, then assembled the 1271 six to blown K3 spec, added a pre-selector box and Dunlop R5 racing tyres. If you've a

taste for irony, you can think of it as a racing K3 dressed up as a K saloon, instead of the usual other way around; entirely appropriate, as the development mule for the supercharged K3 racers is said to have worn saloon bodywork. 'It was a con on William Morris,' Peter smiles. 'He wasn't very keen on racing, so apparently they told him it was going to be a new road model.'

In terms of trim and accommodations the two machines are nonetheless a well matched set, or as matched as limited production automobiles built by a small concern are ever likely to be. Items like switchgear and instrumentation vary among all these cars depending on what was in the parts bin on the day that section was assembled. Peter also notes that there were considerable differences in the bodywork construction and timbering, especially considering the cars were ❯

No external handles for the rear doors gives two-door style.

'If you've a taste for irony, you can think of it as a racing K3 dressed up as a K saloon'

Pre-select gearbox is unusual in having a floor-mounted shifter.

both built in the last 1935 production series and only 69 chassis numbers apart.

But you'd be hard pressed to find any major visual dissimilarity in the pair, aside from the Dublin and Ulster Green versus the Oxford and Cambridge Blue (as they were sold, incidentally). And Mr Kimber's obsession with displaying the company logo leaves absolutely no doubt what you're looking at, from any conceivable angle. There are octagons everywhere; the instrument bezels, courtesy lamps, courtesy mirrors and gear knobs are octagon-shaped, the cam cover fasteners and oil-filler neck are octagon shaped, even the door hinges are octagon-shaped. You suspect that given enough time, they'd have figured out octagon-shaped tyres.

The odd thing is, it doesn't seem odd at all. On the contrary, the effect is really quite pleasing and you find yourself thinking: 'Oh look, I've found another one,' and you grin. For a passenger, too, the distinctive interior detailing helps make the cabin an entertaining place to be. For the driver, there's a surprisingly complete assortment of sporting dials among all those octagons, and the luxuries include a trip odometer and a fly-off handbrake, plus a right fair allocation of personal space, enough for a

plus-six-footer to settle in happily.

A considerable amount of the two cars' twinship goes away, however, once you're on the road. The blue car is quite the little delinquent in everyday driving; it's an experience consisting of soul-stirring bursts of howling acceleration bracketed by grumbling and spitting and loading up. With something over 100bhp in its present state of tune, it doesn't like low speeds or low revs much at all, and requires a good deal of throttle blipping and temperature watching; Peter says it was feistier still before he down-sized the blower: 'The original racing supercharger was just far too big for normal road use,' he explains.

The steering is also comparatively stiff below 20-25mph; Peter puts this down to the racing tyres, and of course the ride is period-firm on both cars, bringing a squiggle and squeak from those pillarless doors. But if the Blue One isn't the choice for a milk and eggs run to the supermarket on a rush hour Friday evening, show it an open, fast road, and it's gone – and with great style and considerable presence.

The Green One, on the other hand, is simply a joy under any circumstances. The engine is smooth, unfussy and flexible, willing to lug in that traditional long-stroke pre-war manner from

amazingly low rpm; the gearbox, once you find your double-declutching rhythm and adjust for first and second being where third and fourth should be and vice versa, is nicely notchy and crisp, and if you play the gears and power in harmony with each other you can make far better forward progress through traffic than most people would expect from a mid-'30s family motor.

Across country the car is admittedly slower than its stablemate, but you can cruise at a steady graceful 60mph, and in the day, from a model of this size, that was most assuredly 'hot stuff'. It took a while, but by 1935, MG was starting to get a grip on this sports saloon idea, and with a lovely combination of pure sport driving pleasure, classically handsome lines and user-friendly civility, the KN was finally coming into its own.

Then the firm killed it off. Blame company politics if you like; when William Morris chose

on July 1st of that year to sell his previously personal holding in the MG Car Company to Morris Motors, Abingdon came under the none too tender mercies of master product rationalist Leonard Lord. Anything of marginal productivity, which described the KN to a tee, and much of MG overall for that matter, was thenceforth expected to stop phaffing about and start contributing to the greater corporate good.

Or you can blame the marketplace, because Len Lord was basically right – playing with racing cars and building niche products at the height of the Depression was economies-of-scale suicide, and the KN had never been especially successful anyway. Never really more, most experts would agree, than a way to use up a stock of saloon bodies. So in truth, nobody killed the KN, they just let it die a natural death. The SA that debuted a few months later, and

was actually instigated by Cecil Kimber himself before the Morris takeover, set the pattern for future MG saloons as totally separate design entities from the sports cars, planned from the outset for mass production.

However you choose to read the history, the last KN rolled through the factory gates in the late summer of 1935. And MG saloons, sometimes for better, sometimes for worse, would never quite so literally be tin-topped sports cars again. **MG**

CONTACTS

Chisbon Restorations
chisbon@aol.com, 01255 862626

The Triple-M Register
www.triple-mregister.org

TECH SPEC

1935 MG KN Saloon

Engine:
1271cc sohc in-line six

Power
56bhp@5500rpm, RAC rating 12.08hp

Transmission
Four-speed manual, non-synchro

Weight
2349lb

Fuel economy
25mpg

Performance
0-50 in 18.4 seconds, top speed 75mph

JACK DANIELS
on pre-war MGs

Interview by Steve Havelock

J ack Daniels devoted 50 years of his working life to the British motor industry. He is best remembered for his close association with Alec Issigonis on the design and development of the Morris Minor and the Mini, but MGs were his true passion. In 1927, at the tender age of 15, Jack joined the fledgling MG Car Company on the shop floor as its first un-indentured apprentice. By the time he retired in 1977 he was Chief Engineer of Advanced Vehicles for BL Cars. When Steve Havelock spoke to him at his home near Christchurch in what's thought to be the last major interview he gave before he died in November 2004, aged 92, he had very clear and fond memories of his time at MG before World War Two.

What sparked your interest in cars and why did you join MG?

'When I was a boy I lived in a village called New Marston, near Cowley, Oxford. The biggest shop in Oxford had a chauffeur who lived along our road and he used to come home with all sorts of different cars. I couldn't resist going and looking at them. My father didn't have a car – he couldn't afford one.

'I was at a commercial school, the Central School at Oxford. I applied to join Great Western Railways to do office work but, as time went by, school holidays went past and I heard nothing from it at all. I'd made no attempt to go for an apprenticeship, largely because my father couldn't afford it. You had to pay for them in those days.

'Then my headmaster came to see me and said: "I've just had a note from a new car firm, MG Car Company, which has just been formed up at Edmund Road, Cowley. They asked if somebody from here could join them, so I put your name forward." Well, I went but, much to my surprise, it wasn't an office job at all. It was a job in the company's works, which would be as its first apprentice – yet un-indentured, which meant that I didn't have to pay anything. I had a doubt that my father might argue about it, but he didn't. Not only didn't I have to pay MG, but I got ten bob a week (50 pence). To be un-indentured in those days was completely new. The pals I had at school who were apprenticed all had to pay – and they didn't get anything back either, not for the first year. The day after I agreed to MG, notice came from Paddington (Railway) for me to go there. I was happy to say that I was not coming.'

What did you do when you arrived at MG?

'The job I had was to dismantle the Morris Oxford chassis, which were brought down from Cowley in a string of five behind one tow car. Those five were a day's work for the factory. It was cheaper to take the complete chassis from Cowley than to have all the separate bits brought down to us. I had to strip them all down, label all the bits and put them in the stores. I had to put the engine into a trolley, strip it down so far and take it to the first of five specialist engine builders. He would take the crankshaft and put brand new bearings in and properly hand fit them – and con-rods he'd do as well. He'd also put in brand new pistons. The MG had special materials and special pistons. We polished all the ports, polished the head, all sorts of things. We changed the valves, the valve springs, pistons and all the bearings were done. We made a hand-fitted, tuned engine. Then I'd take the chassis bits off, even knock some brackets off that were riveted on to it, like for the running boards. I'd also take off the brake mechanism. The Morris Oxford had a twin-shaft brake mechanism, but the MG was different. When all these things were done, they went down a hand-pushed line and the chassis were re-assembled with all the new equipment.

'They then came into a running-in section, which was on rolling roads. We started the cars on petrol and ran them in on town gas. We drove them at different speeds and, after five runs, they were taken to get their bodies fitted. It was quite time-consuming, but when all was finished the cars didn't need running in.

'In those days, the Morris works had a break of anything up to three months in the summer. As we got our stuff down from them, MG had to have a similar break. In my first year, we apprentices were put to work outside, building a road around the factory. I enjoyed it too. In my second year I was putting in, for the first time, a compressed air line all around the factory. So, two years had gone by before we had that. While I was doing it, I was up a ladder overlooking the top of George Propert's open-topped office. He was the General Manager. Cecil Kimber (MG's founding light) came in and said to Propert: "There is a man at Corn Market Garage, which is a Morris garage, named Sydney Enever and I want him brought in here." The very next day, Sydney Enever was a member of the MG camp. [Enever became MGs Chief Engineer 1954-1971.] He was, of course, the one who did all the record speed trials, but he came just as a mechanic, nothing else. Not a designer.

'Around about the same time, we started up a drawing office. We didn't have one before, as we didn't need it. They got a chap named Keith Smith and after about a month he needed some assistance. Propert got all six apprentices together and asked if any of us would like to take it up. Well, none of them was anxious, so I said, "I will try it out if you will guarantee that I can return if I don't like it." Propert agreed, and Keith Smith started off by teaching me drawing. First of all, I was doing a lot of tracing. I was a bloody red-hot tracer! All his drawings were on paper with paper backing, and he wanted them traced on to linen backing as soon as I could. They still have some of those drawings out at the Heritage place. Smith was a good chap really.

'When we first started the drawing office, I had to take the drawings to an architect's office two miles away to do the blueprints for us. Later, we got our own facilities and I had to do them. We were set up in the gents toilet. It was the only place they'd got to put us in. It was a hand-wind machine. We had water there, but drying them was a different matter, so they all got stuck up on the wall in the toilet and when they dropped off, they were near enough dry.

'Smith left and we got a chap called George Gibson. We had to move to Abingdon [1929] and Gibson and I were certainly the first there, about three months before the main works came. The fellows in the MG factory had the ❯

JACK DANIELS

> ### 'Later we got our own blueprint facilities. They all got stuck up on the wall in the toilet and when they dropped off, they were near enough dry'

opportunity of either leaving MG and going to Morris at Cowley or coming to Abingdon. Remember, they were mostly Oxford people and Cowley was at Oxford, whereas MG was six-and-a-half miles away. Hardly anybody left – in fact, I couldn't tell you one. We started at 8am, which was half an hour later because of the travelling time. When I started, the chaps were getting ten pence an hour, in old money, whereas the people at Cowley were averaging about one shilling and three pence an hour – quite a lot of difference, but they still came to MG. There was a spirit in that factory from the word go. Red-hot keen, the lot of them.

'I worked five-and-a-half days a week to 5.30pm with one hour for lunch. Saturday would be up until midday. At lunchtimes we used to play cricket in the factory. We had a large area of concrete floor ready for expansion, usually with cars all around us – and they got hit, too! Damned good games of cricket there.

'We moved into the new office, by which time Hubert Noel Charles came as the boss, the Chief Designer, and things began to happen. There was Gibson, myself and a chap by the name of George Cooper and that, for a year or two, was the total office.'

So Charles came in above Gibson?

'Oh yes, very much above. He came to us from Cowley. He was a company man and a full engineer, no question about it. As far as I was concerned, he was my inspiration. He taught me means of drawing that I didn't know before. He really brought me out in all sorts of directions. Not only drawing but mathematics as well. He was trying to give me a bit of engineering knowledge and took me under his wing (I was still in my late teens).

'We started on the MG C-type, which was engineered right from the word go. We made a unique chassis for it, and the engine was basically a Wolseley overhead-cam unit. From then on, we went until about 1935, through the alphabet to the S-type. We missed the M – that had already gone. They were mainly MG Midgets and 1100s. There were one or two bigger ones, like the Tiger, but there was nothing much made of them.

'In that period, 1933 or 1934, we even had Reid Railton come down to check the design of the R-type Midget, which was all independent suspension and a central box-frame chassis. We were working on big drawing boards in

half scale. He said OK and that was its racing car for 1934.

'Earlier than that, we did the MG Midget single-seater racing car with George Eyston, and the car that was known as the Humbug because of the painting on it [brown and cream stripes]. It was an 1100cc single-seater. Record-breaking cars they were, and I worked on both of those. In that period of four or five years, we would do one production and one racing car. For the production models, we would use as much of the racing car materials that we could possibly get into it. When we improved the racing engines, that went straight into the production vehicles. We couldn't afford to do racing cars on their own.'

So it wasn't a case of making racing cars from production cars, it was the other way round?

'Yes, that's right. We were racing all over the place. There was a works team of three that ran for about three years actually. Mechanics went with the cars. The top bloke was named Freddie Kindell. He was an ex-mechanic from Mercedes. Alec Hounslow and Reg Jackson were the other ones. We had a top team. It was jolly interesting, believe me. I used to go every time to Brooklands, to the pits to view them. On one occasion, we had all the team there but an extra bloke came in. He was a butcher, but I can't remember his name. He wanted to race at Brooklands. He bought an MG and had enough money to arrange for a pit as well and I was put in charge of his pit. But I regret to say that he couldn't have been all that good a driver: on the first day of the Double Twelve he went over the top at the bridge onto the road below and killed himself.

'I'm not sure which year, but it was before the R4 came out. We had just won one of the races, either a 12-hour or 24-hour race, and Alec Hounslow was the chief mechanic for the car that won it. At the end of the race he said: "Do you want a lift home kid?" I of course said yes, so we sat in the same racing car that had just won. I put the wreath around my neck and he drove to Abingdon. He said: "I want to be home within the hour." Well, he was well on the way to doing it and we passed our boss, Charles, on the way. Remember, we hadn't even changed the bloody tyres, which were a bit on the wrong side. In due course we got to within five miles of Oxford, where we had a few spots of rain and all of a sudden, whoosh, we were in the ditch.

'As always happens, a crowd appeared from somewhere and we lifted the car out of the ditch just as Charles came along past us with a critical eye. The wheels were splayed almost at right angles, but Alec found that he could steer it just a little bit, so we drove it the next five miles to a garage. He sent me off home and said that he was going back to the factory for a new axle to bring back and fit. The next morning that same car was in a rally.

'In mid-summer 1935, the MG Company was taken over by Morris. Leonard Lord was put in charge and closed down MG's racing activities. I had to move over to Cowley and that very week I had been scheduled to go along as a passenger in one of the rallies. I had to abandon it, and that annoyed me.'

The takeover didn't go down too well at MG, did it?

'There was nothing we could do about it. We didn't like being taken over, there was no question about that. The atmosphere we had at Abingdon had been so good because we had racing as well. It was a superb working place.'

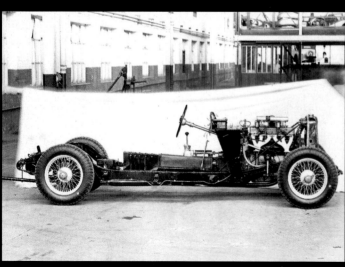

Above: **Jack Daniels contributed to the Abingdon company's large SA saloon.**

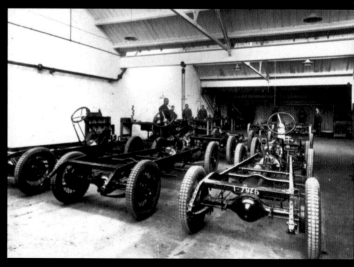

Above: **Daniels began his long working life at MG assembling MG 18/80s....**

Above: The MG
Car Company
drawing office
at Abingdon
shows JD fourth
on the right.

Did attitudes change?

'For a while, yes. It was certainly de-tuned, shall we say. Virtually the whole of our drawing office was taken out. We were clipped down to just three. There was HN Charles, myself and George Cooper, and that was it.'

You went on to be closely involved with the design and development of the Morris Minor and the Mini, but I sense that MGs were special to you?

'I loved my work on the MGs. To me, MGs were my start in life. They were really fine. There were the two record-breaking cars that we built. Single-seater racing cars. Charles was the designer but I was the one who drew the whole things out. We had a whole lot of records from those cars, bit by bit.

'Another thing I was proud of: we were always racing against Austin and we were always after more power. Everybody's idea at the time to get more power was to have a spherical head. Even Charles bought that idea and we designed a spherical head to go on the top of a Midget. But we never made it because you had to put the plug straight down through the middle and, at the time, 14mm plugs were just coming in. Charles was scared of them, and he didn't like them. He went back to a cylinder head shape substantially the same as Wolseley had done, but instead of all six ports being on one side, made it an eight-port crossflow head. I designed that out and he sent me up to Stirling Metals in Birmingham with a drawing of the casting of the head. I went back a week later and brought the head back, still warm.

'You could get things done quick in those days. That head was done in 1934 and went through all the racing. This was the 146bhp 746cc MG engine. There were two record-breaking cars – Sydney Enever did another one later on. They later went to the Jabbeke straights in Belgium because nobody was using those motorways at that time. It was record-breaking, pure and simple. I was proud to do any of those MGs. To pay for the racing we had to put it into production, and it became the standard head on the standard car.'

Do you believe that 'Racing improves the breed'?

'It can do. We were playing that game at MG not because we were trying to, but because we couldn't afford to do otherwise. After one year's racing, for argument's sake, you find that, as we did, the two-bearing crankshaft was a bit inadequate. We'd got to go to a three-bearing crankshaft. That means a re-design and a lot of cost. How are you going to pay for it? By putting it into production. The racing was the test bed. I used to like racing and still do today.'

Have you enjoyed your working life?

'I have enjoyed my life except the last bit. I wasn't sorry to leave at the end of my 50 years because the whole bloody business was being tied up with the cash boys, the economics. Too restricted. In the early days we had the opportunity to do something different every time! As far as I am concerned, I am certain that I had the best part of the motor car industry. It has deteriorated as far as engineering is concerned since. I'm sure of it.'

.Above: ..and he worked right alongside Hubert Noel Charles developing IFS.

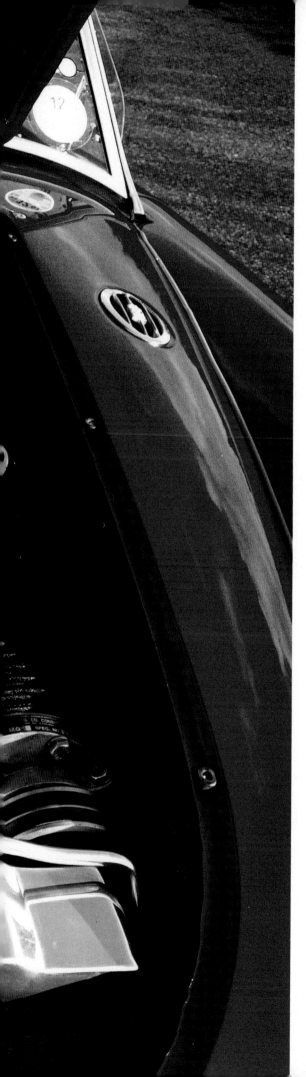

Blown Away

Mark Tossell's supercharged MGA was repatriated to Britain from the USA and perfectly recreates period American tuning practices

Words and pictures: Andrew Roberts

Imagine the clock has been turned back to 1958. The location is a sun-drenched Santa Barbara in California, with the Pacific Ocean lapping the beach. You have just driven your new MGA, top down of course, to the newsstand to collect the latest copy of *Road & Track*. Now, back home with a mug of coffee, your attention is caught by a test of the MG-Judson and what would seem a well engineered supercharger installation for the MGA. There is a power increase of some 25 per cent and an equivalent increase in torque. Reliability doesn't sound like a problem, either. It seems like something you could fit yourself in the garage. And you get to thinking of that club hillclimb a month away. Wouldn't the Judson supercharger give your MGA an extra edge?

Back in the late 1950s such a scenario would have frequently been played out among sports car owners on both the West and East Coasts of the USA. Then, British models from MG, Austin-Healey and Triumph were the choice of literally thousands of drivers. Their imagination was fuelled by motorsport – the Watkins Glen road circuit had opened in 1948 – and American drivers like Phil Hill, Dan Gurney and John Fitch were rising stars. *Road & Track* was the magazine that sporting motorists turned to for news of the European Grand Prix scene and it fired the enthusiasm of owners. Always there was the quest for performance, and there was no shortage of firms keen to cash in on this pent-up demand.

Which is where the Judson supercharger entered the scene. It was the Volkswagen Beetle brigade that took vast numbers of Judson supercharger kits, which explains why few have apparently survived in MG applications. A number are known to the North American MGA Register (NAMGR), while possibly three reside in the UK. So what were the attractions to the American buyers of yesteryear?

Firstly, this was bolt-on performance improvement. According to *Autocar* the MGA 1500 had a top speed of 98mph and a 0-60mph time of 15.6 seconds, while its power output was 72bhp. With the Judson ❯

'The real pleasure is just being able to drive it whenever I choose'

supercharger fitted, *Road & Track* estimated a top speed of 105mph, but more importantly a reduction in the 0-60mph time to 12.5 seconds. Power was increased to 90bhp. Similarly, there were improvements in torque, from 77.4 to 95lb.ft. Secondly, this was performance that did not compromise the driveability of the car, unlike stage tuning or a hotter cam which, while delivering top-end performance, would invariably do so with a loss of flexibility. Thirdly, it was affordable at $260 including a Holley carburettor, exhaust manifold and all necessary parts. Finally, it was within the abilities of a mechanically minded owner and could be installed in around five hours – a comfortable weekend job, with ample time for testing.

Supercharging at high pressures can cause reliability problems, but Judson sensibly set a relatively modest boost figure of 5.5psi. The supercharger is a vane type, which delivers its performance gain at all speeds, unlike a turbocharger with its lag time. To counter the problem of rubbing friction of the vanes, Judson set them at an angle, which resulted in the centrifugal force being virtually cancelled. Lubricant was used at a rate of around two pints per thousand miles and an aluminium rocker cover, which incorporated a metering valve, was supplied with the kit. The lubricant was SAE 10, or Marvel Mystery Oil, which is still available.

The scene now moves forward to 1990. Mark Tossell, whose MG

ownership had included an MG Metro, 1275cc Midget and an MGB GT, decided that an MGA was to be his next project. He sourced a 1958 MGA 1500 that had been purchased from an American dealer and reimported to the UK from Bellevue, Washington State. Its UK owner was in the throes of acquiring a narrowboat and subsequently the MGA changed hands. Ostensibly the 117,000-mile example looked sound, but being a car that had been well used and living in the Pacific Northwest with its damp climate, all was not as good as it seemed. Even so, Mark used the MGA for a couple of years before restoration started in earnest.

Anyone who has seen any of Mark's cars will know that they are always beautifully presented, and the MGA would be no exception. The engine was the first to be overhauled and was fitted with a Stage II cylinder head, a Weber carburettor and an Aldon distributor. This was followed by the gearbox, which was restored in its original four-speed guise, Mark not succumbing to the growing trend to fit a Ford Sierra five-speed gearbox.

Next, the body was completely renovated and painted, while by now the chassis was restored to better-than-Abingdon standard and the steering transferred to the right. MGB shock absorbers were fitted to the front and telescopic Konis to the rear. Brakes remained drum all round, but with competition shoes.

The seats are special but totally in period, being recreations of those

Right: Screen-mounted spotlight recalls rallying days of the era.
Left: Headlamp grilles and spotlights are also period-perfect extras...
Right: ...as are side vents in the wings, though they're not yet functioning.

used in the Works MGAs. Renowned MGA restorer Bob West supplied these, as he did the cylinder head, along with a huge amount of advice. The finishing touch was a set of replica Dunlop knock-on wheels, shod with Firestone Firehawk tyres, that really do set the car apart. Here, by sheer persistence, Mark was fortunate to be able to add his wheel requirement to a batch being made for a Jaguar restoration.

The choice of body colour was seemingly easy, because the car had always been red and it would clearly stay that way. But the hue is not the ubiquitous Orient Red or later Chariot Red used by the factory. Instead, it was specially mixed after Mark, who'd originally fallen for a vibrant colour sourced by his paintshop, demurred when he learned that it was Volvo Truck Red. 'I couldn't have the car painted in a truck colour,' he says. Notwithstanding this, the chosen tint is so perfect for the sweeping lines of the MGA, you wonder why Abingdon didn't go brighter in the spectrum.

So, once again, a pristine MGA was seen on the wonderful driving roads around Mark's Barnstaple home, and further afield, too. For this would be no cosseted MGA that rarely felt tarmac under its tyres. Trips to France, Belgium, Luxembourg and Germany have been regular forays, but the great favourite is the Jersey MGOC event; 7000 miles a year are typical.

Mark had joined and registered his car with the NAMGAR and this not only brought him valuable contacts throughout the restoration, but also alerted him to the existence of the Judson supercharger. A brace of articles in *MG World* and *Total MG* on Judson-supercharged MGAs fired his enthusiasm to follow the same route. 'I loved the neatness of the installation and how well it fitted under the bonnet,' says Mark. 'And because this was an American car, the conversion would be both correct and in period.'

The question was where to start, and inevitably eBay entered the frame. Soon, a Judson was offered for sale complete with its Holley carburettor, but elation quickly turned to despair as the supercharger was not as described. The only solution was to rebuild it completely, a task that would tax everyone involved. Not the least of the problems were the supercharger vanes, which had to be painstakingly remade one by one.

When the supercharger was complete and plumbed in, Mark and his fellow helpers might have expected their problems were over. Not so, for overheating problems now revealed themselves. The bottom pulley that carried the fanbelt turned out to be the wrong size and a replacement had to be manufactured – but not before overheating and a subsequent supercharger seizure had resulted in a blown head gasket. A custom-made gasket, considerably thicker than the original, together with a new radiator from Pro Alloy, finally cured the overheating problem, and with the correct-size pulley the supercharger worked exactly as Judson predicted half-a-century before. For good measure, a Kenlowe electric fan was added to the underbonnet specification to augment the bonnet vents. Operating pressure was, and is, around 5.25psi.

The finishing touch was a finned rocker cover from a 1960s B-series engine that Mark found at the MG Show at Stoneleigh, and this has been superbly finished in a high-temperature crackle black finish that perfectly matches the Judson supercharger. The overhauled chrome Holley carburettor complements the exceptionally neat underbonnet installation, while the Ampco Vapor Lubricator rounds off the period atmosphere. An authentic boost gauge was sourced to complete the installation and then astonishingly an original can of Marvel Mystery Oil was found in Mark's ❯

Above: Despite its pristine condition, Mark's MGA averages 7000 miles each year. Right: Ampco Vapor Lubricator adds authentic period touch, as does Marvel Mystery Oil.

local garage and presented to him. The contents were immediately put to their intended use, while regular supplies are sourced via the Internet to keep the supercharger running sweetly.

Everything about this MGA is in period – something that Mark is very particular about. The radio is one example, picked up for a few pounds at a car boot sale. Similarly the spot and foglamps, when it would have been far easier to buy replicas. The headlamp grilles are period accessories, too, typical of those found on the other side of the Atlantic, as are the highly effective wind deflectors on the screen. The side vents in the wings were fitted Stateside to provide cockpit cooling – an answer to a notorious MGA problem.

Period this example may be, but there is nothing dated about its performance – as Mark proved on the driver's roads of north Devon en route to our photoshoot. Coming back to an MGA after driving an MGB or an MGF, it immediately becomes apparent how compact the car is in relation to its siblings. There is an extraordinarily one-piece feel about this model, with both driver and passenger feeling an integral part of it.

But these are MGA generalities. How does Mark's perform and does the supercharger installation add to the driving experience? The answer in a single word is 'Yes' – undeniably so. The advantage of the supercharger is immediately apparent, the extra torque being evident on the hilly departure from the environs of Barnstaple. Where with a standard MGA 1500 you would be expecting downward changes, the Judson supercharger means this isn't necessary, while the improvement in acceleration is marked.

Coupled to an ideal suspension set-up, this turns out to be a machine that epitomises everything a MG should be. Responsive, predictable and demanding that it be given its head, it is just what Syd Enever and John Thornley envisaged all those years ago when they formulated the design. Pin-sharp steering and roadholding that ensures the performance can be used to the full mean this MGA is a car to be seriously enjoyed, and of all the examples that returned across the Atlantic in the 1990s, this is surely one of the best. The marriage of MGA 1500 power and the Judson supercharger is a well-nigh perfect one and demonstrates that painstaking attention to detail can result in an MG which is greater than the sum of its parts.

There are countless MGs restored to very high standards that scarcely turn a wheel but, as we have seen, this is not the life of this MGA. 'It is a car for driving,' says Mark, not even flinching when a passing vehicle propels a stone towards the pristine paintwork. 'You don't have to worry about things like that. Everything can be put right and I do try to keep the car in tip-top condition.' Is he tempted to show the car? 'Because it is modified it

can only be a Pride of Ownership car and I sometimes enter, but just for fun,' he explains. 'The real pleasure is just being able to drive it whenever I choose and that means throughout the year.'

Bringing any car up to a standard like this MGA is inevitably a team effort and Mark is appreciative of the help he's received along the way. He singles out for special thanks MGA guru Bob West, staunch friends Paul Turner and Dave Boswell, Ben at West Cross Garage, Braunton and Colin at the Carbody Centre in Ilfracombe, together with the NAMGAR, MGCC MGA Register and MGOC members. As this very special MGA celebrates its half-century, it is a credit to every one of them, not least its custodian.

1000MILES
IN AN MGA

Historic Mille Miglia MGAs will turn back time when they return to Italy, restored to their Works competition specification of more than 50 years ago

Words: Andrew Roberts Photographs: Stephen Dixon archive

When Bob West and Steve Dixon drove down the starting ramp in MGA MJB 167 at Brescia on May 11 for the 2006 running of the Mille Miglia retrospective, they were re-enacting history. For back in April 1956 the same car, in the hands of Peter Scott-Russell and Tom Hag, was driven superbly in the worst conditions ever encountered on the 1000-mile Italian road race. They were to finish a highly creditable 70th and were the first all-British crew home. MBL 867, the sister car driven by Nancy Mitchell and Pat Faichney, was 74th and won the Ladies Prize. But what was really noteworthy was that of 365 starters, just 182 finished.

The return of MG as a Works race entrant in 1955 with the MGA, with three EX182 entries at Le Mans and the RAC TT at Dundrod in Northern Ireland, had been overshadowed by tragedy. Le Mans witnessed the most horrendous accident the sport has ever seen and, in addition, Dick Jacobs was severely burned when his MGA crashed and caught fire at White House. The TT saw three drivers killed and BMC decided that no further racing by the Works would be sanctioned. The sentiments against motor racing were running strongly throughout Europe, Le Mans having cast a long shadow over the sport, with effects that are still felt today.

The fact that the Mille Miglia was an out-and-out road race and was the third round of the 1956 Sports Car World Championship should surely have disbarred an MG Works entry, but MG Car Company General Manager John Thornley turned a Nelsonian eye to this and to entreaties from Competitions Manager Marcus Chambers, who had serious reservations about the entry impacting on the rally programme. Had there been repercussions from on high, no doubt he would have justified his decision by arguing that because the cars were started singly the event was akin to a rally, with the results decided on a time basis rather than position on the road.

John Thornley therefore sanctioned the entries, undoubtedly with a view to a strong performance in the newly instituted 'Price Class'. This was aimed at lower-priced sports and GT cars, and the result was a much greater influx of British entries than previously. The stipulation for the class was that the sports cars should be open, and in addition to the two MGAs, Austin-Healey 100M, AC Ace, Triumph TR2/TR3 and Sunbeam Rapier were all represented, bringing a more cosmopolitan feel to the entry. The 1500cc class in which the MGAs ran would also feature Porsche with the 356, while

1000 MILES IN AN MGA

Clockwise from left:
MJB 167 and MBL 867
with their crews in
Abingdon; MBL 867 as
restored today; battling
atrocious weather in '56.

> 'Two Tudor screenwash bottles were fitted behind the crew, their purpose uniquely being to dispense Lucozade as required'

the Osca would also provide stern opposition and astound with a top-ten finish.

Both MGAs were built up by Douggie Watts and Tommy Wellman at Abingdon to long-distance racing (but not Le Mans) specification. Twenty-gallon fuel tanks with their distinctive central filler with double fuel pumps feeding the SU carburettors were the major departure from the production cars. Brakes remained standard drums, ventilated at the front. An anti-roll bar was fitted, with the Andrex shock absorbers retained. The suspension was stiffened and a small amount of negative camber employed. Oil coolers, a higher axle ratio and close-ratio gearbox was also used.

Externally, the cars resembled the EX182 Le Mans cars of 1955, with a single large spotlight mounted in the offside grille and no bumpers. A large chronometric tachometer was installed and twin aeroscreens were fitted, but these provided scant protection for the crews in the constant rain of the event. Twin electric Altette horns were fitted, essential for keeping excited spectators at bay. Two Tudor screenwash bottles were fitted behind the crew, their purpose uniquely being

to dispense Lucozade as required! By far the greatest change to the appearance of the cars was their colour – now red in place of the traditional British Racing Green. Previous events had apparently seen Italian railway level crossing keepers favouring cars in the national racing colour of red, while mysteriously holding up other entrants. The solution was to paint both cars red, and this set the trend for the majority of the BMC Works cars in the future.

The route of the Mille Miglia changed little over its years as a road race, and for its penultimate running in 1956 it was a little over 992 miles, starting and finishing in Brescia. The route took competitors through Verona, Vicenza and Padova, before heading for Rovigo, Ferrara and Ravenna. From here, entrants would run along the Adriatic to Pescara, before turning inland to L'Aquila and Rome, the traditional halfway stage. From this point it was a near flat-out blind to Siena and Firenze, before the Futa and Raticosa passes to Bologna and Modena. Piacenza saw the entry turning eastwards again, through Cremona and Mantova to the Brescia finish.

The selection of MG drivers was an interesting

one, for it was recognised that no reconnaissance could possibly learn the roads. Rally experience would prove a priceless asset, and the choice of Nancy Mitchell co-driven by Pat Faichney proved to be an inspired one, with Nancy's uncanny ability to react to changing road situations, weather and crowd hazards. Peter Scott-Russell, who would later become the voice of Silverstone with his commentaries, was joined by MG Chief Test Driver Tom Haig in the other MGA.

Inevitably, the Ferrari, Maserati and Mercedes-Benz entries were favourite, but in the time-honoured tradition of starting the smaller-capacity cars first, the heavy metal caught up with the MGAs in only the last two hours of the race. Every contemporary account dwells on the weather, which was not only wet but also unseasonably cold. For the crews of open cars it must have been incredibly difficult, being constantly soaked and frozen to boot. Road surfaces were treacherous and any cobbled surfaces swiftly became skating rinks. North of Rome the Futa Pass was shrouded in mist and low cloud, with visibility often down to as little as five yards.

'Earlier this year its ownership changed, but very fittingly into Nancy Mitchell's family, to her grandson Bruce Chapman'

Throughout all of this, the two MGAs ran like clockwork. Marcus Chambers had organised service at both Rome and Florence (Firenze), but there was no time for the crews to stop for anything other than oil and petrol. In the event, it was the Scott-Russell car which finished first, with a time of 15 hours, two minutes and 15 seconds, with Nancy Mitchell just under three minutes behind. Although the Mitchell/Faichney outfit was the first female crew home, the Automobile Club de Brescia did not award a cup for this achievement. It was left to the local MG agent to purchase a beautiful silver flower bowl in lieu. The MGAs were second and third in class, but controversially the winning Porsche had stopped to erect its hood, in clear contravention of the regulations.

Predictably, the race went to the pre-event favourite Eugenio Castellotti in the new V12 Ferrari 290MM, followed by Peter Collins and Louis Klemantski in the Ferrari 860 Monza. Ferrari also took the next three places before a trio of Mercedes-Benz 300SLs. Sadly, it was not a race without its share of tragedy, for John Heath of HWM succumbed to his injuries, together with two other drivers.

The final running of the Mille Miglia as a competitive event came in 1957, but again this would be an event marred by tragedy. Nancy Mitchell and Pat Faichney would return, this time in a Triumph TR3, but be eliminated as a result of a smash. But the appalling accident of the Ferrari

of the Marquis de Portago, which crashed into a crowd of spectators at around 160mph when an axle broke, spelled the end to the Mille Miglia. Open-road racing would linger on the Targa Florio in Sicily, but for mainland Europe it was the end. However, such was the affection for the race that the Mille Miglia retrospective events were born, using the same roads and many of the actual cars that participated in the original events. There is now considerable factory support from the heritage operations of BMW and Mercedes-Benz, while MG has been represented, too, notably with the K3 and the MGA.

Yorkshire restorer Bob West with business partner the late Mike Horner had painstakingly returned the Nancy Mitchell car to its Mille Miglia specification and reunited it with its original driver. In 2001 it gained a much-coveted entry for the Mille Miglia and, driven by West and then-custodian Stephen Dixon, won the hearts of the Italian spectators. Says Dixon: 'It was an unforgettable event with flat-out driving, often with a police motorcycle clearing a path for a group of hard-running cars.' Appearances at the Goodwood Revival (including in 2005 with Rauno Aaltonen at the wheel) and at Le Mans have further added to the vehicle's competition pedigree. It has also been a welcome visitor to the Abingdon Works Car Show and to MGCC Silverstone, but most fittingly MBL 867 was reunited with Pat Faichney back in 2001.

Early in 2006 its ownership changed, but very

fittingly into Nancy Mitchell's family, to her grandson Bruce Chapman. With a post-Mille Miglia Works history that includes the Ladies Prize and a Coupe des Alpes for Nancy Mitchell and Pat Faichney on the 1956 Alpine, and a similarly impressive performance for Mitchell and Doreen Reece on the 1957 Lyon-Charbonnieres Rally, not surprisingly the intention has since been to maintain its high historic profile. Although regrettably no invitation was forthcoming for the 2006 Mille Miglia retrospective, MBL 867, or Mabel as she is known, joined four other Works MGAs, including its Mille Miglia team-mate, on the Alpine Rally retrospective, the Rally des Alpes.

In the meantime, MJB 167 also came into the custodianship of Stephen Dixon and Bob West, who again embarked on the most painstaking of restorations. The specification was back to its original Mille Miglia condition, bringing the first Works MGA to be used in international competition post the 1955 Le Mans to its ex-Abingdon state. The pair fired up the car in time to take part in the 2006 Mille Miglia retrospective – the only MG to do so on that occasion – while on the Alpine Rally MJB 167 donned a windscreen and Works hardtop exactly as it did in 1956, when Bill Shepherd and John Williamson drove it to 18th overall and fifth in class.

At the time of writing, both MGAs have been confirmed for the 2009 Mille Miglia retrospective, in a historic rerunning of that iconic pairing of more than 50 years ago. 🔵

Magnette Attrac

I t's all too easy to forget the impact World War Two had on Britain's automotive industry, on our motoring in general, and for how long the effects were felt. Understandably, the manufacture of munitions, military vehicles and aircraft took precedence, car production took a back seat and every aspect of the business was strictly regulated.

Once the weapons of war finally fell silent in Europe, the British Government certainly encouraged the building of new cars – but manufacturers were under strict instructions to export. Few vehicles were destined for the home market and those that remained in Britain usually ended up in the hands of essential users. These factors, combined with petrol rationing and the paucity of spare parts, saw private motoring grind to something of a premature halt.

Nevertheless, this had been a heavily mechanised war, a war during which for many servicemen and women provided their first experience of the thrill of driving. With the cessation of hostilities there arrived a renewed zest for life and

optimism, and they returned home fuelled with a desire to get behind the wheel of a car in any shape or form. This post-war euphoria was short-lived though, and people soon discovered that peace came at a price.

War had cost the nation dearly, and not just in terms of lives lost. As the only allied country to fight the battle from beginning to end, our economy had suffered hugely. Britain was deeply in the red and had been for some time. Indeed, the second half of the conflict had been fought using funds provided by the USA through its lend-lease agreement. The war may have been over, but the battle to rebuild had only just begun.

The Labour party, led by Clement Atlee, came to power in 1945 and its plans for economic reconstruction were draconian to say the least. Having won the war, it seemed as if the British people now had to pay for it. Rationing remained in place and austerity prevailed. The automotive industry was also struggling to get back into volume production: it was already suffering from a mandatory 50 per cent export quota, and in 1947 the Government raised this to 75 per cent. It was export or die!

ion

With stunning and exclusive photography, this is the story behind one of MG's most accomplished and desirable sporting saloons

Words: Martyn Morgan Jones Photography: John Colley

Marque improvements

Forced to venture overseas for sales, Britain's automotive industry could no longer rely on pre-war designs, or even rehashes. The average 1940s home-grown car simply had not been developed or tested rigorously enough. Reliability in harsher climes, where unmade roads were commonplace, was poor. The market had gone global and vehicles needed to be built accordingly. Needless to say this was no easy task, but it would prove beneficial to those consumers who could not only afford a car but could somehow manage to get their hands on one. As well as vehicles becoming better built, equipment levels improved, too.

Styling was another area to come under scrutiny. In fact, it underwent a sea change. In the late 1940s, car design began to reflect the specific tastes and requirements of the countries where the models were going to be sold. And, with a lot of them ending up in America, designers began penning some decidedly transatlantic shapes. From this time on, cars didn't just have a job to do; they also had to make a style statement.

One of the boldest post-war automotive statements was the sensational Jowett Javelin, designed by one of Britain's greatest production car stylists, Gerald Palmer. Born in Britain but raised in what was then Rhodesia, Palmer returned to the UK in 1927 to start an engineering apprenticeship with the commercial vehicle builder Scammel. He also designed and built a stylish two-seater roadster, which he called the Deroy.

He failed to secure the backing required to put the Deroy into production, but the prototype caught Cecil Kimber's eye at MG and, through him, Palmer ended up in the Morris drawing office at Cowley, where he headed up the design team working on MG's new Y-type.

Palmer left Nuffield in 1942, but was tempted back in 1949 to what was a disparate organisation, where managerial in-fighting and boardroom mistrust were the norm. The company certainly produced a wide range of cars but, regrettably, most were past their prime. A few, notably the Rileys, were extremely good but they were expensive to build and old-fashioned. The only way that Nuffield was going to slough off the past and move with the times was ❯

'Palmer's mind was made up – Nuffield's new mid-sized cars would possess Italianate flair'

to integrate, modernise and produce cars that were up to date. Palmer was one of a small band of visionaries who took on this challenge. He not only took it on, he would soon become a director of Morris Motors. Initially, however, he was charged with the task of designing new MG and Riley saloons.

Y to Z

Of these, the new mid-range saloons were perceived as replacements for the Y-type, a car which had been under development at the outbreak of WWII but whose production had been delayed by the conflict and not gone on sale until 1947. As good as it was, there was no escaping the fact that the Y-type had its roots in the 1930s. What Nuffield needed now were cars that took the traditional MG/Riley virtues of performance, handling and style, and pushed them well into the 1950s.

Palmer was initially hampered in his options by the economic necessity that meant he had to utilise existing engine and transmission set-ups. Luckily, there were no such restrictions when it came to creativity and there was nothing to stop him clothing these mechanicals, some of them pre-war, with stylish and modern bodyshells.

For some time, Palmer had been praying at the temple of Italian styling. He had visited many continental motor shows where he had become enthralled with the way Italian designers managed to make their designs cohesive, flowing and, above all, stylish. His mind was made up; Nuffield's new mid-sized cars would possess an Italianate flair.

Not every aspect of the new models' design should be attributed to Italy however; one or two were home grown. Stan Bletchley had already styled a possible Y-type replacement in 1948, and some of this car's design cues were adopted but shaped by Palmer's rather more delicate hand.

Soon the plans for the MG were added to, as a Wolseley derivative had been proposed. Not that Palmer had an issue with this: the MG and its bigger Riley sisters were to have more sporting engines, lower chassis and bodylines, and better brakes. As a luxury marque, the Wolseley would be biased towards prestige and not pace.

Merger, Magnette and badge engineering

The Magnette name first surfaced, in relation to the new saloon, in the early part of 1950, although it was intended to be affixed to a Riley. By mid-June however, MG and the Magnette moniker had become inextricably linked. The name might have been sorted, but the actual car wasn't given the green light for production until November 1951. It was also announced that it would be introduced at the 1952 Motor Show. No pressure then! The Magnette, which was still being referred to as 1¼-litre, was to be followed by a similarly styled Wolseley saloon in March 1953 to replace the unsuccessful 4/50.

This would all have been well and good, had it not been for the fact that November 1951 was also the month in which the Nuffield/Austin merger was agreed. The new company would be known as the British Motor Corporation and the ripples of change were already lapping at the wheels of the Nuffield marques. Leonard Lord, who would soon become Chairman and Managing Director of BMC, was all for collectively axing Morris, Wolseley, Riley and MG in favour of Austin. Thankfully it didn't happen. Not only would this have crippled the company financially, it would have been a PR disaster.

Lord then put his weight behind the idea of 'badge engineering.' In effect, this meant that BMC would produce basic models which could be adapted with different marque badges and trim for little extra expenditure. The only stumbling block was MG. Many of its models were unique, and loyalty to the marque was considerable. In the end, the MG Magnette was sensitively incorporated. True, it was still badge engineered and closely linked to other BMC models, but thankfully it was also allowed to retain as much of its own identity as practicable.

Subsequent to the merger was a review of all existing and future models, following which it was decided that Wolseley should be allowed to nose its way to the front of the production queue. In all fairness, this was an entirely logical move. The new Wolseley, the 4/44, pipped the Magnette into production only because it could make use of the 1250cc XPAG (XPAW in this application)

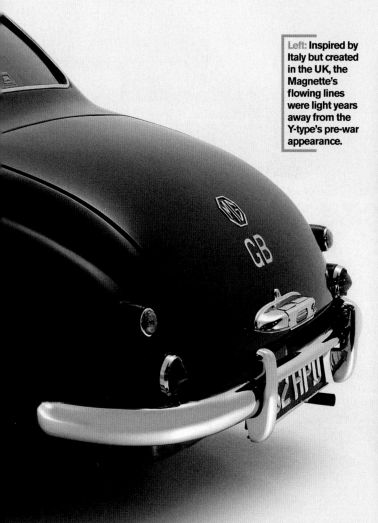

Left: Inspired by Italy but created in the UK, the Magnette's flowing lines were light years away from the Y-type's pre-war appearance.

Above: Sharp steering, good brakes, ample power – a great place to be.
Below: Ample luggage space despite the shapely tail. Switch to radial tyres is highly recommended.

Right top: Door cards are new, but Bob has kept his car looking original.
Right bottom: B-series was a new motor when first used in Magnette. Early problems were soon ironed out.

engine, which was deemed powerful enough for the needs of the typical Wolseley owner. The sporting Magnette, on the other hand, was now being considered as a 1½-litre and required a more powerful engine, such as the soon-to-be-introduced 1.5-litre BMC B-series. There were other changes too: Palmer's preference for a separate chassis is well documented, but despite this, in 1950 the decision had been made to use unitary construction, much of the rigidity being provided by the combined box-section body side members and sills.

The Magnette holds the honour of being the first MG to be built using unitary construction. There were other firsts, too. Coil-sprung independent front suspension was not new, but the Magnette sported a fresh take on it. The upper wishbone was entirely conventional, although from there down things became rather more interesting. The lower link was a single transverse arm. From this spurred a tie-rod which was located to the body behind the axle line, and there were front and rear reaction arms. Dampers were telescopic and mounted within the springs, while the rack and pinion steering drew many favourable comments.

The front suspension worked straight out of the box, but the same couldn't be said of the rear. Palmer had designed the axle to be mounted flexibly on the springs using rubber bushes. To control the torque reaction, he devised a torque arm set-up which may have looked promising on the drawing board, but in practice proved to be an unmitigated disaster. So much so that production was halted while a solution was sought. The answer was simple – mount the axle rigidly to the springs using beefy U-bolts. The telescopic dampers remained, complete with natty cooling fins.

Running with the more traditional rear suspension, the Magnette's road manners were excellent. Not only did it handle well, thanks to a very effective Lockheed hydraulic system with 10in drums all-round and twin-leading shoes up front, braking was first-rate. So too was its on-road performance. Under the Magnette's shapely bonnet lay a brand new 1489cc four-cylinder, the first in what would prove to be a long line of B-series motors. The Magnette was the first MG to be fitted with this type of engine, but before we praise it too highly, it should be remembered that in some quarters it was seen to be a retrograde

step. The first incarnation had split little-ends, split skirt pistons, diagonal big-ends, felt oil seals, poor manifolding and an antediluvian oil by-pass system. These 'faults' were soon engineered out and the engine became the uncomplicated, tough and reliable unit that we know and love. Topped off with two 1¼in SUs, it produced 60bhp at 4600rpm and 78lb.ft of torque at 3000rpm. Mated to this new engine was a slick-changing, all-new, four-speed gearbox. On any reasonable straight, 80mph was attainable and the Magnette's acceleration was equally impressive.

In fact, it was an impressive car all round. Performance, economy, handling, accommodation, quality – the Magnette ticked every box. Especially the one marked styling. The ZA was every inch a modern car, which lifted jaded post-war spirits. It was sumptuously equipped, smartly trimmed, beautifully proportioned, elegantly designed, obviously sporting and unmistakably an MG.

Production proper began in February 1954. Surprisingly, reaction to the new car was at best lukewarm. Worse still, the Magnette moniker precipitated an unexpectedly hostile reaction from some MG diehards angered that the name was now associated with a mere saloon! Thankfully, things soon settled down and the car's true qualities were allowed to shine. Test models were slow in arriving, but brisk on the road. *Autocar* and *Motor* were both impressed and the Magnette was helped on its way by enthusiastic and very positive reviews.

Not so good was the fallout between the autocratic Leonard Lord and the creative Palmer. Sacked by Lord, in 1955 Palmer left BMC to join forces with Vauxhall where he remained, in a mainly managerial role, until his retirement in 1972. The Magnette on the other hand was allowed to mature and develop.

A to B

In July 1956 the ZA received a new high-compression engine, which pushed power to 68bhp with a corresponding increase in torque. Just two months later the ZB was introduced, as was its Varitone sibling. The ZB was mostly about cosmetic changes such as the loss of the front wing hockey stick trim, the move to a dished steering wheel, dashboard changes and so on, although on the mechanical front it did also enjoy the benefit of bigger carbs. In addition to such standard fitment niceties as flashing indicators the Varitone, as its name implies, was blessed with attractive two-tone paintwork. To further emphasise the colour scheme, thin chrome strips ran the length of the car from radiator grille to rear

'The Magnette was the best-looking four-seat sporting saloon on sale at the time'

bumper. As the hockey sticks were now deemed superfluous, these were omitted. Curiously, the Varitone would soon be offered in single colours, too.

The Varitone did have one other distinguishing feature – a larger panoramic rear window. Unfortunately, Pressed Steel had not tooled up for this modification, so bodyshells that had been designated as Varitones were dispatched to Morris Motors' body shop in Cowley to have their rear window apertures enlarged. It would be nice to report that this was a skilled and technical operation. It wasn't. Apparently, the whole process was rather Heath Robinson. Nevertheless the larger rear window, a Varitone hallmark, looked good and was well received.

The same can't be said of the automatic transmission option. Probably with an eye on the lucrative and successful American market, from January 1957 the ZB and Varitone were offered with a clutchless semi-auto. Known as the Manumatic, this didn't prove to be a great success. Less than 500 found homes and it was quietly removed from the options list in 1958. Nevertheless the Magnette was selling exceptionally well, with many finding buyers in the USA, which makes one question why production was stopped so early.

Premature end

There is no doubt that the Magnette should have remained in production well into the 1960s. Not only was it a handsome car, very popular and with scope for further development, but it was by far and away the best model in the entire BMC range. The ZB was also a quick car for its day. Indeed, for a time the ZB was proclaimed to be the fastest 1.5-litre saloon available in Britain. Sadly, and despite the many plaudits, the plug was pulled in December 1958, with the last Magnettes leaving the factory line in January 1959. By the time production had ended, 36,601 had been made.

Rivals

The similar-looking Wolseley 4/44 (or 15/50 from 1956 with B-series power) could have been considered as a rival, but this was really of a very different character. There were continental offerings from the likes of Alfa Romeo and Lancia, but if you were looking for a home-grown alternative to the Magnette, you would have probably visited your local Rootes showroom. Rootes had an impressive sporting pedigree and made much of this. Late in 1955 Rootes unveiled the Sunbeam Rapier, retrospectively known as the Series 1, a car that was derived from the Hillman Minx and used a tuned Minx engine.

Compared to the Magnette, it had some minuses. It was two-door, had a column gearchange, and the styling was a tad too Americanised. There were pluses, though. It had a higher top speed, standard-fitment overdrive and good handling. In 1955, the Rapier retailed at £1044, the Magnette was yours for £1041. The Rapier gained a slightly different engine and twin Zenith carburettors in October 1956, which raised top speed to an impressive 88mph. When the Series II arrived in February 1958, the Magnette had real competition. The Rapier now sported a floor-mounted gearchange, a 1494cc 'Rallymaster' engine, bigger front brakes and could nudge 91mph. It was a big seller.

Some Magnette owners did switch to Rapiers but most would remain loyal to the marque. After all, the Magnette was the best-looking, four-seater, sporting saloon on sale at the time. Its performance was impressive and, above all, it was an MG.

Revival and survival

Thanks to the efforts of the various specialist clubs and spares organisations, the Magnette is surprisingly well catered for. The majority of parts are available, at a reasonable price, and there exists an enthusiastic and knowledgeable following. If you are looking for a taste of the 1950s, then the Magnette must be considered as a sporting saloon to savour. Few saloon cars from this era have aged so well, look so good and drive with such flair. When *Road and Track* magazine tested the Magnette in December 1954 it concluded: *'In short, for a car with individuality, good driving traits and a 'custom' quality, the Magnette just about fits the bill.'* It still does.

Right: The sporting saloon Magnette was sumptuously trimmed with wood, leather and stylish octagonal dials.

Feature car

Bob Hough, who owns this delectable Damask Red ZB Magnette, has been a fan of MGs for quite some time. When he relocated to Dorset, one of the first things he did was to buy a rather nice Midget. This suited him well, but it was the Magnette that was starting to tug at his heart strings, as he admits: 'I intended keeping the Midget, but I'd seen a number of Magnettes at club meets. I thought that the lines were lovely and being a four-seater, it was a very practical classic.'

Practical, but out of his reach, at least for a while. Then: 'I'd been left some money, enough for a Magnette,' Bob explains. 'Of course, I had to convince my wife that it was a good idea. Luckily, she didn't need too much persuasion.'

After looking at a few, he found 932 HPD. Owned by Malcolm Kimberley, this car was the perfect partner for the Midget. Some time back, Malcolm had done a rebuild/restoration and generally the car was in good condition. There were a few areas that needed attention though, as Bob recalls. 'I took the car to a specialist in Poole who stripped the old underseal from the underside, repaired the floor to make it as per original, and then bodyschutzed it. The sills were fine ❯

and just needed some minor work. I removed most of the chrome, which was then refurbished. The Mazac rear number plate/reversing lamp cover is new. These are exceptionally rare, but Malcolm managed to find one.'

Bob got all of the other parts he needed from MG specialists, with most being obtained from Lou and John Shorten. 'Lou has been a Magnette owner since 1957,' says Bob. 'She is President of the MG Car Club Z and Farina Magnette Register. John is a highly skilled panel maker, metalworker and restorer. Among the items the Shortens provided were the aftermarket rear flasher plinths, which have been painted body colour. The flashers are on a separate toggle switch and there are hazard lights, too. The control box is original, but the innards are new. I did have a replica period battery, but it now has a plain black one from, of all things, a Nissan 4x4. I fitted tripod headlights that have the sidelight incorporated. The original sidelights are now flashers fitted with orange bulbs.'

Having finished the exterior, Bob moved on to the interior. There is something rather special about the cabin of a Magnette with its octagonal instrumentation and luxury appointments, so Bob has kept it looking almost original and it is stunning. The door cards have been replaced, as have the carpets, front squabs and the carpeted sections on the rear of the seats. Broadland Upholstery Services undertook these repairs and the recolouring, while the Shortens provided the new boot card, mat and hinge kit. Seatbelts are a relatively recent and very sensible addition. Inertia-reel units, they were professionally installed by Quickfit Safety Belt Services. No radio is fitted, although Bob has considered one as it would help while away the hours on the many long runs this car undertakes. Bob believes in using his MGs and he insists on keeping them in A1 condition mechanically.

The braking system sports new hoses, linings and copper pipes, while the master cylinder has been overhauled and fitted with stainless steel inserts. Magnette brakes are good, if a little on the heavy side. Bob reckons that adding a servo, fitted using existing but superfluous holes, has made all the difference. He also uses synthetic brake fluid. The dampers are the originals, but they've been overhauled. However, as far as the tyres are concerned, Bob's eschewed originality and the crossplies have made way for Michelin ZX radials. The engine's been converted for unleaded, but Bob feels it's probably due for a check over, as is the gearbox which has a slightly weak third ratio.

'MG ownership is rather special,' says Bob, 'and the Magnette is a rather special car. It's a joy to own, a full four-seater. The big plus, of course, is that MG badge. The Magnette is a proper MG.' ⊕

**Above: Palmer's design also wore a Wolseley grille, but MG badge was the sporting choice.
Below: Bob Hough, with the ZB Magnette that brings him so much pleasure.**

TECH SPEC

932 HPD – 1958 MG ZB Magnette

Chassis

Unitary construction body, welded steel.
Wheelbase: 8ft 4in
Track: 4ft 3in
Suspension: Front: coil, upper wishbone, lower transverse link, front and rear reaction arms.
Rear: live axle with semi-elliptic leaf springs.
Dampers: Girling finned telescopic front and rear

Steering

Rack & pinion
Turning circle: 37.5ft

Brakes

Lockheed hydraulic 10in drums front and rear

Wheels

Ventilated steel disc bolt-on
Rim size: 4J x 15
Tyre Size: 5.50 x 15

Engine

Four-cylinder in-line, pushrod ohv
Twin SU 1¼in H2 carburettors (ZA)
Twin SU 1½in H4 carburettors (ZB)
Cubic capacity: 1489cc
Power output: 60bhp@4600rpm
– 68bhp@5200-5400rpm
Torque: 78lb.ft@3000rpm, 83lb.ft@3000rpm

Gearbox

Four-speed manual, synchro on top three ratios
Mph/1000rpm: 15.25 (ZA) 16.32 (ZB)

Performance

Max. speed: ZA 80mph, ZB 86.5mph
Acceleration: 0-50mph ZA 15.6secs, ZB 13secs
Overall fuel consumption: ZA 24-32mpg,
ZB 23-30mpg

Numbers built

ZA 18,076, ZB standard 10,722, ZB Varitone 7803, Manumatic 496

Naylor Brothers

RESTORATIONS

'When Only The Best Is Good Enough'

For over 40 years the name of Naylor Brothers has been synonymous with the very finest standards of craftsmanship. From Triple M, T-Type, MGA, MGB and C, and through to Austin Healey.

Restorations that undeniably stand the test of time.

Specialists in:

- Bodywork & coachwork restoration
- Mechanical & electrical renovation
- Chassis renovation & manufacture
- Competition preparation

If you are looking for the best for full or part restoration, or routine service, contact the team.

Tel: +44 (0)1274 585161   Fax: +44 (0)1274 532772
Email: alastair@naylorbrothers.co.uk

www.naylorbrothers.co.uk

Airedale Garage, Hollins Hill, Shipley, West Yorkshire BD17 7QN England

Open 8.30am - 5pm Mon-Fri. Saturday by appointment

A Spritely ma

no-frills sports car? Already we are thinking Austin-Healey Sprite and MG Midget, because nothing before or since has so perfectly encapsulated low-budget, wind-in-the-hair motoring. It was in May 1958 that the Sprite was launched to a world which was familiar with cheap sports cars – but usually associated them with flawed specials, flexible chassis and wayward handling.

Compared with its contemporaries, the Sprite was virtually perfect in every way. You wouldn't think so from the spec, though. A 948cc BMC A-series engine. Front suspension from the Austin A35. Drum brakes. Quarter-elliptic rear leaf springs. An A35 gearbox and rear axle. A

Morris Minor steering rack. A body so basic that it didn't even include a boot lid. Tiny sliding side windows and the most primitive hood possible. Talk about the sum being greater than the parts!

How did this work? By being stitched together around a monocoque body/chassis so stiff that it took even its own designers by surprise. With little in the way of body roll and a wonderfully precise, high-ratio steering set-up, the Sprite would react to a driver's every input.

Later Sprites and the similar MG Midgets that followed were granted larger engines, more fulsome interiors and much-improved weather gear. But for character, for unadulterated fun, it's the early cars that win – and we have three of the best for you here.

chine

Celebrating the best low-budget, mass-production sports car ever made with three of the most important examples in existence

Words: David Lillywhite Pictures: John Colley

Clockwise from below: **Pre-production Sprite; Midget coupé was one of three racers; Super Sprite is unique.**

PBL 75

'This must be one of the most photographed cars of all time'

Below left: The Sprite was a real exercise in going back to basics, not even a boot lid being provided.
Below centre: Minimalist theme continues inside, with hollow door shells adding to limited elbow room.
Below right: By accident or design, it is that cheeky nose which gave the Frogeye its memorable nickname.

Sprite

This is the one. The most important Sprite in the world. It's a beauty, perfectly restored and only recently arrived back in the UK after over 40 years in relatively quiet exile down under. We're glad to have PBL 75 (chassis number AN5/507) back.

Leaf through original Sprite publicity material and you'll find PBL popping up with remarkable regularity – but there's much more to its history than being a mere camera star. It was one of a small batch of Sprites built between November 1957 and early January 1958, the first true examples to be produced after testing of Q2, which itself was the second of the only two Sprite prototypes built.

No one has been able to confirm how many cars were built in this first batch, but we do know that PBL 75 was registered in January 1958 (along with sister car PBL 74) and went on to be used as a test and development car in the French Alps and at MIRA, where it was subjected to 1000 miles of the dreaded pavé. It was this testing that led to the discovery of a weakness in the chassis (see *Productionising the Sprite* on p32), rectified in production by welding plates into the rear inner wheelarch and floor area. The plates in PBL 75 are bolted in rather than welded, though, just one of several points that identify it as something special.

Meanwhile, PBL 75 was on its way to stardom, being photographed by BMC's Head of Publications Ron Beech, with a pretty blonde in both left- and right-hand seats. Ron's pictures were widely used across adverts, posters, postcards, books, press packs and magazines, making PBL 75 a real star. Sadly, efforts to track down the blonde model have so far failed.

Roy Salvadori was also filmed in PBL 75, with ex-racer John Bolster doing the commentating. 'You will never tire of driving the Sprite' was one of his suitably plummy proclamations, and the stills from the resultant publicity film showing the car again appear across all manner of PR material. From there, PBL 75 was prepared for the press launch of the Sprite at Monte Carlo in 1958. It is suspected that this particular machine didn't actually make it to Monaco though, but instead stayed behind for yet more magazine road tests – so many, in fact, that Geoffrey Healey later commented that 'PBL 75 must be one of the most photographed cars of all time'.

Once the fuss of the launch had died down, PBL was relegated to a more sedate life as a Healey family runaround, before passing through numerous owners. But in 1965 it was bought by Phil Evett who, two years later, emigrated to Australia, taking PBL 75 with him. The car was restored between 1973 and '84, and then again between 1998 and 2006. Early in 2007 it was sold to its current owner and shipped back to England, coincidentally and fortuitously just in time for the model's 50th birthday celebrations in 2008.

Of the other early Sprites, PBL 74 is known to exist but is hidden away in, apparently, a very poor state and unseen in public for years. Another early car, chassis AN5/505, is in Mississippi, USA. Prototype Q1 has been lost, while it is thought that Q2 was used to build the Super Sprite, which we feature overleaf.

So you see, PBL 75 is still quite a star.

❯

Right: Chassis was recycled Sprite prototype, but every exterior panel was extensively altered for the Super Sprite.

364 EAC

Super Sprite

With hindsight it seems an odd project. But ensconced in London's infamous Steering Wheel Club in 1957, Donald Healey and Leonard Lee, Chairman of engine manufacturer Coventry Climax, clearly thought differently. There they conceived the idea of a lower-cost successor to the successful Austin-Healey 100S sports racer. It would be based around the soon-to-be-launched Sprite, but would be powered by a Coventry Climax FWA engine.

And so was born the XQHS Super Sprite, as its works designation went, chassis number ST469 (ST stood for Special Test). Almost inevitably, the project was delayed by the launch of the Sprite and the early production problems that went with it, but by late 1958 a unique lightweight alloy body had been fashioned by the Donald Healey Motor Company's chief panel man Bill Buckingham, working from a design by Les Ireland.

As you can see, the styling was strikingly different from the Frogeye's, with a deep swage line, conventionally positioned headlights and a front-hinged bonnet for improved engine access. It was a full four inches wider than the Frogeye, with every exterior panel – even the sills – completely different. There's nothing in the way of weatherproofing, though, and the windscreen is a cut-down Sprite item.

Under the skin, it was all conventional Sprite. The chassis is almost certainly that of the prototype known as Q2, as confirmed by chief experimental engineer Roger Menadue and backed up by the many handmade sections still visible – for example, the unused bonnet hinge boxes on the bulkhead are riveted in rather than welded, and the inner wings are clearly not machine-pressed.

Coventry Climax had provided one of its R&D engines, which was mated to the stock BMC gearbox. All the same, the front crossmember and the battery tray had to be altered to accommodate the longer engine, but the only other serious mechanical change over the Sprite was the four-wheel disc brakes, a first for the model and a big improvement over the tiny drums used all round on the road car. The Super Sprite consequently served as a test bed for the disc-braked Sebring Sprite works race cars.

The Healeys had big plans for the Super Sprite project: big enough to require BMC funding. Full costings to build an initial production batch were handed over to BMC, but (perhaps not surprisingly) to no avail. In his book *More Healeys*, Geoff Healey explained: 'BMC would never agree to it being put into production and finally squashed the project, telling us not to work with engine manufacturers from outside the group.'

So instead, the Super Sprite became a mobile test bed and general fun car, run by the Healey family on trade plates until finally being road registered in September 1962 and sold on. It passed to club racer Barrie Hart for £625, who raced it until 1966. At some point before 1970 the Coventry Climax engine was replaced by a tweaked 1098cc A-series, never to return – the Super Sprite's current owner would love to track down Coventry Climax serial number FWA/ET/515/6156.

By 1974 the Super Sprite had covered 24,000 miles and had gained the rear lights it currently wears rather than the individual Lucas units with which it started life. It went through a variety of custodians, gained a respray, and eventually ended up with its current keepers in 2006. It's never been restored and even now the mileage is a mere 30,100. Just as the Healeys did, the present owners use it as a fun car – and being 150kg lighter than a stock Frogeye, it sure is a lot of fun...

›

Right: Profile was supposedly inspired by the Aston Martin DB4GT.

Midget coupé

Yes, this is a works-built MG Midget, even if it does look more like an MGB. No, it's not one of the famous 'Jacobs Midgets'. In fact, it's the little-known third of just three coupés built by the factory in 1962, designed for racing and successful thanks to reduced weight and improved aerodynamics.

Former works MG driver and later private team entrant Dick Jacobs had been left without an MG model to campaign following the demise of the MGA. And then, the story goes, he was sat at his desk contemplating a side profile of the new Midget in the launch brochure, while also flicking through an issue of *The Motor*, which happened to include a similar side profile of the Aston Martin DB4GT. Jacobs superimposed one on top of the other, had his eureka moment and sped off to the BMC competitions department, where his enthusiasm infected General Manager John Thornley and Chief Engineer Syd Enever.

And so Jacobs got his two Midget coupés (the Jacobs Midgets as they're now known), while a third, near-identical coupé – this car – was driven by John Milne, an MG works driver based in Scotland and well connected in the Scottish motorsport scene. Milne later bought the car, and it's now campaigned by stepson James Willis and is a familiar sight at European circuits.

The three coupés were true giant-killers, with the Jacobs cars achieving great success in English club racing and Milne's doing the same north of the border – but also in the famed Nürburgring 500km, where it raced in 1963, '64 and '65, achieving strong class results (third, fourth and fifth respectively).

The secret of these cars' many successes was their clever construction, using the steel chassis of the Sprite and Midget with a lightweight aluminium body attached by rivets and epoxy resin. This lowered weight to 1232lb, but it was the reduction in drag by adding the droop snoot and coupé roof that really made the difference – it was reckoned that at 100mph the coupé needed 13bhp less than the standard car.

Every additional horsepower counted, for the engine was a mere 995cc initially, derived from the maximum-capacity overbore of the standard 948cc unit. In 1963, though, the Milne car ran with a supercharger, but this caused the motor to become so hot that it would overheat if it remained stationary for more than about 30 seconds. Torque was impressive, however, for it was Enever's intention that the car would be able to lap Brands Hatch almost exclusively in top gear.

Then came a normally aspirated 1293cc A-series, followed by an 1138cc in 1965, but things were moving on and the coupé's last gasp was in Modsports in the late 1960s, briefly sporting nasty wheelarch extensions. Then it sat around, making occasional appearances, until a restoration and racing resurrection in the 1990s. James is planning a supercharger next, but this time with more efficient cooling. Now that will be impressive!

Below: Reinstating a supercharger is on the jobs-to-do list – bonnet already has a bulge to accommodate SU.
Bottom: Midget heritage is clear, but coupé weighed far less thanks to lightweight aluminium body panels.

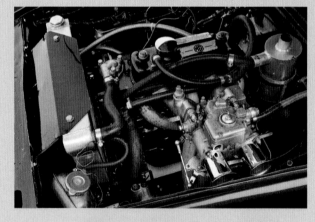

Below: With its light weight and aerodynamic body, the coupé could almost lap Brands Hatch in top gear.

'MG had always maintained no sports car cheaper than its £900 MGA was viable'

Above: Miss World, Penny Coelen, perches on a Sprite at '58 Motor Show.
Left: Sprite prototype Q1 pictured in 1964 – where is it now?
Below: Super Sprite being hand-crafted in aluminium.

Productionising the Sprite

Rivalry, jealousy and revenge: the plot of a Shakespeare play? No, just the story of how that other Warwickshire-born national treasure, the Sprite, reached production in the late 1950s. The problem with the British Motor Corporation was that it never really existed: the 'merger' in 1952 between Austin and the Morris empire – actually an Austin takeover – left deep and lasting resentment on both sides. The former bitter rivals started co-operating only when they perceived the outside threat from Triumph and Leyland, by which time it was too late.

Within BMC, the MG Car Company managed to carve itself a niche as the group's specialist sports car factory. But it didn't help that BMC's abrasive chairman Leonard Lord had crossed swords with MG people many years before, when he was working as Morris's right-hand man. A subsequent row between the two men had seen Lord leave to join Austin, vowing to take his revenge on Morris.

Since the formation of BMC, the MG factory had been making the Austin-Healey 100, designed by the small independent Healey firm and adopted by Austin. This led to a long delay in MG receiving approval for its own medium-sized sports car, the MGA. So when Leonard Lord met up with Donald Healey at the 1956 Motor Show and asked him to design a 'little bug', the kind of cheap runabout a chap could keep in his bike shed, he knew there would be jealousy at MG. But Healey is said to have costed the new model at £300, whereas MG had always maintained no sports car cheaper than its £900 MGA could be economically viable.

The Healey factory had the first prototype running by Christmas. It was designed by Gerry Coker, who had styled the 100, with Donald's son Geoffrey overseeing the chassis. Code named Q1, it was presented to the Austin top brass at Longbridge, receiving the go-ahead for production on

February 20, 1957. Further development followed, after which the tooling for the body panels was made. A second prototype, Q2, was built, seemingly from production panels, probably in late autumn 1957.

When production began at MG's Abingdon factory is a moot point – records give the lowest chassis number as AN5 501, built on March 31, 1958. Actually, the first cars made are likely to have been 503 and 507 (PBL 75), which were registered in January 1958. The earliest build dates recorded in the production trace are for chassis number 556, built February 21-25 and marked 'Vienna Show', and chassis 526, built February 26-27, labelled 'Geneva Show'. Neither car made it to these events, and it seems likely they were diverted to development and tested to destruction, as both were later rebuilt. Structural problems had surfaced.

MG man Don Hayter, designer of the MGB, took part in the testing. He said: 'The Sprite came to us having supposedly been fully tested, but I think it had only ever been driven on the road. I don't think it had been on the pavé at MIRA and perhaps hadn't been driven at all fully loaded. I took one of the very first models off the MG production line and the first thing I did with it was to fill the tank, pack the boot and attach a luggage rack with a 35lb load, just like owners would. Problems soon showed up – the cars were folding apart along the rear bulkhead.' The production line was put into reverse and trim removed from the 80 or so examples built, for strengthening plates and brackets to be added. March 31 is probably the date the production line restarted.

So, if the way the Sprite reached production was occasionally a comedy of errors, it certainly wasn't a full-blown Shakespearean tragedy – that would come later with the Leyland years.

Tom Coulthard

Above: Wearing a modern MG shade of Tahiti Blue, Mike's Sprite has married the best of old and new into one great package.

Reinventing the wheels

This Sprite had reached not so much a mid-life crisis, but more an end-of-life crisis. With its future hanging by a knife-edge, it took some radical changes to keep the spirit alive Words and pictures: Simon Goldsworthy

his is a tale that will unite and divide our readers in equal measure. Certainly there are elements in it that will strike a chord in each of us. So when we say that Mike Harrison bought a ten-year old Sprite in 1977 and used it as everyday transport, we are sure that most of us have fond MG memories of doing something similar. When we add that he ran it on a shoestring while at university, a few more heads will be nodding in recognition. And when we mention that the Sprite took Mike and his wife Ann around Devon on their honeymoon and all around Ireland and Cornwall on their holidays, we reckon that most readers will understand exactly how this car became a part of the family, to have and to hold long after it had fallen into seemingly terminal disrepair.

But not everything is quite as simple and straightforward as it appears. The car that Mike is driving today is indeed that same Sprite, but in many ways it is also a different vehicle. In part, that is because it has acquired a new Heritage bodyshell along the way, but there is a whole lot more besides. For example, it is somewhat quicker off the mark than it ever was in Mike's shoestring days – hardly surprising when you learn that it now has three times as much power as it had back then. Yep, that's 210bhp under the bonnet! Back in the late 1970s, Mike would have needed to buy both an MGB and an MGB GT V8 to get that ❯

Above: **Mike has no regrets about the many changes he has made to his Sprite, saying that it is now the car he always wanted to have.**

sort of power!

Obviously those are not the sort of power gains that can be wrung from the original A-series engine, so we'll stop teasing and reveal that Mike has had his car converted to K-series power. At which point, all those readers who had been nodding in sympathetic agreement earlier on will split into two distinct camps: those who want to know how the conversion was done and whether it was worth all the effort, and those who fail to see why Mike was not satisfied with the car that Abingdon saw fit to offer.

Well, we'll get to the technical details shortly for those who want to know, but first let's fill in some of the background that may help explain why the car turned out the way it did. For starters, what I haven't mentioned is that Mike used to be heavily into motorsport, helping his twin brother Doug to build various road and rally Minis and the like, and then navigating on road rallies while his brother Doug drove, finally co-driving on stage rallies in a Peugeot 205 for his good friend Russell. Mike also used to take the wheel for autotests, car rallies and the occasional treasure hunt. So he's a man who likes speed and isn't afraid to tinker.

Mind you, the only place his Sprite was going quickly was downhill. It had been taken off the road in 1983 and stuck in a garage. Mike used to pull it out every now and then, sweep up the rust and then push it back in. Each time, it was a little bit lighter, and the temptation was to get rid of it and free up some garage space.

> ## 'An alternative route was moving up the alphabet from A-series to K-series'

It was Ann who wouldn't let him do this, saying the Sprite was part of the family. So in 2005, Mike pulled it out of the garage for the last time, determined to make a decision. At first glance it looked reasonable, but poking it with a screwdriver revealed just how little metal there was left. Clearly its resurrection was beyond Mike's welding skills, so he took plenty of pictures and sent them off to some specialists. They came back with restoration quotes of £8000-10,000.

That was too rich for Mike. But a new Heritage bodyshell cost around £3500 [current retail price is £4700], and Mike reckoned he could build his car into one of these himself. That would mean, though, that it would no longer be exactly the same Mk3 Sprite as Heritage only offered the later Sprite MkIV/Midget MkIII and 1500 bodyshells, which came with the shaped rear cockpit to accommodate the folding-hood design. That sowed the seeds of change in Mike's mind. It just happened to coincide with a feature in *Practical Performance Car* magazine looking at modifying options for the Midget. As that article pointed out, tuning the A-series to 100bhp is feasible, but going much deeper into three figures can be cripplingly expensive and leave you with power characteristics that are fine on track, but next to useless on the road.

An alternative route was moving up the alphabet from A-series to K-series. This was an approach being championed by Tim Fenna at Frontline Developments in Bath, and the article spelled out the options in great detail. Here was a car that could hold its own with Porsches and Subarus, and while it was still not cheap to build it was certainly far cheaper than either of those alternatives. Yet what really sold Mike on this conversion was not the fact that PPC's test car was good for 0-60mph in just 4.6 seconds, but that it was even faster from 60-0mph. In rallying, you soon learn that good brakes can be even more important than outright power.

The conversion process is not especially dramatic, the main chopping consisting of taking a couple of inches out of the heater tray. Frontline also bolts on some additional suspension mounts to allow upgrades to suit the power, and strengthens the front chassis rails and the sills. The gearbox tunnel required

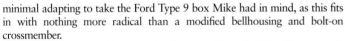

Above: Finished machine owes much to the engineering and vision of Frontline.

Above: Racy bonnet pins keep everything fixed in place when the going gets heavy.

Above: Leather-clad MGB seats bring with them the bonus of good head restraints.

Above: This is a car that is equally at home being driven to the shops or on track.

minimal adapting to take the Ford Type 9 box Mike had in mind, as this fits in with nothing more radical than a modified bellhousing and bolt-on crossmember.

With the decision made to go for change, Mike called Tim Fenna to ask whether he would want a new shell before or after painting to carry out the necessary modifications. As it turned out, Tim had a brand new shell in the workshop that had already been converted and was looking for a new home. Mike had it resprayed in MGF Tahiti Blue and took delivery of a bare shell in September 2005.

He also bought Frontline's modified suspension to put on it. In this case, that consisted of vertically mounted rear telescopic dampers, one-inch lowered springs, RTL (Rear Traction control Link) and eight-inch disc brakes on the back, Frontline telescopic conversion with reinforced upper wishbone in place of the old lever arm dampers up front, uprated one-inch lowered springs and 10in vented discs. Plus an 11/16-inch anti-roll bar to improve roll stiffness and Polybushes all round. More money was spent on Frontline's unique fine-spline uprated half shafts with matching limited-slip diff, and on its double hub bearing kit.

Mike then set about transferring whatever bits he could from the old Sprite, having them refurbished or exchanged when necessary. As will be clear by this point, there was not an endless supply of bits to transfer, but the list of admittedly minor pieces that made the migration was still fairly lengthy. Mike found it was a real pleasure to be working on what was effectively a new car fitted with new parts, although it also helped to have the old shell alongside as a reference guide. But there was a tear in his eye when he had finally taken every last widget off and it was time to have the old shell hauled away.

In January 2008, the now rolling shell was packed back off to Frontline to have an engine fitted. Mike had been put off doing that himself by the fuel-injection and engine-management systems, but he also wanted Frontline to road test the car as he had little idea where to start on fine tuning the suspension to get the most from it.

Above: Doing without the bumpers has given the Sprite a more competitive air.
Right: Single-box exhaust and Frontline 4-2-1 manifold help the K-series to breathe.

'I couldn't rebuild my old car, nor could I build it as a Mk3 Sprite with a new shell'

that he worked out with Tim are a compromise between road and competition use, giving a slightly firm ride in normal conditions but not requiring him to grub about changing settings for autotests and track days. The result is a slightly choppy ride at low speeds, which Mike assures us smooths out once you hit 70mph. At these speeds and when braking hard, the solid top link in the front suspension makes itself most noticeable, the Sprite feeling far more stable than it ever did before. The steering seems pin sharp too, not so much because of modifications, but because everything old and tired has been replaced.

So does Mike have any regrets about making such a radical transformation to his faithful Sprite? 'Absolutely none,' he declares with conviction. 'It is the best thing I have ever done. The thing I love about this car is that it is docile and tractable enough to drive down to the shops if you want, but you can also drive it to a track and put in a very creditable performance without lifting a spanner. I've already booked a couple of track days, as well as a training day to teach me the basics of hillclimbing. I've never done that form of motorsport before, but now I've got the car to tackle it and I will be giving it a go next spring.'

So Mike clearly loves his new Sprite, as do the rest of his family. But where does that leave the two camps we talked at the beginning of the article? Well, the modifiers are probably thinking already of which changes they can make on their own particular budgets. Those who prefer originality may be impressed with the end result, but probably remain unconvinced this is in fact the same car. I guess that since it has a new bodyshell, a new engine and a new gearbox you can understand where they are coming from, but I will leave the last word on this particular subject to Mike:

'I knew I couldn't rebuild my original model, and neither could I build it as a Mk3 Sprite using a new shell. And since there are lots of very fine restored cars around already, quite frankly, what was the point? I now have the machine I always wanted, and you know the funny thing? Despite the radical and extensive modifications, getting behind the wheel still feels as comfortable and familiar as putting on an old pair of shoes. An old pair of shoes and a huge grin, each and every time.'

Originally Mike had planned to fit a 1.6 engine. By the time he had finished talking to Ed Braclik at Frontline, though, he had gone for a 1.8VVC, rebuilt to 1900cc with a fully ported head and fitted with solid cams, solid lifters, large injectors, forged rods and pistons, strengthened main bearings and a lightened flywheel – Ed is obviously a great salesman! Not that Mike is complaining: even running the car in for 900 miles at no more than 3000-3500rpm, it was faster than his old model had been and just as much fun to drive.

After a trip to BETC Racing in Oxfordshire for final tuning on its rolling road, Mike was finally able to start exploring the limits of his revitalised Sprite. Straight-line speed is, as you would expect, absolutely stunning, but the suspension is equally brilliant. Mike had worried that the LSD could make the back end a little skittish, but this is not the case, even in the wet. That rear axle is already located by Frontline's RTL installation to stop all the K-series power from winding it up, and Mike has since also added anti-tramp bars to keep the back axle firmly in its place under heavy acceleration. The suspension settings

■ **For helping to make his dream car a reality, Mike would like to thank Tim Fenna and Ed Braclik at Frontline Developments (01225 852777, www. frontlinedevelopments.com) for help and enthusiasm, as well as Sussex Car Parts (01403 711551, www.sussexclassiccar.co.uk) and Moss (0800 281182, www.moss-europe.co.uk) for their ready supply of parts. For availability and prices of Heritage bodyshells, contact sales@bmh-ltd.com or call 01993 707200.**

MG 1100

MG 1100
Historic race car

In its time, BMC's 1100 range was the country's best selling car. The MG model was deemed to be the 'sporty' version but, unlike many other top sellers, the 1100 was not a frequent visitor to the racetrack. This is one of the few that is still being raced in historic events

I n the summer of 1962, regulations for the Motor Six-Hour race were announced. After reading them, Dick Jacobs of Mill Garage, who had previously raced MGAs, Magnette and a brace of special bodied Midgets, decided that the MG version of the Morris 1100 that was due to be announced three days before the race would be in with a chance of a Class win.

Stuart Turner, BMC Competitions Department Manager, provided some technical help based on the existing Morris model which itself had only been out for two months. University Motors, the distributor that supplied cars to Mill Garage, let them have an MG version two weeks early, registered JWC 111.

This enabled Dick to run in the MG 1100 before the car was race prepared. The compression ratio was increased and the 1¼in SUs were replaced with 1½in versions. Dick calculated a careful fuel strategy, which meant the MG could skip the final fuel stop. On Saturday October 6 1962, Jacob's drivers Alan Foster and Andrew Hedges did indeed win the 1300 Class in this prestigious race having covered 157 laps of Brands Hatch.

Fast forward 42 years and another racing competitor sat down and started a thought process that would also conclude with an MG 1100. In September 2004, CCK's Shaun Rainford wanted an unusual saloon car that he and John Rhodes could share in the next year's Top Hat series, a vehicle so different that it would be invited to race at the Goodwood Revival Meeting. The search for an MG 1100 was on.

After several blanks had been drawn, a 1966 example turned up in

Right: John Rhodes brakes for the Goodwood Chicane.
Below left: JWC 111 on its way to a Class win in the 1962 Motor Six-Hour Race.
Below right: Shaun Rainford at Goodwood.

nearby Seaford. The vendor had bought the car from a friend who had shipped it back from Arizona before converting it to right hand drive. Finding the car was exactly as described, Shaun bought it on the spot and, after a fish and chip supper, drove GUF 960D home.

Once in the workshop, the 1100 was stripped and work started in earnest. The car was virtually free of corrosion, just requiring one tiny section to be welded into the floorpan. The shell was then seam welded before they designed a roll cage, which was then made for them by Fabricage. This incorporates a front crossmember on the floor to prevent the engine coming back into the cockpit and thus protect the driver's legs. There are two front door bars and a crossmember which runs across the back seat, which also provides the rear mountings for the safety harness.

Heeding stories of the odd transverse engine shedding a flywheel under extreme circumstances, Shaun got the lads to weld a sheet of ¼in steel plate onto the bulkhead. The extra weight was worth it just for the peace of mind.

Following meticulous preparation, the shell was painted in its Connaught Green over Old English White livery, with the cage also finished in matching green before being bolted in place. Front quarter lights have been retained and all the window winders operate correctly.

The suspension was 'dried' for safety reasons, then both subframes overhauled and trued along with the rear trailing arms before being bolted direct to the shell. The rear anti-roll bar was removed as it would have hindered sensible cornering on the track.

The transverse A-series engine was stripped and cleaned, then rebuilt to racing tolerances with Omega pistons. After it had been wedged and bladed, the original cast iron crank was polished whilst the conrods were lightened and polished. The whole bottom end assembly was then balanced. Piper ground a race cam to what has become known as CCK1 spec, and this runs with lightened followers and 1½:1 ratio rockers. A Morspeed cylinder head was bolted on using a copper competition head gasket. A 12.5:1 compression ratio sounds high, but is safe when run on leaded four star.

The original radiator cools sufficiently – export versions were uprated. The fan is driven by toothed belt and pulleys – at high revs, standard V-belts can turn themselves inside out and come off. A 13-row oil cooler has been fitted in the grille aperture, offset to the driver's side so as not to interrupt the air flow to the radiator. Breathers from the rocker box and gearbox discharge into a custom made aluminium catch tank bolted on the inner wing adjacent to the oil cooler. To prevent oil blowing out, a spring holds the dipstick in place.

Above: **John Rhodes (left) and owner Shaun Rainford with the car (top); engine bay looks fairly standard except for the breathers, catch tank and larger SU carbs.**

GUF 960D

'Today's tyre compounds will restrict the tyre smoking antics he was so well known for'

A Jack Knight straight-cut close-ratio set has been fitted in the gearbox, which has a 1:1 straight cut drop gear and a 3.7 limited slip diff. Standard driveshafts are coupled to the stronger Cooper S CVJs. BMC's original steel fuel tank is retained under the boot floor, and a boot mounted Facet Red Top pump feeds the 1½in SU carburettors fitted with Pipercross socks. The three-into-one exhaust manifold runs into a racing silencer and exits via a 2¼in tailpipe. Whilst the note is rorty, it satisfies the noise scrutineers.

Like most competition cars, the fuel and brake lines run along the floor inside the car. Brakes are standard with 8in discs at the front and 8x1.25in drums at the rear. Pads are of harder material but rear linings are standard on the basis that they do very little anyway. The servo that came with the car was discarded to allow the driver to experience maximum response through the large aluminium brake pedal. Besides this sits a period Paddy Hopkirk throttle pedal.

To help balance weight distribution, the battery has been moved from the boot and is housed in a sealed box behind the passenger seat. This also means it is further from the fuel tank and the shorter leads minimise voltage drop.

A spares car provided a set of original Dunlop aftermarket alloy wheels. The refurbished 12x5in rims now adorn the MG fitted with Dunlop 4.5x12 L-section, CR65 racing tyres, a requirement of the regs. Experimenting with pressures has resulted in running 36psi all round with negligible understeer.

To race at Goodwood, the 1100 retains original trim, including rear seats. Corbeau specially made the four slot, high back driver's seat with its Luke four point, 3in strap safety harness. Other safety requirements include a laminated windscreen, front and rear towing eyes and a Lifeline 2.4-litre fire extinguisher. There is also a high intensity brake light mounted on the rear parcel shelf. The bonnet remains hinged, but is now secured at the front by two pins, while the original boot lid is retained by three Dzus Fasteners.

An 8000rpm electronic rev counter sits on top of the dashboard, with a combined oil/water gauge and the obligatory cut-out switch bolted on brackets below. Key start has been retained; the only other switches are lights, wiper washers and indicator stalk. The large steering wheel has been replaced with a 13in leather rimmed version, which provides more cockpit space. It was not necessary to prune the length of the gearlever, still complete with its well-worn wooden knob.

Following testing by both John Rhodes and Shaun Rainford, the 1100 is beautifully set up. The owner comments: 'It is totally neutral, just like sitting in your armchair – point and squirt. It is a car that you can attack the bends in.' Power comes in at just a shade under 4000rpm and the tacho is red lined at 7250. On CCK's rolling road it showed 80bhp at the wheels, which equates to around 120 at the flywheel.

Rhodes is very complimentary about the car and is genuine in his belief that the preparation is up to the standard of those John Cooper Minis he raced in the 1960s. With a smile on his face, he also admits that today's tyre compounds are harder and stronger than those of that era, which should restrict the tyre smoking antics he was so well known for in those days. Many will no doubt recall his 'Smokey John Rhodes' nickname.

The atmosphere at the Goodwood Revival Meeting is unique, Jean Rhodes commenting that it was particularly poignant for them as her husband was such a regular competitor at the circuit in its original hey-day. Throughout the weekend, the car did everything he asked of it and John's best lap during the first part of The St Mary's Trophy Race was 1min 45secs.

During his race, Shaun got his lap times down to 1min 44secs and enjoyed great dices with the Mercedes-Benz 300SE, Toyota Corona, Ford Anglia and Vauxhall VX 4/90, all of which he passed, only to lose the places again as the result of a gremlin in the fuel system. Despite this, Shaun summed up the weekend by saying: 'It was fabulous. I would like to thank Lord March for inviting us to take part in what is undoubtedly the best motor racing event in the world.'

CHROME-BUMPER MGBS

Driving the I, II and MkIII of MG's shining star

Words: Martyn Wise Photography: Paul Harmer

I f only one model could be regarded as the epitome of the classic car, then surely the evergreen MGB would be amongst the front runners. With more than 500,000 examples built over a production run that lasted nearly 20 years, the MGB is regarded by enthusiasts around the world as the definitive classic car.

Spawning a specialist supply, restoration and service industry, the MGB has become an icon of the classic car boom years of the late 1980s. The clean lines of Syd Enever's design, mated to simple but effective vault-like mechanicals in a comfortable two-seater package have provided the MGB with an endearing quality which has not only stood the test of time, but also transcended the generations to attract admirers who appreciate MG's sports car for the common man.

Although a product of the swinging 1960s, it was during the Thatcherite boom years that the B scaled new heights as a growing and increasingly affluent middle-aged and middle-class market turned to the classic car scene to recapture their youth. And where better than the aspirational 'B roadster, which was once unattainable but now affordable in their bid for wind-in-the-hair motoring?

Encouraged by a growing band of wannabe owners, a whole industry appeared to spring up overnight to cater for the insatiable demand for a classic ›

MGB. Rust-free examples were repatriated from the States in their droves, while rotten home-grown examples could be refettled with new bodyshells and panels made on the original presses. Suddenly, immaculate MGBs restored to original as-new standards were changing hands at more than ten times the 1962 car's original £949 asking price.

The boom years couldn't last but, when the classic car bubble burst in the recession-hit early 1990s, the MGB fared better than most. If anything, the burgeoning prices had taken this humblest of roadsters once again beyond the reach of those to whom it had appealed and the enforced repositioning in the marketplace returned the sports car back to real devotees.

Today the MGB roadster continues to be the first choice for many looking to get on the classic ladder. Restored examples abound, and for all but the most committed DIY restorer, purchasing an original or renovated car is the most sensible and cost-effective route to ownership. Selection is also relatively easy. The shape and look of the MGB roadster remained almost unaltered during its 18-year production run, save for the 'rubber-bumper' model which was introduced in late 1974 in a nod towards US market safety requirements.

But while even the least informed buyer is aware of the simple choice between 'chrome' and 'rubber' MGBs, few appreciate the subtle differences which separate the three – or some may argue four – variants spanning the 'chrome' era from 1962-1974.

Introduced at the 1962 Earls Court Motor Show alongside the MG 1100 saloon, the MGB was well received by the motoring press of the day, who appreciated the new, modern design afforded by the monocoque shell. Replacing the successful MGA was never going to be easy, but chief designer Syd Enever and his team proved successful in producing a combined package of looks, performance and handling which were right for the space-age 1960s just as its predecessor had been for the 'never-had-it-so-good' decade.

In an overall package which was shorter than the MGA, the B was far

> **'Few appreciate the subtle differences which separate the three (or some may argue four) variants of the chrome era'**

roomier inside the two-seater cockpit as well as offering greater luggage capacity. Construction was pretty well straightforward, with the Pressed Steel body/chassis structure giving the MGB its inherent strength. Following the conventional front-engine, rear-wheel-drive format, the flat floorpan rose over a central transmission tunnel which was joined to the front bulkhead with a box-section. A rear box-section ran across the car behind the seats, while side members ran forwards to bear the engine and front suspension and rearwards over the back axle to act as spring hangers. Front wings were then bolted on and rear wings welded, essentially leaving the outside bodywork unstressed.

Although the MGB carried over the live 'banjo' back axle from the MGA, which sits on semi-elliptic leaf springs, the front suspension was a direct descendent from the Y-type and TD with independent wishbones and coil springs mounted on a detachable sub-frame. With hydraulic lever-arm dampers fitted both front and rear, the MGB afforded a softer suspension than the outgoing MGA.

Power came from the four-cylinder overhead-valve pushrod B-series engine which had been gradually modified over the years and stretched to 1798cc. Producing 84bhp, this gave a 0-60mph time of around 12 seconds while the

Spot the difference

MGB MkI (GHN3) Sept 1962-Oct 1967
- Three-synchro gearbox
- Three-bearing engine (up to Oct 1964)
- Pull door handles (up to Oct 1964)
- Rear 'banjo' axle
- Narrow transmission tunnel
- Wider gap between front sidelights and grille
- No reversing lights
- 'Curved' rear tail-light lens covers
- Chrome quarter-lights
- Strap-on fuel tank (up to March 1965)

MGB MkII (GHN4) Oct 1967-Oct 1969
- Four-synchro gearbox
- Rear 'tubeless' Salisbury axle (NB – also available on some late production MkI cars)
- Pre-engaged starter motor
- Reversing lights fitted
- Reclining seats available on late cars

MGB MkIII (GHN5) Oct 1969-Sept 1974
- New recessed grille in black
- Smaller drilled, three-spoke steering wheel
- Revised dash/fascia air vents (from Oct 71)
- New vinyl reclining seats
- BL emblems on front wings
- Rubber inserts on chrome over-riders
- 'Straight' rear tail-light lens covers
  Production changes from October 1972:
- New grille with chrome surround and centre bar together with black plastic 'Honeycomb' mesh
- Padded wheel (with three slatted spokes), centre console, door pulls and armrests

Below
MkI cars gained a five-bearing engine in October 1964, but never lost the three-synchro gearbox.

'It is possible to change the heart of an MGB without affecting its look, but it is a matter of individual preference'

MGB went on to a top speed of more than 100mph. Not scintillating figures by today's standards, but more impressive if viewed over 40 years ago. On the road this translates into a pleasant driving experience, with reasonable performance allied to predictable handling. Those looking to extract that bit more from their B are well catered for with a host of aftermarket products designed to improve both power and handling.

Today it is possible to completely change the heart of an MGB without affecting its aesthetic period look, but such alterations are a matter of individual preference. And while enhanced performance may appeal to owners already familiar with the MGB package, first-time buyers tend to be swayed more by originality.

For the earliest models – MkI MGBs manufactured 1962 to 1967 with chassis numbers beginning with GHN3 – that means the three-synchro gearbox and, with examples produced up to October 1964, the three-bearing engine. Other distinguishing features include, again on models up to October 1964, pull door handles and a strap-on fuel tank. All MkI MGBs come with a wider gap between the front grille and sidelights when compared to later cars, as well as a narrower transmission tunnel with a different-shaped speaker housing.

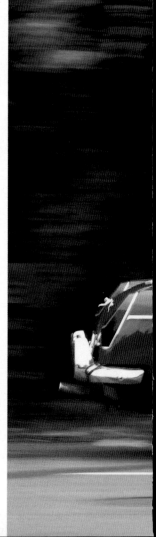

The attractive fascia features the larger, three-spoke steering wheel with centre horn push, while externally MkI cars are not fitted with reversing lights and the rear tail-lights feature 'curved' covers. Side quarter-lights are also fully chromed as opposed to the stainless steel variants which followed.

MGBs manufactured between October 1967 and October 1969 which begin with a GHN4 prefix are regarded as MkII models. The major change is the introduction of the four-synchro gearbox and the tubeless Salisbury axle. An improved starter motor was also fitted and reversing lights added. In addition, late MkIIs also featured new black reclining seats, but without headrests.

MkIII models followed in October 1969 with GHN5 chassis numbers and

changes to the cosmetics. A new, smaller, leather-bound drilled three-spoke steering wheel was introduced, while leather seats were discontinued in favour of a vinyl pattern. Externally, cars were offered with new 'Rostyle' wheels and the plastic rear tail-light covers featured 'straight' edges. For the 1971 model year, a new fascia with face-level air vents and rocker switches was introduced, along with a new lift-up armrest and brushed-nylon facings to the seat covering. The most striking changes, though, came with a revised grille. Up to late 1972, this featured a black recessed version which, it may have been felt, was complemented by the black rubber inserts on the front bumper overriders. However, the change must not have proved popular as the more traditional chrome grille re-appeared, although with a black plastic 'honeycomb' insert.

On the road there is little to choose between the three models although, as with any car which features non-synchromesh on first gear, the three-synchro examples need a little more care when changing down if the driver is to avoid the embarrassing 'crunch' at road junctions. Early models also tend to feel they have a longer throw between gears, which can sometimes delay quick changes until the gearbox is mastered.

Handling is in the true Safety Fast tradition, although sudden changes in direction and undulating roads which feature changes in camber are best taken at a more sedate speeds. The larger three-spoke steering wheel with its narrow rim is also not suited to an aggressive driving style, and perhaps it should be remembered that whilst sporting cars in their day, these early examples of the MGB are best regarded as touring cars and 40-year-old models should be treated with the respect the marque's status has earned.

Later MkII and MkIII models obviously benefit from the more familiar four-synchro gearbox, which makes for less stressful changes, while mechanical modifications also mean less general maintenance. But which is the preferred choice for the would-be buyer? Top London dealer Nigel Guild of Former Glory has sold hundreds of MGB Roadsters during his two decades in business, but he maintains there is no particular example to which buyers gravitate.

'Demand for chrome bumpers and tax-exempt cars has always been high, but beyond that people do not really show much preference,' he

Left: Wire wheels were always a popular option. Below left: Automatic gearbox was rarely selected. Below: British Racing Green remains one of the most popular colours (along with red) for chrome-bumper MGBs.

Automatic choice?

At the time of our photoshoot we were fortunate that Nigel had acquired a 1969 model with the ultra-rare automatic option. Nigel reckons this auto 'B is perhaps the finest driving example of any Roadster he's come across in 20 years trading.

After a brief test drive, it was easy to see why. The auto box was very smooth, just a slight tendency to snatch between first and second when attempting quick getaways. Once familiar, the auto made for very smooth progress through the gears, hanging onto ratios to change up at optimum revs. For a nigh-on 40-year-old car the auto offered surprisingly good acceleration, pulling strongly and evenly in response to throttle input. Ideal as a long-distance tourer and perfect in urban driving, this particular example comes with originality that is hard to find thanks to its modest 27,616 recorded miles.

Above: Leather was standard on early cars, but piped covers are a popular mod for all models.

Above: Auto gearbox isn't the only rarity on this car: original leather seats are unusual today.

Above: The MkIII saw a switch to vinyl seat facings with a knit-backed pattern in the centre panels.

Above: Upright rear lights conformed to BMC style, and were shared with contemporary Midget.

Above: MkII kept the rounded style of lens, but gained a pair of reversing lights on the tail panel.

Above: Squarer light was introduced with MkIII and lasted through rubber-bumper production.

'While sporting in their day, the earliest MGBs are now best regarded as touring cars'

says. 'They tend to come to us looking for a nice example not requiring any work other than general maintenance, and are not too interested whether it is a MkI, II or III model. Years ago everyone wanted Tartan Red or British Racing Green. These colours are still the best sellers, but they have been used on so many restorations that some buyers want something more individual.'

Having driven thousands of MGBs, what remains the dealer's choice when looking for a classic MGB Roadster? 'I like the look of the very early MkI models but prefer the driveability from the early 1970s,' says Nigel. It seems that if even one of the most experienced MGB devotees cannot make up his mind then, if you're in the market for a classic 'B Roadster, the best advice is to consider all the options and enjoy your search for that perfect car.

Buying tips

Inspect bodies, particularly sills, door bottoms and wing joints for rust, even on restored/Heritage-shell cars. Replacement panels are reasonably priced, but the cost of professional fitting soon adds up. If originality is your thing, the British Motor Industry Heritage Trust at Gaydon can, for a modest fee, provide a build certificate detailing the car's chassis and engine numbers, colour, trim and any extras supplied at the time of purchase.

Cars being sold privately by club members are likely to have been looked after, especially if they have been owned for a number of years. But some private sellers overestimate the value of their cars, especially if they were expensive rebuilds of a few years ago. Many dealers have a better understanding of today's market value, and give the benefit of a warranty and other statutory purchase rights. Expect to pay between £5000-£10,000.

Thanks

Our thanks to Nigel Guild at Former Glory for supplying the test cars featured. For further details on other stock MGB Roadsters and GTs, contact 0208 991 1963 or visit www.former-glory.com.

MGB – the past reinvented

Martyn Morgan Jones revisits the MGB story and looks at the contemporary
setting that inspired this most iconic of MG sports cars

Words: Martyn Morgan Jones Photographs: John Colley

L ife seemed so much simpler back in the 1960s. Perhaps it really was. Often permissive, frequently carefree, sometimes superficial, this was certainly a transitional decade, a period of great social, cultural and economic change. Employment levels were generally high, most people were bringing home a reasonable income, and there was more free time available. It is hardly surprising then that the 'swinging 1960s' witnessed a sharp rise in consumerism and widespread enjoyment of leisure activities. At the top of many people's ever-lengthening shopping lists was a new car, and included among their leisure activities was motoring. And why not?

Britain had a car industry, roads were far less busy and, for an increasingly large number of people, driving was a pleasurable pastime.

However, at the core of all the changes the 1960s ushered in was a drive for higher standards. Expectations were shifting. What was deemed 'good enough' in the 1950s was not longer going to make the grade – the acceptable had become unacceptable. This was certainly the case with the motor industry. One of the many cars that would fail to make the transition from the 1950s to the 1960s, although it had many virtues and remained in production until June 1962, was the MGA.

The MGA was an achingly pretty model with flowing, almost organic lines. Indeed, it was so delicately drawn it was hard to believe that beneath that exquisite

Above: MGB was first open-top MG to feature door locks. The pull-handles were replaced by push-button versions and revised doors in April 1965.

exterior lay an enormously strong, heavy, but well designed box-section chassis. It was this which helped provide the MGA with its exceptionally fine handling – characteristics that elevated it above its contemporaries. The MGA didn't just handle well; it was reliable and had good performance. Plus, when driven with reasonable restraint, it proved economical. In fact, the MGA ticked every box bar one – refinement. At low-to-medium speeds, the trade-off for the delectable handling was a ride quality that could be harsh and unforgiving. What's more, noise levels were relatively high and the level of trim was quite basic.

There is no doubting the fact that the MGA set new standards in the mid-1950s, but by the 1960s the benchmark was considerably higher. Prospective buyers still coveted the traditional sports car virtues of performance and handling, but these had to be packaged together with a much higher level of comfort, sophistication and refinement.

BMC realised that if the model's MGB successor was going to succeed, especially in America where the bulk were headed, it needed to be a more contemporary design. Of course, with such a vast and oft-unwieldy organisation, many cars weren't as 'new' as they appeared. They were often the result of packaging changes, badge engineering and different marketing strategies, rather than the product of major design differences. In many ways, this was true of the MGB. It was born out of a corporate DNA, but it was always better than the sum of its familial parts.

'The MGB was a happy
marriage of looks, refinement,
performance and tradition'

Something old, something borrowed, something new!

In an ideal world Abingdon's engineers would've liked to have pushed the technical boundaries, but they were hamstrung by fiscal and bureaucratic constraints. Despite having trialled coil-sprung rear suspension, they had no choice other than to fit cost-effective and workable live axle and leaf springs to the production cars. This was basically the MGA set-up, although the emphasis was placed on ride quality rather than outright handling. The front suspension was also essentially MGA, albeit with minor differences. Not that this was an issue: this system was a delight and it endowed the MGB with finely tuned responses.

The power unit was also umbilically linked to the MGA, although there had been much in the way of experimentation first. A prototype V4 had been evaluated in an MGA and this was factored into the MGB's development. Unfortunately, BMC then abandoned its plan to introduce V4 and V6 engines. The highly strung MGA Twin-Cam was also considered, but due to poor servicing and misuse, a litany of well publicised problems led to it being dropped in 1960, well before it and the MGB could be united. This left just the 1622cc motor. Testing had shown that so equipped, the performance of the weightier MGB would not be up to par and more pulling power was needed. Fortunately for MG, BMC's new mid-sized saloon, codenamed ADO 17, was on the drawing boards, and this space-efficient, roomy, but heavy car was definitely going to require a bigger unit.

In what had become almost standard practice, BMC used Abingdon as a product-testing department and on this occasion the MGB was the guinea pig. In a very short space of time the 1798cc three-bearing 18G engine was created. Equipped with twin HS4 SUs, the 18G produced a healthy 94bhp at 5400rpm. This may have been only 1bhp up on the 1622cc, but torque had climbed from 97 to 107lb.ft (110lb.ft from 1964 on), which came into play lower down the scale, too. Thanks to this 'new' and lusty motor, the MGB could hit 0-60mph in 12.2 seconds – quick enough to quieten, if not quite silence, any criticism.

The engine may have been a redesign, but the bodyshell was all-new, a unitary construction whose box-like structures gave it immense strength. And, despite the car being a smidgen shorter than the MGA, due to the unitary construction the engineers had managed to glean much more interior space. This allowed the fitment of larger, more comfortable seats and provided extra legroom. There was also additional instrumentation, the quality of trim was better and wind-up windows were standard. In a word, the MGB possessed what its predecessor lacked – refinement.

It looked good, too. Although Don Hayter penned a number of quarter-scale drawings, his final design was a full-size layout from which a wooden pattern was made. It was from this that the prototype and production tooling were created. The MGB may have lacked the catwalk beauty of the MGA, but it was undoubtedly a happy marriage of looks, refinement, performance and tradition. Launched at the Earls Court Motor Show in September 1962 at a cost of £690 plus £259 purchase tax, it had a very positive reception.

Rivals

There were a number of cars on the market, including hotted-up saloons, which could equal and sometimes better the MGB's performance, but few possessed its charm, heritage and classic appeal. If the MGB had a nemesis during its formative years, it was the Triumph TR4. The two had much in common. Like the MGB, the similarly priced TR4 was blessed with a brand-new bodystyle. It was also more refined, had extra room over its predecessor and the revamped chassis provided better handling. It even used a revised and larger-capacity

Left: 808 JEA has body-coloured filler pieces. Bumper filler pieces switched to bright alloy in May 1963.

Above: Chrome door handles were fitted only on the pull-handle cars.
Below: Pack-away hood sticks and jack are secured by straps which are riveted to the body of the car.

version of a much earlier engine. Plus, depending on which road test you read, it could at least equal the MGB's 103mph top speed and was definitely quicker from 0-60mph. It sold exceptionally well in the USA, too.

As fate would have it, by the end of the decade the MG would still be slugging it out against a Triumph, although the TR series had evolved into the TR6 and the MGB had morphed into the MkII. And, by a quirk of fate, both cars now belonged to the same parent company, British Leyland, whose allegiance was firmly on the side of Triumph.

Another MGB challenger was the good-looking Sunbeam Alpine, which had reached its third incarnation by March 1963. With its 1592cc engine it wasn't as accelerative, but it could almost touch 100mph and its handling was up to the mark. Nevertheless, it was designed and styled with the US market in mind. As a result it tended to appeal to a different kind of buyer. If you were in the market for an MGB, a more traditionally styled car, you might've contemplated a TR4 but, as good as the Alpine was, you probably wouldn't have considered one.

Despite the competition from Triumph, the MGB had a relatively easy and successful passage through the 1960s. In the 1970s however, it came under increasing pressure from younger and more vigorous opposition. BL was on a road to nowhere and, by association, so was MG. Despite BL throwing its corporate weight behind MG's 50th anniversary bash in September 1979, days later chairman Michael Edwardes announced plans to close the Abingdon factory the following year. MG's workforce, who had worked tirelessly and with great loyalty, were stunned and deeply saddened. At least they could resign themselves to the fact that they had been instrumental in creating a legend. At its peak, some 50,000 MGBs were leaving Abingdon each year, and by the time production ceased in 1980, 512,112 had been built. This still ranks as one of the largest production runs of a single design of sports car in the world.

Right: The three-bearing engine was only ever fitted to the MGB and was replaced by a five-bearing 18GB unit in October 1964.

Revival and survival

The fact that the MGB exceeded its expected seven-year production life by eleven years was surprising enough, but its subsequent longevity has been astounding. It is an endearing and enduring car which has spawned an industry to serve its every need, and is one of the most widely supported and universally recognised classics that money can buy.

By its very nature the MGB is non-threatening. It was not a risk-taker or a boundary-pusher. Think evolution not revolution. In many ways, the MGB has even more charm and appeal now than it did in the 1960s. It is an attainable classic, rooted in the past but comfortable in the present, and this only adds to its attraction – an attraction that shows little sign of diminishing.

When *Motor* magazine reported on the new MGB in 1962, it was moved to write that it was 'a delightful modern sports car with a marked bias towards the grand touring character, and a pleasure to drive'. Nearly 50 years on, this still-delightful sports car and grand tourer remains a pleasure to drive.

Feature car

There is a school of thought, one that we subscribe to, that the purest cars, and the ones which are as the designer intended, are the very earliest examples. This is certainly true of the MGB and our feature car in particular. Devoid of superfluous detail but blessed with an understated style, 808 JEA, a January 1963 example and one of the earliest RHD cars, is as minimalist as it is magnificent.

It belongs to long-time MG enthusiast Rob Symonds. Rob still has a 1972 MGB GT which he bought in 1976, but he did have a brief flirtation with a Rover P6 3500S in the 1980s. The Rover was fast-living and fun, but would ultimately prove to be an expensive mistress and the two eventually parted company. He hadn't intended getting another MG until he spotted 808 JEA on a classic run. ' It was for sale,' Rob remembers. 'I really liked the look of it, but it was my wife who encouraged me to get the details. I learned from the owner, Derek Price, that it had previously been restored to a high standard by a friend of his and the bodyshell was reputed to have been galvanised. Even though the restoration had been undertaken some years back, the car still looked really good, so I decided to buy it.'

What attracted Rob to 808 JEA most of all was the fact that the restoration had been done sympathetically. In fact, it looked like an original, unrestored car. There were a few little things that needed doing, of course, but Rob didn't rush out and buy new parts. 'I decided that as the car was so original in appearance, I'd continue this theme and return it to as near showroom condition as possible. I used as many of the original parts as I could and refurbished or repaired them.'

It's likely that the three-bearing engine has been rebuilt at some time, but it's the original unit and has covered just 81,000 miles. To create the correct period look, among other things he has done Rob has painted the engine and dynamo red and replaced the Jubilee clips with wire ones. For practical reasons a stainless steel exhaust has been fitted, but that's the only deviation from standard. Rob runs the engine on Shell V-Power, which he doses with Castrol Valvemaster. 'I don't get any problems really,' he admits. 'The combination of V-Power and Valvemaster works well and smoothes the engine out.'

The four-speed gearbox is also pretty much as it left Abingdon, although it was rebuilt last winter as it was beginning to feel and sound rather agricultural. Of course, due to its vintage it doesn't have synchromesh on first gear, but what

Above: Until late 1964 the grille had 36 stainless steel slats (all of them individually riveted), and indicators that are positioned very wide.

it does have is overdrive. This became an option in January 1963, although Rob thinks that his was not fitted at the factory but some time later. As he reasons: 'By rights, cars that left Abingdon with overdrive would have had a cranked gearlever fitted. This one has the standard lever.'

808 JEA has also undergone something of a styling makeover and it is now dressed as it left Abingdon in 1963. 'When I bought this car it came with black carpets, hood and tonneau,' says Rob. 'But, when I received the Heritage Certificate and a photo that had been taken by a previous owner, I became aware that 808 JEA had been an all-red car and was fitted with disc wheels. This prompted me to return it to original trim, and I went for steel wheels, too.'

Don Trimming provided the new hood and tonneau, but as for the mats? Well, Rob had to get creative, as he recalls. 'It should have been fitted with rubber mats and not carpets. I managed to find some secondhand sill mats, but the floor ones I got from Australia. They are very good reproductions but are available only in black. Undeterred, I bought some flexible red paint from a yacht chandler and painted them with this. I was surprised at how good they turned out. The paint has worn well and with age the mats look even more authentic! The seats have been recovered, but the rest of the interior is original, even down to the chrome insert in the binnacle and the Jaeger instruments.'

The swap to steel wheels was easy at the front, but much more involved at the rear, as Rob recounts. 'To fit the rims up front just involves removing the bolt-on adaptor. For the rear I needed a steel wheel 'banjo' axle. Luckily, I managed to do an axle exchange with a chap in Belgium who was converting his car to wires! The disc wheels actually came from Birmingham and were originally fitted to the TV project car that featured in *An MG is Born*. To complete the car's return to original specification, I managed to locate a set of 5.60 x 14 crossplies.'

Rob is a genuine MG enthusiast who takes a delight in being part of a global movement which recognises the importance of the marque, the part the MGB has played, and the role it is still playing. Out of all the cars he owns (and has owned), 808 JEA remains his favourite.

'I get such a buzz from owning it, even when I just look at it in the garage. The changes I have made have been to 1963 factory specification and they have been carried out on a reasonably tight budget. I think they have improved the car. It is a very easy motor to live with and an even better one to drive – better than my GT even.'

**Above: Rob Symonds and the Roadster he has tried to keep close to original specification.
Below: 4x14in steel wheels were standard until 1969, when width increased to 4½in.**

TECH SPEC

808 JEA – 1963 MGB Roadster

Chassis

Unitary construction body, welded steel, front suspension on subframe
Wheelbase: 7ft 7in
Track: Front: 4ft 1in Rear: 4 ft 1¼in
Suspension: Front: coil and wishbone
Rear: live axle with leaf springs
Dampers: Armstrong lever arm front and rear

Steering

Cam gears rack & pinion
Turning circle: 32ft

Brakes

Disc size front: 10¾in
Drum size rear: 10in
Hydraulic, cable-operated parking brake

Wheels

Steel disc bolt-on
Rim size: 4J x 14   Tyre size: 5.60 x 14

Engine

Engine prefix: 18G
Four-cylinder in-line, pushrod ohv
Twin SU HS4
Cubic capacity: 1798cc
Power output: approx 94bhp @ 5400rpm
Torque: 107 lb.ft @ 3500rpm

Gearbox

Four-speed manual, synchromesh on top three ratios with overdrive
MPH/1000rpm: Manual top: 17.9, o/d: 22.1

Performance

Max. speed: 103mph
Acceleration: 0-60mph 12.2 seconds
Overall fuel consumption: 22mpg
Numbers built: 1963 – 23,308

MGC power &

Forget the armchair critics – the MGC was a good car waiting for that last little bit of development to make it great. David Marsh's much-modified example makes the most of this MG bruiser's great potential

Words: Paul Wager Photography: Richard Meadows

The MGC is one of those cars that tends to divide opinion. Some love it simply for its rarity and underdog status, while the armchair experts will always deride it because they once read in a magazine that it was an understeering lash-up designed by committee.

Me? I've always had a soft spot for the six-pot MGB if only because it's not a V8 and well, I just love the sound of a good straight-six. True, an extra pair of cylinders hanging over the front axle line didn't do the handling any favours, but the reality today is that with just a few tweaks in the right places, the MGC can be turned into a seriously capable car.

Proof of this comes in the shape of David Marsh's Tartan Red 1969 example,

Sebring style

originally modified by MG Motorsports' Doug Cook as a road car demonstrator and acquired by David in 1998. Doug is a well known advocate of the C and had built this car as his own personal rendition of what the MGC would have evolved into if it hadn't been axed by the product planners: modified engine, Sebring-style wide arches and simple-but-effective suspension mods designed to dial out the infamous understeer.

After running the MGC for a while, David felt the need for more power and took the car over to motor builder Lester Owen with a view to reworking the C-series lump. Lester of course is the 'L' behind legendary engine genius LH Owen, famed in particular for its exploits with BMW's 'M10' four-cylinder as found in the 2002 model of the 1970s – and in modified form in the 1500bhp Grand Prix cars of the

1980s. Despite his claim to Bavarian fame though, Lester apparently remembered working on MGC engines way back in the days of his apprenticeship and relished the chance to get stuck in once again.

In true race engine builder fashion, however, he refused to modify the top end until the bottom end had been sorted to his satisfaction. 'Do it his way or he'll show you the door,' laughs David, who of course was only too happy to do it Lester's way if that meant taking advantage of the steel crank handily provided by Dennis Walsh. The full specification includes a 3003cc overbore, that steel crank, Cosworth rods and pistons and a '641' camshaft boasting normal lift but wider overlap.

On top of this sits MG Motorsports' original big-valve head, running a 10.5:1 compression ratio and sucking through triple

Above: Sebring-style modifications including the lack of bumpers and those fat arches give MGC a purposeful and aggressive presence on the road.

Weber 45 DCOEs fed by a custom cold-air intake. The exhaust is Doug's original MG Motorsports' system, while an LH Owen modified distributor allows the use of 95 RON Premium Unleaded fuel. In the interests of longevity, there's now a one-way anti-drain valve in the oil filter set-up, while the cooling system has been completely renewed and runs with the popular Water Wetter additive and a pair of electric fans, one of them blowing over the Webers to keep them nice and cool: the MGC isn't a crossflow design, remember, so the exhaust and carbs live very close together.

The result of all this work was a conservative 238bhp at the flywheel on LH Owen's rolling road, corresponding to 198bhp at the rear wheels. In a car which weighs around 1200kg, that makes for an entertaining package, and it sounds absolutely glorious, too. 'She's a bit grumpy,' laughs David, backing the crackling and popping C out of the garage. But once warmed up and on cam, the shriek of the straight-six through the triple 45s is half-way between a vintage Bentley and a D-type Jaguar. 'I did try a single-tailpipe silencer,' he explains, 'but we lost 45bhp and went back to the twin-exit MG Motorsports' system.' Proof indeed that the two sets of three cylinders really don't like being joined up.

Right: **MGC is no fair-weather cruiser and gets used year round.**

The original gearbox also came in for some attention while the car was in LH Owen's hands, receiving a full rebuild with new bearings and a general freshening up, while the MG Motorsports' competition overdrive unit has been retained.

Handling of course is a very personal issue, and after trying the car as acquired David found he wanted to do things differently. Doug's preferred approach was a softer rear end, allowing the MGC to lift a front wheel in tight corners just like the works racers in period photos, but David preferred a stiffer tail. The solution? David enlisted Warwick-based Techcraft, who retained Doug's 25 per cent stiffer front torsion bars and clever negative-offset front wishbones, but added a one inch solid anti-roll bar and Spax adjustable dampers all round.

Together with the uprated rear leaf springs and radius arms to prevent axle tramp, the result was a complete dialling out of the infamous understeer. 'Doug hated the idea of the radius arms,' laughs David. 'He just doesn't believe in

Above: **Engine makes 238bhp at the flywheel – that's 198bhp at the rear wheels.**

Above: **Leather-trimmed MG Motorsports' Sebring-style interior is very smart.**

'It wouldn't take much more than a roll cage and stickers to turn it into a proper race car, but this would be a shame'

them. But once he'd tried it, he loved it.' Modern rubber helps of course, and the C sits on 225/50 Bridgestone SO-3s – although David rates them as being 'good for the road but nothing like as good as the S-02'.

Hiding inside the period 15-inch Minilites are a set of AP discs and four-pot calipers, which bring the C's stopping power neatly into the 21st century, while the Mercedes master cylinder was a mod suggested by Lester when David complained that he kept locking up the front wheels. It's an elegant solution which simply allows more pedal travel and hence a more progressive feel than the original. Since this car was originally a wire-wheeled model, the rims themselves are fitted using period Tech Del centres which adapt the Minilite wheel to the splined centre-lock hub.

Inside, the car is still much as it came, which means an MG Motorsports' Sebring-style interior complete with leather-trimmed seats, a period reverse lock-out bar, fly-off handbrake and everything nice and new looking. In the traditional Sebring fashion there's no glovebox, although David did have the heater reinstated in the interests of usability. He's more than happy to take ❯

Above: Boot-mounted badges are extremely subtle, but they say a great deal.

Above: After nine years of development, the MGC is now spot on. But with two other competition cars in the family jostling for attention, it is also up for sale.

the MGC out in the winter and it sees action at least once a month.

Warming the engine up gently before heading out for our photoshoot, it's obvious that David looks after his expensively built motor, but he's not averse to using the car hard and has been an enthusiastic competitor in the Paul Matty Sportscars hillclimb series since 1998. A personal best so far is a 65.3-second run at his local climb Loton Park, although a 53.5-second result at Prescott is no mean feat, either – and all from a car which people like to tell you is famous for its handling problems. In fact, David reckons it wouldn't take much more than a roll cage and stickers to turn it into a proper race machine, but after a blast round the local B-roads, I'm tempted to agree that this would be a shame. The MGC was always intended as more of a fast touring GT than an out-and-out racer, and despite a relatively uncompromising specification, this one is still a car in which you could tackle long distances. With the overdrive box, it's surprisingly civilised in fact, and David admits to having found his wife fast asleep beside him on at least one late-night trip. At 80mph the overdrive knocks the engine down to just 3000rpm, which is the equivalent of many a modern executive cruiser and reduces the exhaust note to a comforting rumble at motorway speeds.

Motorways aren't what you build a 200bhp MGC for though, and on the back roads

David's C is a far more entertaining proposition than the hottest of hot hatches. From a vicious standing start on a wet road, it will snake its way up to third gear, but it is all nicely controlled and the reworked suspension remains compliant enough to keep rubber in contact with tarmac and let the driver get on with the important business of pointing it in the right direction. The torquey powerplant makes it easy to drive fast, yet it's happy to rev hard if you let it – and the generally sorted feeling of this C makes it extremely easy to forget that you are in a 38-year-old car.

In spite of all this however, at the time of writing the car is for sale for the simple reason that with David also running a competition-prepared Merlin kit car and son Richard starting to compete in his own BMW M3, the family are running out of time and space. 'Three competition cars is a bit much really,' laughs David, who has the C on the books at Sussex Sports Cars for £19,995, a pretty reasonable sum when you consider the time which has gone into getting it just right – nine years, in fact.

'Yes, it's been a gradual development,' admits David when I ask him if it will be a wrench to let go of a car into which he's clearly put so much of himself. 'That's the best way if you don't know what you're doing,' he jokes – but on this evidence I'd have to say that he does know very much what he's doing when it comes to making the MGC go and handle like it should. ⓜ

Eighteen years is a long time for any car to remain in production, and the two MGB roadsters featured here represent the first and the last of this esteemed line – a pull-handle from 1962 and a 1980 LE

Words & photographs: Dave Bowers

FIRST *and* LAST

The two cars you see here are a so-called 'pull-handle' model dating to 1962, the first year of MGB manufacture, and a Limited Edition model dating to 1980, the last year of production. As suggested by the name, early MGBs had a different type of door handle fitted to the press-button items on later examples. The Limited Edition MGB, abbreviated to LE, was a run-out model of 1000 cars: 420 roadsters in Bronze Metallic and 580 GTs in Pewter Metallic.

Throughout its extended production run, the MGB retained much the same mechanical specification, the only real significant difference being the adoption of energy-absorbing bumpers and raised suspension in 1974, which also applied to the MG Midget. This was a necessary concession to new American regulations, which aimed to reduce the cost of collision repairs.

However, complying with this requirement for the all-important US export market proved to be doubly unfortunate for MG. Fitting rather ungainly bumpers (soon inaccurately termed 'rubber bumpers') detracted from the car's appearance, while raising the suspension so that said bumpers were at a uniform height to those

fitted to all other makes affected its poised handling. It was a supreme example of the blind pursuit of one objective failing to take account of another that was far more important – road safety!

Undoubtedly, the introduction of the rubber-bumper models didn't do MG any favours, although we shouldn't forget that these modifications enabled sports car production to continue at Abingdon for a further six years until 1980. If the factory had closed in 1974 due to the loss of the lucrative North American market, what chance would there ever have been of resurrecting a volume sports car range with the MGF in 1995 after such a lengthy intermission in production?

No doubt the virtues or otherwise of the rubber-bumper cars is a topic that will remain a subject of heated debate in MG circles for ever more, although this certainly doesn't apply to the owners of the pull-handle and the LE featured here. They are in complete agreement that these are both really great cars.

Stephen Mitchell of Northowram near Halifax, West Yorkshire, is keeper of the pull-handle roadster in Tartan Red, and he also owned the LE until recently before selling it to his friend, Graham Austin, who lives

Few visual clues betray the passage of 18 years of MGB production..

RFX 133W

331 XUD

nearby in Haworth.

I first met up with Stephen on the Bradford to Morecambe charity run, and after chatting about the two machines the prospect of bringing them together to appraise their respective merits was discussed. It was a project that would involve Graham taking a test drive in the pull-handle model, to which he readily agreed – and who wouldn't, given this car's remarkable condition?

Stephen bought the LE in 2000 in almost factory-fresh condition, with only 2200 miles on the clock as it hadn't been road registered until 1996; the first owner preserved it in aspic as part of his private car collection. Stephen commented: 'The car was first sold by Kennings of London for £5110.01 on January 23, 1981, to a chap in Middlesex who owned the collection. I had an MGA at the time that I'd restored, but due to advancing years, I needed something more comfortable. Initially, I was after a chrome-bumper MGB, so I attended an H&H auction at Buxton in 2000, but the three chrome cars on offer didn't meet with my expectations. The LE was prominently displayed beside the auctioneer's rostrum. What really caught my

attention was the low mileage. Although it had a reserve of £11,000, I paid only £9500, a good price for me as the Panorama Bay Motor Company of Poole in Dorset had previously sold it for £14,995 in 1996.'

Being in the motor trade and owning a garage business obviously confers a few advantages when it comes to buying and selling cars, as Stephen outlined concerning an MGA that he bought as a half-completed restoration project. He said: 'My 1959 MkI roadster was acquired in 1995, my first MG indulgence. I bought it from a friend, John Hopkinson, after an evening at the pub. Earlier that day I'd sold a secondhand Citroën, and I still had the cash at home. So I was in a position to offer John a wad of readies for the car which, much to my satisfaction, he promptly accepted.

'After collecting the car the next day, I then ran into a bit of a problem – I didn't dare tell the wife what I'd done. However, she found out after spotting the money for the Citroën wasn't in the stock book. Which was followed by: "You haven't gone and bought that old wreck standing outside, have you?" My name was mud!'

Whereas the MGA required lots of work before it was roadworthy, the LE was a complete contrast, a car Stephen could admire, polish up and take it for a drive when the fancy took him. The only attention it required was cleaning the underbonnet area – a film of clear lacquer had been applied to the engine which didn't meet with Stephen's approval at all.

Keep the mileage low and preserve the car's value, or throw caution to the wind and enjoy the vehicle by using it for its intended purpose, is a dilemma that the buyer of any low-mileage

MGA was Stephen's first MG indulgence, and a bit of a wreck when he bought it.

Left: Re-imported and converted to rhd, car's few modifications include five-speed box.
Above right: Facia and instruments are obvious distinguishing marks between old and new.
Below right: Three main bearing engine was rebuilt (inset), but is now beautifully finished.

machine then faces. Stephen commendably went for the latter option and drove the LE regardless of the miles clocking up on the odometer. This included attending many shows, including the MG Car Club Spring Rally held on Jersey, which is about as far as you can travel from Yorkshire without having to drive on the opposite side of the road. It was a long journey that was rewarded in April 2006 when his MG won the coveted Prix d'Honneur Trophy.

However, when Graham borrowed Stephen's LE and took it to a car show, he was rather puzzled when the judge started jotting down notes on the score sheet that didn't bode well. Graham remarked: 'The judging was being done by a young chap who may not have even been born when this car was built. The MG's body had been rust-proofed using the Tectyl method before Kennings sold it, as was done by many dealerships in those days, and I could see he had noticed the car had been undersealed. I tried explaining this was common practice at the time when this model was new, but then he mentioned the quality of the paintwork in the boot was pretty poor, as evidenced by run marks. I then

tried explaining that the car was still in totally original condition, and it had received no work whatsoever after spending much of its life in a collection, but he wasn't having any of it. So that was that. Clearly, he had no comprehension of BL's standard of workmanship in those days, with the result that valuable points were lost.'

You have to wonder whether, if Stephen took his 1962 pull-handle MGB for judging at this show by the same person, the upshot would be a loss of points due to the door handles being replaced with incorrect items.

After enjoying the LE for seven years, Stephen got wind of the pull-handle car that was being offered for sale locally. 'I'd always wanted a pull-handle, and this was the nicest that I'd seen so far, so I bought it,' he explained. 'Like my MGA, it was an American car which had been converted to right-hand drive.

'The body was in an excellent state and completely original other than the front wings, which had been replaced. I then arranged for the three-bearing engine to be rebuilt by Stephen Clegg of AMK Engineering of Earby, Barnoldswick. The motor was fully balanced

and the carburettors refurbished, tasks that Stephen carried out to the very highest standard, so my car now goes like stink.

'I replaced the clutch and fitted new brake parts, which altogether totted up to £5000 including body repairs and the engine rebuild. Since then, I've done 500 miles and the engine's now nicely bedded in. I recently changed the Castrol running-in oil for Duckhams 20-50, and the high oil pressure is fantastic.'

As the car left for America with a red hood fitted, this is what is installed today. Stephen also replaced all the seat covers and interior trim that hadn't fared well in a sunny region of the USA.

After sampling the LE on a number of ❯

Above left: Flatter dash, smaller instruments and padded wheel are all features of late MGB.
Below left: Engine was unaltered in capacity, but did gain two extra crank bearings in 1964.
Right: They may be controversial, but black bumpers suit Bronze Metallic paint well.

occasions, Graham was doubly keen to buy when Stephen announced his intention to sell the car. Particularly as he'd received a handsome insurance payment following a road accident that hinted quite strongly at the need to adopt a new kind of motoring hobby. 'I was out riding my BMW R60 motorbike when a Fiat Punto crossed my path. I went over the car's roof, damaging just about every panel on the way before I finally hit the ground,' said Graham. 'I

'Despite all the points I have raised, I'm amazed just how similar these two cars are'

was in a bad way and vowed never to ride a bike again. So when the insurance payout arrived for the motorcycle and my injuries, I decided to treat myself as compensation for the physical injury and suffering I'd endured – and Stephen's LE came up for sale at just the right time.'

With the sun shining and a rambling country route decided upon that avoided meeting up with Sunday drivers, Graham was ready to climb into Stephen's pull-handle car with a view to assessing how it performed and compared with his LE. Somewhat predictably, Graham's initial remarks before starting off followed the conventional wisdom that later cars weren't a patch on the earlier ones due to the much-criticised and much-maligned rubber-bumper modifications, with the result that the true sporting spirit of the MGB had been lost.

After setting off and changing up a few gears, Graham concurred with Stephen's comment that the gearboxes on earlier cars were a lot smoother to operate than on his LE, which was slightly notchy, a characteristic which also applied to other rubber-bumper cars he'd driven:

one clear point ahead for the pull-handle then? Well, not exactly, as Stephen then confessed that his car benefited from a Hi-Gear five-speed Ford Sierra gearbox conversion.

However, Graham was then able to assess the merits of the non-original five-speed gearbox against the LE's overdrive unit, which operates on third and forth. 'Using overdrive on my car feels a bit antiquated compared to a five-speed gearbox,' said Graham. 'Although I have to say, this probably has a lot to do with driving modern cars all week, as slotting into fifth does comes naturally and seems a lot more flexible in operation. But given time, I hope using overdrive becomes second nature, and it does provide a far more classic driving experience.'

Beside the pull-handle's gearbox, both cars veer from standard spec in having polyurethane suspension and steering bushes, which Stephen fitted after a set of rubber bushes that he'd put on the LE failed in under a year. So both cars were well matched in this respect, and any differences in the way that they handled was purely down to the inherent characteristics of

Stephen (on right), Graham (standing) and Graham's partner, Lorraine O'Brien.

the suspension and steering rather than worn, 'soggy' bushes.

Graham commented: 'The pull-handle seems so direct to drive, which may in fact owe quite a lot to the way it was put together, although I can't say that my LE performs all that much differently. You'd have to take both cars to the limit before any differences were appreciable. However, this model's steering seems a lot lighter than on the LE – you can really flick it through the corners. This may have something to do with the lower driving position, but setting the car up for corners seems a lot easier, and sitting lower offers a straightforward, directional view of the way ahead. What's more, the windscreen top rail isn't directly in the line of sight as it is when I'm driving my LE.'

Surprisingly, considering the pull-handle doesn't benefit from brake servo assistance and the LE does, Graham observed that the braking efficiency was much the same for both cars.

The route he had chosen travelled up and down dale around the fringes of Haworth, a route that he travels on a daily basis. Graham

commented on the pull-handle's performance: 'This car seems to have much more urge, which may have a lot to do with the care that went into putting the engine together. I would like to explore the motor's full performance, but with only 500 miles since the rebuild, it needs to be treated with respect.'

Graham also observed that the powerplant felt remarkably unstressed when travelling along a flat road in fifth gear, with the tacho and speedo reading a leisurely 1500rpm and 30mph respectively. In addition, he said that the throttle response was reassuringly immediate, even when accelerating away in the same high gear.

He summed up his observations after pulling to a halt: 'Strangely, this car seems a bit quieter than mine, and it's so rattle-free – the hallmark of a very well restored vehicle. The engine's very responsive, and taken overall, this model seems more vital in the way that it picks up speed compared to my LE. What's more, you never feel as if it's rolling about; mine tends to pitch about, which no doubt has something to do with the suspension being lifted.

'Taken overall, I'd never have thought this car was first sold in 1962, although despite all the points I've raised in its favour compared to my LE, I'm amazed just how similar these two models actually are; I still can't quite put my finger on why this happens to be so.'

Asking Graham which of the cars he would have preferred taking home seemed rather unnecessary, and if Stephen ever decides to sell his car, he won't have to search all that far before finding a buyer. And should this ever come to pass, Graham will surely not have all that much trouble selling his LE to make room for it, particularly as he has vowed to maintain the car in its original untouched condition from now on. Other than running up a few more miles on the clock, of course. *MG*

High C

Abingdon's Competition Department evolved a handful of super-lightweight MGC racers alongside the production models. We encounter the best-provenanced of these in its California retirement

Words: Phil White Photography: Jon Hill

I f they had made the MGC in this configuration,' yells Henry Camisasca over the din, 'they'd have had a winning combination. In many ways the firm brought the car out too early and missed the lessons they learned developing the race machines.' As if to underline his point he selects third gear and buries the throttle. The fantastic roar that results is unmistakably the product of a British straight-six, dominated by exhaust note because we have the windows open. 'She really wants to go,' Henry shouts delightedly as the car accelerates round the on-ramp and onto a sun-drenched, virtually empty freeway.

Fourth gear is slotted and our onward progress continues unabated. This is a very torquey engine indeed, and although it feels tall-geared, it gains speed rapidly. The impression is heightened by the sheer mechanical noise of motor and drivetrain, the rush of induction and the whine of straight-cut gears. Having just stepped from a hired SUV we feel very close to the ground, and the speedometer is wildly overconfident. 'It's way off,' says Henry as he points to the needle, which waggles optimistically between 80 and 90mph. 'We're doing about 70.'

Actual speed is mildly irrelevant, because the overriding emotion is excitement at travelling in a fairly prominent piece of motorsport history. MBL 546E straddled the transition from MGB to MGC, posting some pretty respectable placings in international races as it did so. It is also MG's last hurrah in works racing, before BMC closed its competition department at Abingdon. Having decided to give its road cars a sales

push by competing in big international long-haul races, Abingdon created a lightweight version of the then-nascent MGC bodyshell. It involved collaboration between Abingdon, BMC's colleague Pressed Steel in Swindon, Morris Bodies and Jaguar's favourite panel supplier, Abbey Panels in Coventry. Specially made aluminium outer panels were married to the steel substructure of the MGC GT body, while bonnet, boot and doors were also aluminium.

It is known that of the 20 sets of panels pressed, six shells were created. Two became works cars, while two were later built for competition by racer John Chatham. He also constructed a pair as road cars, for WH Gardner and BL Motor Sport Press Officer Alan Zafer. The machine in which we are hurtling loudly through the California countryside is the first works model, and officially the best-provenanced MG of its kind on the planet. MBL 546E – the car is referred to almost universally by its registration number, although occasionally the affectionate derivative 'Mabel' is employed – was entered in the 1967 Targa Florio as a Prototype. Although the MGC's torsion beam suspension and competition-spec all-disc brakes were present and correct, the engine was a 2004cc rendition of the MGB's four-cylinder. Thanks to spirited driving by Paddy Hopkirk and Timo Makinen it finished ninth overall, and third in class.

The press referred to it as an 'MGB lightweight', missing the discreet gap in its badging – to this day the tailgate wears the legend 'MG GTS', with nothing but holes where a B or C might be mounted. Although either letter might pass muster, it is the latter that would have more weight. Because at its ❯

MG GTS

Above left:
Cockpit has been occupied by many an illustrious racing name.
Right:
Extensive use of aluminium panels keeps weight down.
Below left:
Red engine bay reveals the original colour.

next outing in the following year's 12 Hours of Sebring race the MG sported a new, bulging bonnet with a six-cylinder engine beneath. Hopkirk, this time teamed with Andrew Hedges, took it to 10th overall and a class win. Back in the UK, it was prepared for the 84-hour Marathon de la Route at the Nürburgring, gaining Lucas driving lamps mounted on a front valance painted orange to differentiate it from its yellow-valanced teammate RMO 699F.

Although it may have run 15in Minilite alloy wheels on the Targa Florio, the cars changed to 72-spoke wire wheels at this point. Henry has a set of both and infinitely prefers the model's ride on the alloys. 'They favoured the wires,' says specialist Doug Smith of MG Motorsport in Bovingdon, Hertfordshire, 'because the Minilites were coming loose. There is a picture somewhere of the octagonal centre with a steel washer around it to stop it growing and coming off. It's said that for the Marathon they practised on Minilites, but had to fly out a consignment of wires for the race.'

In Germany, Andrew Hedges, Tony Fall and Julien Vernaeve achieved sixth place. They had at one point been in third place, when after 67

hours the front brake pads fused to the discs. The car entered the pits, yet because pit stops longer than 20 minutes resulted in disqualification it had to go out with no brakes when time ran short. The next lap it clipped two minutes off its best time, then re-pitted. But unable to stop, it missed its pit slot and went out once more. A lap later it was finally halted and repaired.

MBL's final big works race was the 12 Hours of Sebring in 1969, where Craig Hill and Bill Brack struggled to 34th place. This said, it did win the prototype class. The same year it was sold through British Leyland's US base at Leonia, New Jersey. Its new owner was Bruce McWilliams, President of the Rover Motor Company and the man who discovered the Buick engine which became Rover's long-lived V8. Over the next 36 years it had six more owners and resided in both the USA and the UK. Henry Camisasca acquired it in 2005, and exported it to live a pampered life in California.

'When my wife and I bought this house,' Henry says as he opens a door, 'it was because the garage was tall enough to get a lift into.' In fact there are two lifts, and the large, neat space accommodates five cars. There are currently

'It is important to maintain a balance between patina and restoration'

two MGs among them although one, a very credible Sebring replica, is about to be sold to make way for an even more credible E-type replica. Having worked hard for success, Henry spends his money wisely even when buying toys, and acquired the MG under the guidance of Doug Smith. The 'illness', as Henry describes it, was inherited from his father. 'He had so many British cars, from an A40 to an E-type. He thought they handled better, gave better gas mileage and were more intriguing than US iron. He was the laughing stock of the coffee room at work.' Decades on, British classics are cool in California and Henry is surrounded by admiring spectators whenever he takes any of his UK

playthings to a car show or gathering.

But then this model is in a stellar league of coolness, being a machine of extreme historical interest. Its completeness underpins its importance too, something Henry has been acutely aware of when renovating it. 'In many ways, restoring is too strong a word. I've had to replace a lot of perishable items inside, but I have kept all the original stuff. It's an ongoing project, as we source more original parts. It's important to keep a sense of its history, to maintain a balance between patina and restoration.'

Originally the car was finished in red. But shortly before the start of the '67 Targa Florio the Italian authorities decreed that cars should run in national colours. So French models should be blue and Italian machinery, obviously, red. The MG was given a hasty coat of very British dark green. But lift the bonnet or a piece of trim and the original colour will show itself.

Like restoration, research continues. There is still the occasional mystery to clear up. Henry points to a grommetted hole in the Perspex-cowled headlamp area: 'We don't know what the holes are for.' The car did a stint in the New York area, and we conjecture that perhaps it wore

marker lights at this time. Doug Smith later scotches this theory, saying that they were for additional back-mounted Lucas 576 spotlamps on the Nürburgring event. Henry also has a shopping list of desirable items he is yet to discover. On the bonnet are more holes, where a plaque was mounted for the 1968 Nürburgring event. 'That is something I'd really like to have,' he breathes with a collector's enthusiasm.

In the years after its works activities the car had, in the words of preeminent MG specialist Ron Gammons, 'a very active competition life prior to our first seeing her back in the early 1980s.' He believes that it had at some point been on its roof, which is partly why the original works roll cage was no longer present. In any case, subsequent outings included events such as the Liège-Sofia-Liège rally, Targa Espana and the 1996 Coys race at Silverstone. In this latter, despite a small hole in a piston, it managed to finish fifth overall. But through all this it was left very much

Top: MBL 546E rode on both wire wheels and alloy rims.
Middle: Quick and simple solutions for period problems.
Bottom: Basic trim – comps cars were built to do a job.

No B or C on tailgate – MBL 546E switched from B to C-series power during period.

MBL 546E GB

Left: Original competition touches abound, including a 24-gallon tank with huge filler for long-distance race endeavours.

as it was raced by Abingdon. The original motor is present and correct, having last been rebuilt in 1994 by Brown & Gammons.

As a glance through the sheaf of papers in Henry's files reveals, this is quite an engine. A trio of 45 DCOE Weber carburettors feed a ported, polished alloy intake manifold and head. Fully lightened, balanced and blueprinted, the motor gives around 200bhp at 6000rpm, a useful 55bhp up on the all-steel version in the road-going MGC. With endurance racing and the thirst of a racer in mind, Abingdon provided a 24-gallon fuel tank accessed by the huge four-inch aero filler on the offside C-pillar. The gearbox, as Ron Gammons puts it, 'is the original MGC non-overdrive four-speed syncro, straight-cut, close-ratio box, the diff ratio 3.7:1 and the diff unit a ZF LSD, all original factory. I believe it was fitted temporarily with a standard overdrive box for the Liège.' As can be

expected, a parts schedule for Sebring lists a variety of differential ratios. Back then the MG ran a 3.9 gear, with 3.3 and 3.7 as spares.

Outside, the car is an essay in period racing. The deep front valance is pierced by two air ducts to provide brake cooling. Their fairings, like the brackets locating the Plexiglass headlamp covers, are riveted in place more for function than form. 'When considering these cars,' says Smith, 'it's worth remembering that the BMC Competition Department was building models to compete and throw away, not for lasting value. If you put yourself into that frame of mind you understand how they did things. These weren't passionate enthusiasts, they were working men producing something for their boss, making a living. So the most efficient route was always taken, usually involving the parts bin.' Doug points out that the hardware holding the spare wheel straps in place is actually part of the MGB seat retainer. Continuing the same theme, the marker light on the roof looks remarkably like the tail-lamp from a Morris Minor Traveller, and the light illuminating the driver's door number is a fairly universal number plate item.

What dominates the car is not the details, but those hand-formed alloy wheelarch extensions, blisters that have launched a thousand replica bodykits. They transform it, combining with the bulge-laden bonnet to give a sense of purpose the original MGB could never dream of. For many, Henry Camisasca included, this is the stuff of fantasy. His custodianship of the real thing is made all the more special because of the years spent waiting for it to turn up. This, and the lightweight Jaguar he's about to take delivery of, represent the high point in a British car ownership career that began two decades ago with a 1967 Mini Cooper S. He smiles a happy smile when he opens up the door to extract the MG. 'It's a dream garage come true,' he says. MG

TECH SPEC

MG GTS

Engine

2968cc straight-six BMC Competitions unit. Triple 45 Weber carburettors, gas-flowed alloy head. Lightened, balanced, blueprinted. Compression ratio 10.25:1. 24-gallon fuel tank

Power

200bhp @ 6000rpm

Torque

Unknown

Transmission

MGC four-speed synchromesh, straight-cut gear set. Borg & Beck clutch. ZF limited-slip differential. 3.7:1 differential ratio

Suspension

MGC system, utilising torsion bars. 7x15 wheels

Brakes

Girling solid discs all round

Body

Alloy outer panels, steel substructure. Alloy wheelarch extensions and front valance. Lucas driving lamps. Perspex headlamp covers. Painted dark green

Weight

1000kg (est)

THANKS TO:

Doug Smith of MG Motorsport, Bovingdon, Herts, UK. 01442 832019, www.mgmotorsport.com
Ron Gammons of Brown & Gammons, Baldock, Herts, UK. 01462 490049, bg.mgcars.org.uk

MG ENTHUSIAST

THE WORLD'S BEST-SELLING MG MAGAZINE

Celebrate 85 years of MG with the world's best selling MG magazine

■ All the latest news from China and Longbridge ■ Stunning photography
■ Technical advice and products on test ■ Comprehensive event coverage
■ In-depth features and drive stories from Old No 1 to the latest TF

If you are interested in MGs then you will be delighted with MG Enthusiast magazine

Available at WH Smith and all good newsagents from the second Wednesday of every month.

For the latest subscription offer, please call 01778 392 490
Or subscribe online at www.mgenthusiast.com

JUST WHAT MADE ABINGDON GREAT?

Tucked away in a Thames-side town far from the hub of the Midlands motor industry, the MG factory was small, lacked investment and in later years was seriously out-dated – but the dedicated local workforce ensured that MG was the top export earner, the most efficient factory in the BMC group and, above all, a very special place to work. Peter Browning recalls his time at Abingdon

Left: John Thornley was driving inspiration to the whole of the Abingdon workforce.

Above: Factory visits were actively encouraged and regular gatherings were organised by both the MG Car Club and the Austin-Healey Club.

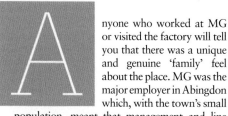nyone who worked at MG or visited the factory will tell you that there was a unique and genuine 'family' feel about the place. MG was the major employer in Abingdon which, with the town's small population, meant that management and line workers were all local people drawn from a small and closely knit community. The works bicycle park was more crowded than the car park as most of the employees lived that close to the factory, and the Cemetery Road exodus at clocking-off time was like the start of a stage on the Tour de France.

I arrived in the late 1950s as a young motor sport enthusiast and stayed until the British Leyland closure. My first job was working in the Car Club offices. I then joined the staff of Safety Fast!, moving on to be Competitions Press Officer and finally BMC (later British Leyland) Competitions Manager. Significantly, it was a series of jobs detached from the mainstream production side of the factory, where I had a roving commission and was certainly in a privileged position from which to observe life at MG during the period.

Despite in later years being an outdated plant lacking in investment, Abingdon was always an extremely efficient unit – one car per employee

per week was an oft-quoted figure, possibly never achieved by any other factory. And when production targets had to be increased to meet a special export shipment, the workforce never failed to respond with an appropriate step up in effort.

This was perhaps possible only because of the method of building the cars, which had not changed much since M-type Midgets rolled off the same lines in the 1930s. This was unique at the time and, right up to the close of the factory, MGs were manually pushed down the line and there was no automated track. I am sure that this contributed to the high build quality – if assembly problems occurred, the line could be temporarily slowed down and the problem solved with the help of department heads, (most of whom were steeped in MG history and, in particular, pre-war racing and record-breaking achievements) rather than passed on to the rectification department.

All MGs were taken on a road test, a tradition that was continued right up to the last of the line of MGBs and Midgets, and which did not happen at other factories. One former road tester told me that he considered this a vital part of maintaining the build quality and ensuring that pre-delivery checks by the dealers were minimised. The test routes are well documented and driven by many owners who visit Abingdon today, and I am sure that the fact they were fast, country roads – classic going for the keen sports car driver – accounts for

something. Meanwhile, the strong family spirit throughout the factory meant that union problems at Abingdon were minimal – certainly when I reached the management stage I was never aware of any serious issues despite the fact that our activities within the Competitions Department (late night and weekend working, special overtime rates, generous overseas travel expenses when on rallies) were probably not strictly in line with union practice. The rest of BMC and later BL were, of course, riddled with union unrest at this time. At Abingdon I got the feeling that if young militant blood thought of causing trouble, wiser heads usually prevailed.

I recall a classic example of this when I had to arrange for an American film unit to do some filming on the production line for a TV programme promoting British sports cars in the USA. As usual the film company had erected batteries of arc lights on the scene, it was a hot summer's day, and things were getting a bit warm on the line. And, as usual for film crews, they took their time over getting exactly the shot they wanted. One young lad finally downed tools and walked off complaining that it was too hot to continue working. The youngster was taken aside by his supervisor and quietly reminded that the American market basically paid his salary and perhaps it would be a good idea if he were to get back to his job. It was probably relevant that the ❯

'Surely no other factory in the world could boast a senior management line-up of such experienced people who lived and breathed sports cars?'

Left to right:
Syd Enever's estimates for droop-snout MGB were spot on; the author driving a GT at Silverstone was pushing his luck when borrowing a press fleet car; vehicles were always pushed manually down the lines.

supervisor happened to be his father!

The workforce always seemed adaptable to new or temporary working conditions. In the early 1960s there was a serious slump in the American market and some 1000 unsold cars were stuck in the collection compounds. The workforce saved what could have been a serious blow to the future of the factory with an immediate plan to convert the vehicles for European markets. In addition, the spare MGB and Midget lines were temporarily turned over to the production of Morris Minor vans and Travellers, which would have earned the factory brownie points at Longbridge.

The strong social side of the workforce has been mentioned, and in 1963 the MG Social Clubhouse was built in the town promoting sports and social activities. Its 250-seat ballroom was the biggest facility in the area and was regularly used for many non-MG occasions. The MG Auto Club was born around this time and later formed the basis for the present MGCC Abingdon Works Centre.

All of Abingdon's heads of department were immensely proud of the marque and were steeped in octagonal history. These people would not stand for any inefficiency and the workforce would, quite rightly, give them great respect. Above all, they were practical people who could roll up their sleeves in an emergency and sort out the problem themselves.

Heading up the design side was Chief Engineer Syd Enever, who started work as a tea boy in the MG Cowley works, came to Abingdon in 1930

working in the Experimental Department and later moved on to be Chief Planning Engineer. Syd penned the MGA and MGB, and was renowned for his inventive ideas usually sketched on the back of a fag packet. Typical of Enever's talent was his response to the request from Competitions for more top speed for the MGB at Le Mans. Enever sketched out the famous droop-snout nose and worked out that it should be good for a 140mph top speed. On the event the MGB clocked 139mph through the speed trap!

Enever was succeeded by the young Roy Brocklehurst, an approachable and humorous fellow and a former draughtsman. When Roy was sadly despatched to Longbridge, he was succeeded by Don Hayter, ex-Pressed Steel and Aston Martin, who was to be the last of Abingdon's Chief Engineers. Talented top draughtsmen at the time were Jim O'Neill (bodies) and Terry Mitchell (chassis).

Key department heads included Cecil Cousins, who reckoned that he was MG's first employee working on the MG-Six. He was much involved in pre-war racing activities, foreman of the Experimental Department and later Works Manager from 1944. Meanwhile, Reg Jackson joined MG in 1928, was the legendary head of the pre-war racing department and was later appointed Service Manager and all-round factory trouble-shooter.

There was surely no other factory in the world which could boast a senior management line-up of such experienced people who lived and breathed sports cars. And, of course, the

outstanding leader of the team was Mr MG himself – General Manager John Thornley.

My first encounter with John was when he called me personally on the phone and invited me to come and talk about working in the Club offices. It was typical that when I mentioned my father had come to Abingdon pre-war to collect his M-type, John himself went to look through the chassis files to see if he could find the records!

John's enthusiasm for MG was infectious; he was a wonderful leader and a fatherly figure to us youngsters at the time. It was well known that every week he would pay a visit to the Personnel Department to get up to date with any personal problems or news about people in the factory. On his regular walk-about sessions down the line, he had thus acquired the perfect chat-up lines: 'How's the new baby?', 'Good score in the cricket last weekend', 'Sorry to hear about your squashed foot'. It was no wonder that when John asked for production to be stepped up to meet a shipping target, the workforce responded.

Thornley maintained very firm ideals on sports car development and design, and fought many battles with his bosses at Longbridge. He also personally sanctioned a number of development and competition projects of which Longbridge certainly would not have approved. The entry of a pair of MGAs in the 1956 Mille Miglia, despite the Longbridge ban on BMC racing after the Le Mans disaster the previous year, was sanctioned as just another 'rally'. When the successful cars returned to the UK and someone suggested they be put on display in the London Piccadilly BMC

showrooms, John immediately had them returned to Abingdon and quietly disposed of, less Longbridge found out.

Similarly, in 1960, when Thornley found out that Longbridge had got wind of the secret plans for the exciting EX 186 racing version of the MGA Twin Cam with de Dion rear axle, it was crated up, sent to the USA and never seen again.

I always felt that the boardroom lunch was another significant factor in creating the Abingdon touch. It was attended by all the senior staff, with regular guests and visitors. Naturally, the topic of conversation was almost exclusively MG and current Abingdon business, a daily clearing house for progress reports on projects, matters of the moment and future plans. Confidentiality was respected when new projects were discussed and outside opinions were particularly welcomed. Dealer principals were regularly invited and, quite rightly, made to feel very much part of the MG family. On the rare occasion when an unhappy owner came to the factory with a complaint, they were often invited to lunch – where I am sure their problem was rectified and confidence in the marque restored.

Overseas visitors to the factory, usually arriving unannounced, were always welcomed. And, if they happened to be MG Car Club members, Thornley usually took them on a guided tour of the Works and insisted that they were invited to lunch. Imagine today the awe-inspiring experience of finding yourself seated amongst such legendary characters.

As the founding General Secretary of the MG

Car Club, John Thornley was very much a 'club' person, realising that badge allegiance was not only good for sales but also that Club activities promoted the best qualities of the marque. Thornley himself, of course, held the position of Chairman of the MG Car Club, and his behind-the-scenes work for the Club is well documented. I came to Abingdon to start up the Austin-Healey Club alongside MGCC, and his support and guidance for AHC was equally generous. Both outfits received significant financial support from BMC (which was not always appreciated by the members) and Chief Accountant Norman Higgins was a very good friend who I know channelled more funds towards the clubs than ever showed up in the accounts!

At an early stage Thornley saw that every MG and Austin-Healey leaving Abingdon had a Club membership application form tucked in the glove pocket, which at the time brought a significant boost to membership. I recall that Longbridge refused to have my Austin-Healey Club brochures put in the cars as it had not been agreed by the Austin dealership network. Typically, Thornley said: 'Bugger them, I'll fix that for you.'

He encouraged all of the senior staff to take a serious interest in 'the art of driving MGs'. Abingdon had its own Advanced Driving School run by ex-police driver Harry Shillabeer, and we were all sent on courses and shown how sports cars should really be driven. This was not pussy-footing around and polishing up our hand signals – there was advanced fast-road driving, skid-pan experience and on-the-limit circuit driving. I was

not the only one who never missed an opportunity to borrow any car from the press fleet and give it a good thrashing! It was all about getting everyone in the team to be enthusiastic and knowledgeable about the product, because we were all salesmen for MG.

The activities of the BMC Competitions Department based at Abingdon did a lot to further the awareness, recognition and fame of the MG factory and the Abingdon name worldwide. The rally team blazed a trail across Europe, and the fact that the works MGs, Austin-Healeys and Mini-Coopers came from this small Thames-side town was well known.

It has been said that the strong emotional local feeling about the closure of MG by British Leyland in 1980 was that it was not only the loss of jobs for the then-current workforce, it was the feeling that part of the town's family heritage had come to an end. Mums and dads, brothers and sisters, long retired but who had worked at MG for so many years, joined the protest and made their feelings known.

Finally, from talking to many former senior MG workers and reading stories written by others of the period, it is clear that the spirit at Abingdon at the time when I was privileged to work there was not new, but had been inherited from pre-war times when the factory was the mecca for sports car enthusiasts.

It was the people who worked there that applied the 'Abingdon touch' to the production of the world's most popular sports cars through more than half a century. ⬡

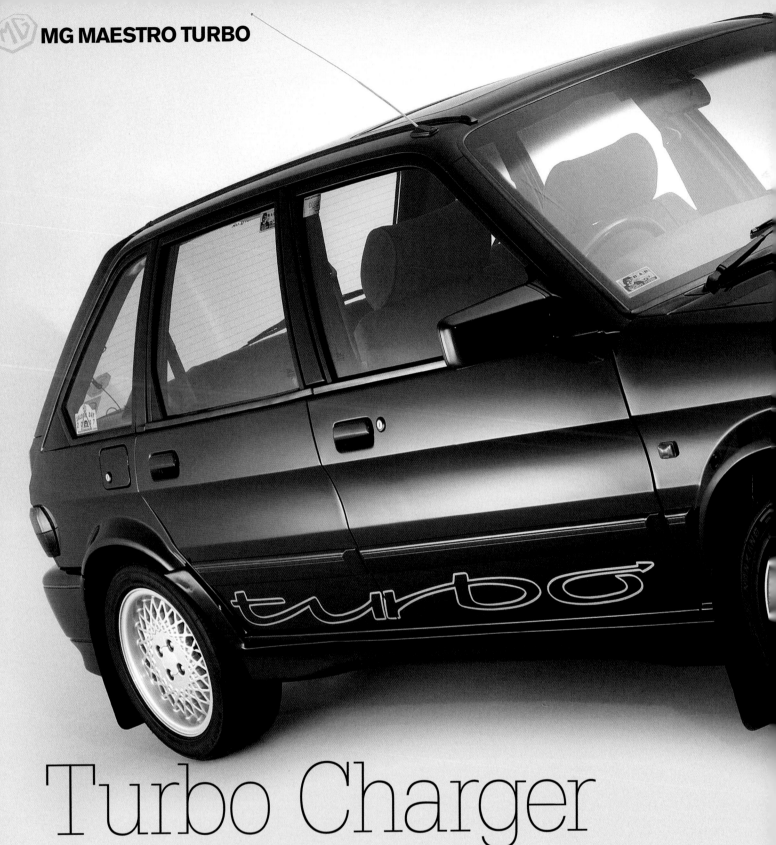

Turbo Charger

With just 504 cars produced and possibly as few as 200 survivors, the Maestro Turbo is an exclusive MG that packs a mighty performance punch

Words: Martyn Morgan Jones. Pictures: John Colley

he 1980s brought us the compact disc, camcorders, 3D video games, digital mobile phones and Microsoft Windows. It was also the decade when Englishman Tim Berners-Lee started turning one aspect of science fiction into science fact. The World Wide Web was on its way…

So too was the mass-marketing subsidiary of British Leyland, the Austin Rover Group. BL had undergone a dramatic and far-reaching re-organisation. The company had been split into several independent and autonomous divisions and when Austin Rover arrived in 1981, the re-organisation was complete. Sir Michael Edwardes, a diminutive but big-hitting South African, had managed to drag BL out if its self-generated mire; not an easy task. There were a number of minuses during Edwardes' tenure at BL, such as the loss of the Triumph assembly plant at Speke (the first major car factory closure since WW2). This was followed by the closure of Triumph's Canley plant and, of course, most tragically of all, MG's factory at Abingdon in 1980.

When Edwardes departed BL in September 1982, there were still many issues that needed resolving. Nonetheless, he left behind a streamlined and healthier company that not only exhibited a more positive image, but which had become a global player. He'd even managed to forge a partnership with Honda, whose expertise and engineering resources would help greatly in the near future. What he hadn't managed to do was get the Maestro into production. Harold Musgrove, who took over from Edwardes as chairman, would shoulder this burden.

If the Maestro was needed for Austin-Rover (and BL) to prosper and grow, then the Metro had been essential to the firm's survival. In the late 1970s and early 1980s, when the Maestro should have been occupying much of BL's time, the Metro took precedence. In many ways it was the Maestro's nemesis, holding it back. The latter's launch was also delayed by the BL/Honda collaboration, resulting in the introduction of the Triumph Acclaim in late 1981. In all, it took seven years for Austin-Rover's new mid-sized contender to reach production. Codenamed the LM10, the Maestro finally debuted in March 1983.

When VW had unveiled the Golf, this capable and very well-engineered model became a template for its market sector. Having adhered to a design brief to produce a mechanically simple, straight-forward, mid-sized family car, Austin-Rover unveiled an entirely conventional vehicle inspired by the Golf. Not only

did the Maestro mirror its FWD hatchback format and MacPherson strut and trailing arm suspension layout, the 1.3-litre versions would use the Golf's five-speed gearbox. On the whole, the Maestro was greeted with enthusiasm.

Enthusiasm was fine, but what was really needed was excitement. There was no doubting that the Maestro was competent; it just wasn't a car to get animated about. Company restructuring, problems with finances, setbacks and styling issues had taken their toll on the model, which had aged prematurely. While it had a fine handling/ride balance, plenty of space and performed well enough, the conservative design in an era that welcomed in Ford's Sierra was a disappointment.

The Maestro's appearance had long been a contentious issue. Even its most staunch protagonists had to concur that it looked old before its time. Harris Mann's more modern proposal had been passed over in favour of a Bache/Beech design. David Bache, BL's chief stylist and head of design, has been credited with penning the shape. He'd been involved with the Range Rover and Rover SDI, but clashed with Harold Musgrove over the Maestro. In doing so, he lost his job.

While there was certainly much of Bache in the Maestro, the core of the design can be traced back to one of his team, Ian Beech. The design Beech penned in 1976 had looked fresh. By 1983 it had not only dated, it had been tweaked by the engineers. To make production easier, they had emphasized the car's sharp

'The hot hatch market was hot, very hot. Austin-Rover just could not overlook this'

Above: Maestro Turbo was a car that wore its MG badge with pride and total justification.
Below: Despite subtle red touches, plain interior gave little clue to the beast within.

features. Roy Axe, who took over from Bache as head of design, was dismayed with these looks. He even tried to stop production so he could do something about them. With just four months to the launch, the management wouldn't sanction this and the Maestro went ahead unaltered. It wasn't a bad-looking car; it was just that its design was somewhat compromised and clearly rooted in the 1970s.

Nothing could be done about the styling so, to modernise the car, Austin-Rover looked elsewhere. In an attempt to move the Maestro into the 1980s, a number of technological ingredients were added to its mix. Body-coloured bumpers were an industry first, certainly in this class of car, but the biggest talking point was the dashboard – literally. Although the dash housing was an anonymous and poorly executed affair, at least it was home to a neat digital display. What's more, it communicated with you. In those pre-sat-nav days, a synthesized voice (actress Nicolette McKenzie) telling you when the oil level was low or your seatbelt wasn't fastened proved to be a novelty. Sadly, it remained just that: a novelty. Early reliability woes led to Nicolette's untimely silence and the return to an analogue display late in 1984.

Things weren't much better under the Maestro's bonnet, either. The trusty 1300cc A-Plus, with its electronically controlled SU carburettor, proved to be a willing and able partner. Released from the shackles of its transmission-in-sump, this engine (which could be traced back to the 1950s) enjoyed a new lease of life. The stop-gap 1.6-litre R-series engine, a lightly modified E-series, was less good and was soon replaced by the 1.6-litre S-series engine with its belt-drive OHC, advanced ECU and better induction system.

Although in many ways an improvement over the Maxi and Allegro, the Maestro, a product of computer-aided design and computer-aided manufacturing, would always be playing catch-up. Despite initially sprinting out of the showroom, as the months passed, sales slowed. By the end of 1983, the Maestro's best year ever, still only 101,000 had found homes. Even the arrival of the S-series engine didn't help. And too much of the product testing was still being undertaken by customers.

Fortunately, Austin-Rover threw its weight behind the Maestro and numerous improvements were wrought. But, as always, it was a case of too little, too late. The Maestro and its soon-to-arrive booted stablemate, the Montego, weren't bad cars. Far from it, they had just fallen victim to circumstances and poor timing. Even the MG Maestro, a model with masses of potential and real flair, fared little better in its early days.

Left Production delays meant that the sharp-edged Maestro shape dated very quickly, but this only adds to the model's charm today.

Hot enough?

The hot hatch market was, as its name suggests, hot. Very hot in fact. Austin-Rover couldn't overlook this fact, although the MG Maestro had only come about due to the surprising success of the MG Metro and the existence of the VW Golf GTI and Ford Escort XR3i. The MG Metro was doing very well and had shocked the management into realising just what an asset it had in the MG marque. They also came to the realisation that the Golf GTI and Escort XR3i were running away from what little competition there was. Something had to be done. Cue the MG Maestro, which was to be available from the start.

It'd be nice to report that when the MG moniker was applied to the Maestro, it effected a magic transformation. It didn't. Whereas the Golf and the Escort were fuel injected, the MG Maestro got a brace of Webers. Hasty development and a poor installation resulted in hot starting woes, fuel starvation and a voracious thirst. The MG Maestro was clearly going nowhere on carbs, even when its R-series was replaced by the slightly more refined, belt-driven S-series. Austin-Rover realised that this range-topping and significant car needed more power and better reliability. So, out came the S-series and in went the Montego's 115bhp 2.0-litre O-series EFi engine. Equipped with this strong and torquey four-pot, a Honda five-speed PG-1 gearbox and blessed with fine handling, the MG Maestro EFi delivered on its promise. As would the yet-to-arrive MG Maestro Turbo.

Boosting the appeal

Some doubted the practicability of a turbocharged Maestro, feeling whatever benefits it brought would be, at best, limited. Harold Musgrove was especially concerned about just how much work would be involved. Indeed, when pressed, he admitted to the fact that some testing had been undertaken but added that Austin-Rover had no plans to put such a car into production.

Nevertheless, the firm drove the project forward. Only it was the Montego, not the Maestro, which first benefitted from forced induction. The MG Montego Turbo, a 150bhp road-rocket, was blessed with neck-snapping performance. Sadly, it was also plagued with arm-snapping torque steer. Here was a car that played fast – and loose. It took until 1987 before the chassis engineers were able to tame the beast, by which time the car had garnered a reputation for its unruly behavior. On the other hand, important lessons had been learned. When the MG Maestro Turbo arrived, all things considered, it proved a well-behaved car.

Rivals

The mid-to-late 1980s and early 1990s were a halcyon period for the hot hatch. In terms of outright performance, the 16-valve Golf ran the MG Maestro Turbo very close indeed. Equipped with a 16-valve cylinder head and Bosch K-Jetronic fuel injection, the Golf 16V could nudge 129mph and reached 60mph in just over seven seconds. In August 1989 big bumpers arrived, complete with front fog-lamps. So too did BBS alloys and power steering. The five-door version was added in January 1990. By this time, VW possessed an image that every other car manufacturer coveted.

Ford produced the XR3i of course, but it also marketed the Series 2 Escort RS Turbo. Nicely styled and well-packaged, it also handled very well. The Garrett T3-equipped 1600 CVH engine generated 132bhp and 133lb/ft. Unlike the Golf and MG, it was never offered as a five-door.

Vauxhall's take on the hot hatch was its Astra GTE 16V. Under the bonnet was a peppy 2-litre engine that produced an MG Maestro Turbo-matching 150bhp. Torque was impressive, too, with a peak of 144lb/ft. This was one of the quickest cars in its class, which had plenty of street cred. Well equipped, with a neat bodykit and even boasting a digital dashboard, the GTE 16V was a serious competitor – although, like the Escort, it was available only as a three-door.

Each of these cars had lots to offer and much to commend. They were certainly class rivals but not really direct competitors. If you were in the market for an MG Maestro Turbo, it's unlikely that you would have been tempted by other marques. The MG Maestro Turbo was a rather special car, which was made all the more attractive because of its exclusivity.

Late developer

Change was a way of life at BL. In 1984 the Morris name had been dropped and Jaguar was floated on the market. Then, in 1986, Austin-Rover was renamed the Rover Group PLC, while 1987 witnessed the demise of the Austin name and Unipart, BL's spare parts division, underwent a management buy-out. The following year, the Rover Group would be privatized and sold to British Aerospace. Somehow, there emerged from all this confusion one of the fastest, meanest-looking and most underrated hot hatches ever. Unlike other models in the Maestro/Montego range, the MG Maestro Turbo actually benefited from its belated arrival. The delays and outside input meant that it was simply better ❯

Feature car

G733 TBD, build number 345, belongs to father and son duo Frank and Chris Lovelock. When Frank retired from the motor trade, it was Christopher who suggested that they should buy a modern classic. As Frank recalls: 'I didn't want to go down the route of taking up golf as a hobby. I'd enjoyed my time in the trade and when Chris suggested getting a project car, I agreed'.

The MG Maestro Turbo seemed to fit the bill nicely. Frank wanted a relatively modern car, it had to be a saloon or hatch, and it had to be different. It also had to be quick and it most definitely had to have a comprehensive history. G733 TBD ticked all the boxes and, it has to be said, was a very lucky find. 'It was my job to locate the car,' says Christopher. 'Dad said that I'd never find one – I did though! I posted a request on the MG Maestro Turbo Register's website. A month later I received a reply. This was back in April 2006'.

When Frank and Christopher went to see the car, they were stunned at just how good it was. Not only had the seller owned G733 TBD since new, he had also maintained it meticulously, as Frank explains: 'It had a full service history. What's more, he kept a log of everything that had been done to the car and every gallon of petrol used. He really didn't want to sell and would

only let it go to someone he knew would look after it. Luckily, he could see just how keen and enthusiastic we were'.

There is absolutely no doubt that G733 TBD is in the very best of hands. Frank and Christopher are passionate about this highly original, immaculate and exclusive MG. They may be its new keepers, but they are patently aware that they have a duty of care.

Frank and Christopher have become this car's custodians. G733 TBD is without doubt one of the very best examples to have survived. Unmolested, unmodified and complete with all of its original factory fittings, this model is in as good a condition today as it was when it left Tickford nearly 30 years ago.

Running on unmarked alloys, this gleaming and low-mileage gem is a regular prize-winner at concours events and classic shows. Long may this continue.

developed than the MG Montego Turbo. To ensure it wouldn't torque-steer itself into an early grave, the MG Maestro Turbo was fitted with its stablemate's improved suspension. The firm had also employed specialist company Aston Martin Tickford, whose engineers fined-tuned the suspension so that it provided the optimum handling and ride balance. They had also done some development work on the engine. The improvements were subtle and, in essence, the Montego Turbo and Maestro Turbo engines were one and the same.

Based on the 2.0-litre O-series, the engine was equipped with a Garrett T3 turbocharger, sodium-filled valves, a decent-sized intercooler and a single SU carburettor, to which was added the idle control/electronic choke control from the 1.3/1.6 models. Mated to this rather potent powerplant was a slick-shifting Honda five-speeder. With 150bhp and 169lb/ft. of torque, performance was electrifying. The all-important (in marketing terms) 0-60mph dash was dispatched in just 6.7 seconds, which was a tad quicker than a Ferrari and many other supercars, a fact that Austin-Rover made great play of in its advertising. Top speed wasn't quite in Ferrari territory, but a figure of 128mph was impressive.

The MG Maestro Turbo was a bona fide hot hatch and, to ensure that everyone was aware of this fact, it was suitably adorned. Power dressing was all the rage in the 1980s and this was certainly true of this machine, which sported a rather aggressively styled and in-your-face bodykit. Although the three-piece rear spoiler from the MG Maestro EFi was carried over, it was supplemented by a roof-level tailgate spoiler. There was a beefier moulded rear bumper and the deep front bumper was a chisel-jawed affair that was also home to a pair of rectangular driving lamps. Full-length side skirts were fitted, and the mirrors, door handles, grille and side rubbing strips were colour coded. To complete the makeover, decals were added – a small and discreet tailgate 'turbo' graphic and the somewhat emboldened versions that ran along the doors.

Tickford produced the bodykit, although it was actually an Austin-Rover design. Every MG Maestro Turbo was built at Cowley, except that they left the

Due to the efforts of organisations such as the MG Maestro Turbo Register, Maestro and Montego Owners Club and the MG 'M' Group, this charismatic and capable MG is well catered for. With the exception of the original Tickford-produced bodykit and certain body panels, the majority of parts are available at a reasonable price, and there exists an enthusiastic and knowledgeable following. Owners tend to fall into two camps: those who modify and those who keep it standard.

If you don't want to follow the hot hatch herd, then the MG Maestro Turbo offers a great deal for such a small outlay. Expect to pay just £3000 for a top example. Of the 504 cars, around 200 are thought to have survived, of which probably between 50 and 75 are on the road.

TECH SPEC

G733 TBD – 1989 MG Maestro Turbo

Chassis

Unitary construction body, welded steel
Wheelbase: 8ft 1.7in
Track: front: 4ft 10.3in; rear: 4ft 9.3in
Suspension: front: MacPherson strut, coil springs, lower wishbones, and anti-roll bar. Rear: trailing arms linked with semi-independent torsion beam axle, coil springs, telescopic dampers and anti-roll bar

Steering

Rack and pinion, PAS. Turning circle: 33.8ft

Brakes

Front: 9.5in vented discs. Rear: 8.0in drums. Cable-operated handbrake

Wheels

Cast alloy. Rim size: 5.5J x 15. Tyre Size: 185/55 VR15

Engine

Alloy head/cast iron block, four-cylinder in line, OHC, eight-valve. Single SU HIF 44E with variable choke and electronic idle. Intercooler. Garrett T3 turbo
Cubic capacity: 1994cc
Power output: 150bhp @ 5100rpm. Torque: 169lb/ft @ 3500rpm

Gearbox

Five-speed manual. MPH/1000rpm: 25

Performance

Maximum speed – 129mph. Acceleration 0-60: 6.7 secs
Fuel consumption: overall 20.9mpg, touring 31.6mpg

Numbers built:

Flame Red – 215, British Racing Green – 149, White Diamond – 92, Factory Black – 49 (these figures include the original show car, making 505 in total)

Above: Garrett T3 turbo blew 150bhp out of the 2-litre O-series engine.

production line without bumpers and graphics. They were then transported in small batches to Tickford's Specialist Vehicle Production Centre at Bedworth, where they received the bodykit and graphics, and were assigned a unique Tickford build number. The completed cars were given a short road test before being returned to Austin-Rover for distribution to dealerships.

The MG Maestro Turbo was launched at the 1988 Birmingham International Motor Show. This was car number 1. Differing slightly from the production models, it was actually registered as an MG Maestro EFi. Compared with its predecessors, even the very capable and well styled MG Maestro EFi, the MG Maestro Turbo was in every way exciting. Exclusive too, as just 504 would be built. Four colours were offered: Flame Red, British Racing Green, White Diamond and Factory Black. Except for the Flame Red cars which had a black insert on the rubbing strip, each had a contrasting red insert. Despite a good number being registered in 1990 and 1991 and Rover featuring it in brochures until mid-1991,

all MG Maestro Turbos were converted between January and November 1989. The model was well received by the press but regrettably not so by the motoring public – it took quite some time for all cars to be sold. For example, our feature car, which was delivered to the dealer in September 1989, didn't sell until March 1990. And that was only after a sizeable discount had been agreed to – the list price was a hefty £13,529 and rivals could be obtained for less.

Unlike other MGs, the Maestro Turbo might not make you go all dewy-eyed, but it's well worth consideration. Together with the MG Maestro EFi, it helped keep the MG name in the public domain. There is much to like about the MG Maestro Turbo. It is a serious performance car. Possibly the only aspect of the model that doesn't quite measure up to today's standards is the braking system – the stoppers are adequate, but not massively confidence inspiring. Fortunately, plenty of well engineered upgrades are available. In just about every other respect, the MG Maestro Turbo can more than hold its own. It is an intriguing fusion of different ideas, styles and engineering solutions. It was a good car in its day and makes an even more compelling case for itself now. Blessed with unique styling, fine road manners, sledgehammer performance, masses of charisma and the all-important MG badge, this model certainly provides a taste of the period, one that is sharp, but definitely not sour.

Contacts

■ **MG Maestro Turbo Register** – www.maestroturbo.org.uk
■ **Maestro and Montego Owners Club** – www.maestro.org.uk
■ **The MG 'M' Group** – www.mgcars.org.uk/mgm

National treasure

Feisty, pugnacious, ever so slightly barmy and nearly a winner, it is no wonder that the MG Metro 6R4 holds a special place in British hearts

Words: Martyn Morgan Jones Pictures: John Colley

The 1980s can be summed up in one word: Thatcherism. Prior to the arrival of the Iron Lady and the Conservative Government, Britain had been all about heavy industry, blood, sweat and tears. Thatcherism ground the unions underfoot, wiped the grime from our faces and swept away the dirt. Where the workplace had been three-dimensional and tangible, it became two-dimensional, clean-cut and increasingly privatised.

Britain had also become a dichotomised society. On the one hand there was Thatcher's trumpeting of family life, marriage, fiscal stability and good manners, on the other hand there was easy credit, rampant consumerism and increasing drug usage. Life for some had little purpose, moved too fast and changed too quickly. For others, it had become as vibrant and colourful as the jackets worn by the new breed of city traders.

Not only was Britain changing, so too was rallying. In 1982, FISA (the *Fédération Internationale du Sport Automobile*,) restructured rallying's rules. The fastest category of cars (Group 4) would now become Group B, and

manufacturers were astonished to discover that FISA had been unexpectedly charitable – only 200 identical examples had to be built within a 12-month period. The new rules even sanctioned the building of a further 20 'evolutions' for motorsport. There were few restrictions placed on what could be done and what materials could be used, especially with regard to the evolution models.

The new rules were a sea change. So too was the arrival of the quattro. Although a rallying newcomer, through its adoption of permanent four-wheel drive, Audi led the way. Left reeling by the quattro's prodigious pace, especially when the going was slippery or loose, the opposition crumbled. In 1981, the quattro's first full season, Hannu Mikkola claimed third place in the drivers' ranking, winning two events. Michelle Mouton triumphed on the San Remo, becoming the first woman to win a world championship rally. On the 1981 RAC Rally, in torrid weather conditions, the quattro was in its element. Even though Mikkola deliberately backed off during the final stages, he finished over 11 minutes ahead of reigning world champion Ari Vatanen in the David Sutton Ford Escort.

Left: The 6R4 may be longer, wider and a tad more powerful, but somewhere in there you can still see lurking the basic Metro DNA.

This wasn't a gap, it was a chasm – and yet some manufacturers still considered four-wheel drive to be too heavy and complex to be viable. Seemingly, at this stage, only Peugeot-Talbot and British Leyland truly grasped the significance of four-wheel drive. Jean Todt, Guy Frequelin's navigator on the 1981 RAC, had witnessed the quattro's devastating ability. He persuaded Peugeot-Talbot that its next rally car had to be four-wheel drive and turbocharged.

Over at Leyland, John Davenport, director of the company's competition arm, had planned to replace the TR7 V8 and TR8 with something akin to Ford's RS1700T. He changed his mind. Impressed by the quattro, he too was convinced that four-wheel drive was the way forward. Davenport, like Todt, didn't need a crystal ball to glimpse rallying's future. The thought of what could be achieved with a purpose-made rally weapon had him, enthusiasts and some engineers and designers salivating.

Just Williams
Among those relishing the opportunity to move rallying up a gear was Williams

Grand Prix Engineering's Technical Director, Patrick Head. Davenport had paid Williams a visit to discuss building a four-wheel-drive Group B rally car based on the Mini Metro. Over in Didcot, drawing boards were readied and Rotring pens were poised as Head and his team prepared to apply their knowledge of FI to the world of rallying.

The decision to work with Williams was pure genius and the resolution to base the new rally car on the Metro made perfect sense. The Maestro had been considered, but discounted. John Davenport later said that 'a small car makes a small track look bigger!'

The Metro itself had been warmly received by the buying public. Other new models were in the pipeline, Rover's SD1 was performing well in the British Touring Car Championship and there was a spirit of optimism within British Leyland. Capitalising on this, Davenport gained approval for the project with the initial development to be undertaken by Williams.

Brian O'Rourke, working under Patrick Head, was given the job of designing it. His background was in the aviation industry and the Metro was his first car

'The car was built to cope with everything that a rally could place in its path'

Right: **V6 engine wouldn't fit up front; placing it amidships was a defining moment, though wheelbase still needed stretching.**

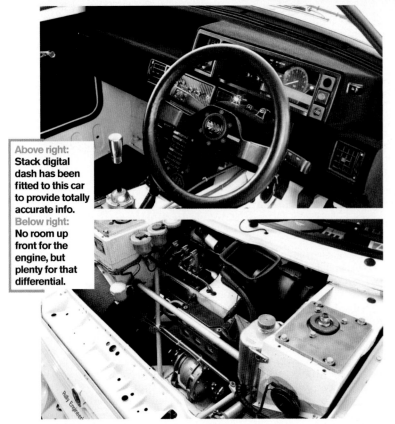

Above right:
Stack digital dash has been fitted to this car to provide totally accurate info.
Below right:
No room up front for the engine, but plenty for that differential.

project. It was also Williams' first non-F1 venture. By pushing even the very liberal Group B regulations to the limit, the links with the road car would become more and more tenuous. That said, early on, the rally Metro retained a number of ties with its production counterpart. For one thing, it was still being considered as a front-engined machine.

After mooting the soon-to-be-introduced Honda Legend/Rover 800 V6, focus shifted to the lusty Rover V8. Too big to fit within the Metro's engine bay, the decision was taken to lop off two cylinders thus creating a 2.5-litre V6, dubbed the V62V. With judicious welding, a purpose-made crank, Vitesse racing internals and a trio of deep-breathing Weber carburettors, the V62V produced 240bhp.

Alas, even in its truncated form the engine's bulk compromised the driving position. Viewing drawings of the proposed layout, works driver Tony Pond was dismayed to discover that the pilot's seat was where the rear chair usually resided. Unwilling to adopt the role of 'back-seat driver', Pond made his feelings known. Unsurprisingly, the team had a rethink. The V62V was retained, only this time the longitudinally fitted engine was mid-mounted, the gearbox ahead of it, with drive going to front and rear wheels. This was the project's Eureka moment.

Impressed, the powers-that-be gave the project their full backing and approval. Williams pulled out all the stops and three prototype/development cars were delivered, two in kit form, one fully finished, in December 1982. Designed from first principles the completed car, which was painted red and sported an Austin badge, was built to cope with everything a rally could place in its path. Impressively tough and immensely rigid, the modified bodyshell was a design strong point. Its floorpan had been cleverly fashioned into what was effectively a seam-welded tubular chassis and the roll cage was built in. The V62V engine was mated to a Williams-designed transmission system.

Austin-Rover take-over

December 1982 is an important date on the 6R4 timeline as it's when Austin-Rover (as it was now called) assumed the mantle of responsibility. Development

continued apace. The 6R4 first turned a wheel at Chalgrove Airfield, Oxfordshire, in February 1983, although Austin-Rover Motorsport didn't unveil its most gifted progeny until February 1984. Only then, confident that it had a potential winner on its hands, did the team go public.

Much of 1983 had been spent testing at Gaydon, Cadwell and in MIRA's wind tunnel. But, in what was a rather bold move, Austin-Rover Motorsport announced plans to trial the machine under competition conditions in national rallies and the team entered a 6R4 on the 1984 York National Rally. Having posted fastest times on eight of the 11 stages and leading by almost three minutes, the car's alternator cremated itself, bringing the 6R4 to an untimely halt. The team had actually planned to withdraw Pond at the end of the event, as he was needed at Silverstone to qualify his Rover Vitesse in the British Saloon Car Championship. Even so, there was no doubting that the 6R4 had the makings of a world-class rally car.

Further competition outings would accelerate its development considerably and gradually the specification and performance were honed. Most obvious was how the 6R4's appearance changed. Although it was never destined to be a sleekly styled Metro rehash, marketing and in-house politics dictated that it should nevertheless be reminiscent of its showroom counterpart. Wide arches aside, the first incarnation was not too far removed stylistically from a production Metro.

However, as development gathered speed and boundaries were approached, the umbilical tie between the road car and its rally sibling was stretched to the limit, then severed. In the end, the only obvious familial commonalities were the front grille, windscreen, headlamps and part of the doors. Only 16 panels/items had been carried over from the Metro, the remaining 347 were unique. The front and rear suspension had also been relocated, stretching the wheelbase by 5½in in the process. This, plus a widened track, taller struts and an effective aerodynamic package, improved handling and stability greatly.

Engineering

Engine development had also continued apace. Patrick Head advocated the use of a lightweight, compact motor. John Davenport agreed and, as has already

been mentioned, Honda's V6 had been considered. Indeed, the dimensions of the 6R4's engine bay are supposedly attributed to this unit. As it transpired, the decision was made to go for a bespoke build. Convinced that a normally aspirated 3-litre engine would deliver the ideal combination of low-speed torque, throttle response and driveability, Davenport eschewed forced induction.

The new powerplant was, in concept, designed by Austin-Rover Motorsport's chief engineer, David Wood. Designated the V64V, it was a compact, 90-degree V6, 3-litre, quad-cam, 24-valve beauty. Wood, who'd plenty of experience with the BD engine range as well as the DFV, had no hesitation in involving Cosworth, which supplied the pistons, valves, guides and springs, all DFV items. Cosworth wasn't involved with the actual build, but it did cast, machine and assemble the 6R4 cylinder heads. This design, which utilised DFV-type porting, was in essence a three-cylinder Mercedes 190E 2.3-16 head. The V64V engine is still the only ❯

Right: This Clubman-spec 3-litre now produces 350bhp; originally cars ranged from 250bhp to 410bhp.

engine designed specifically for rallying; all others are production based.

To cope with the vagaries of rallying, and to handle the power of the V64V, the four-wheel-drive transmission was also rather special. Ahead of the main gearbox, more or less central in the car, were a pair of step-off gears and a Ferguson Formula viscous-coupling centre diff. Running forward and backward from this were propshafts, the final drive of the rear prop being housed in the engine sump. The transmission was robust and relatively easy to work on. Depending on the event, different step gears could be fitted and the torque-split altered.

Despite there being a genuine, albeit commercial, connection with Cosworth this was barely alluded to. Much was made of the association with Williams, but it was the MG heritage that received top billing. In reality, the 6R4 had little to do with MG, but at least Austin-Rover appreciated the potency of the name. MG's sporting tradition and lineage was actively promoted, but quite what MG enthusiasts thought of it at the time is best left to conjecture.

The homologation specification was announced at Knebworth House in May 1985, where it was immediately obvious that the car bore little resemblance to the Metro, or indeed the prototype 6R4. The 200 Clubman cars were built by

Austin-Rover in a corner of the Longbridge factory. The V64V engines were assembled at Standard Triumph's former machining plant, Capmartin Road, Coventry, and the evolution (International) models were completed at Cowley. Checked by FISA, the cars were homologated for Group B from November 1.

Clubman models ran with a simplified inlet manifold, single throttle butterfly, less exotic internals, 250bhp and a synchromesh box. International cars would eventually have the benefit of 410bhp engines, dog-engagement gearboxes, ultra-lightweight body panels and many other options. It had been a real race to get the cars built and inspected in time. Had Austin-Rover Motorsport failed, the next available inspection date was December 1, a week after the RAC Rally.

Rallying to the cause

In November 1985, on the Lombard-RAC and the 6R4's World Rally Championship debut, Tony Pond set nine fastest stage times and finished third overall, a brilliant international debut. Interestingly, this car ran with a synchro box. Its Clubman/International hybrid engine had around 360bhp. Encouraged, Austin-Rover Motorsport announced a full World Rally Championship

In 1987 a group of owners concerned about the 6R4's uncertain future, and keen to tackle the problem, formed the 6R4 Owners Club. Subsequently, in '88, Rover instigated the multi-discipline one-make Esso Metro Superchallenge, which was a great success.

In rallycross, Will Gollop, Michael Shield and Barry Hathaway's 6R4s battled the Group B Fords, Audis, Peugeots and Lancias. Still at a power disadvantage, the 6R4's forte was tight, twisty circuits. Later, many resorted to turbocharging, quoting figures of up to 700bhp. Gollop's 2.3-litre bi-turbo-powered 6R4 netted him the coveted European Rallycross Championship in 1992.

Over the years the 6R4 has been handicapped by various means, including reducing its capacity to 2.8-litres, and then 2.5. Some championships penalised it by one to six seconds, but still 6R4s won. It's not just in rallies that this car excels. From circuit racing to hillclimbing, autotesting to drag racing, the Metro 6R4 has done them all. It's even competed on the Pike's Peak Hillclimb and Paris-Dakar.

The opportunities that once existed for the 6R4 have certainly diminished. Nevertheless, there are still many competing. And, they are not just making up the numbers, they are winning, too: Lawrence Gibson won the 2008 British Rallycross Championship in his Goodman-powered 6R4.

There are few cars that possess this ability and longevity, and there are few that are so well loved and respected. The 6R4 is a charismatic, multi-faceted and hugely talented machine.

'They're still competing – and not making up the numbers, but still winning, too'

TECH SPEC

1985 MG Metro 6R4 – Build Number 196

Chassis

Chassis-less construction with multi-tubed underframe, suspension subframes, integral rollcage, steel and aluminium stiffening panels, aluminium and GRP body panels (Clubman)/carbon fibre and Kevlar (International)
Wheelbase: 8ft 7.1in
Track (front): 4ft 11.5in
Track (rear): 4ft 11.7in

Suspension

Front and rear: coil springs, MacPherson struts, lower wishbones, adjustable anti-roll bars

Steering

Rack and pinion

Brakes

Front and rear: 305mm ventilated discs, four-pot alloy calipers, hydraulic handbrake

Wheels

Dymag magnesium alloy. Rim size: 8J x 15
Tyre Size: front: 225/45/ZR15, rear: 245/40/ZR15

Engine

90-degree, V6, quad-cam, belt-driven, 24-valve, Lucas electronic fuel injection, Lucas/Micos electronic engine management
Cubic capacity: 2991cc
Power output: 250bhp@7000rpm (Clubman)
Torque: 225lb.ft@6500rpm
Power: 380-410bhp@9000rpm (International)
Torque: 270lb.ft@6500rpm

Gearbox

Five-speed manual, synchromesh (Clubman)/dog-engagement (International), centre viscous-coupling differential, front/rear spiral bevel drives, with limited-slip differentials, 35/65 torque split (optional 45/55 and 25/75)

Performance

Max. speed: 140mph (Clubman – the International's top speed was dependent on its gearing)
0-60mph: 4.5 seconds (Clubman), 3.2 seconds (International)
Numbers built: Clubman – 200, International – 20

programme for 1986, with 380-410bhp cars for Tony Pond and Malcolm Wilson.

Sadly, the 6R4 would be outgunned by the opposition, which soon overcame most of the lag problems associated with turbocharged engines. The 6R4's ever-increasing deficit in performance, coupled with camshaft belt and valve guide woes, hindered progress. Nevertheless, it wasn't all heartache. An encouraging seventh, eighth and tenth on the 1986 1000 Lakes Rally was followed with fourth on the San Remo. Hopes were high for the home event, the Lombard-RAC. Sadly, and despite the support of thousands of patriotic and flag-waving supporters, the team couldn't replicate its 1985 performance. However, with cars finishing sixth, seventh, eighth and ninth, Austin-Rover clinched the Team Award. First in the French National Championship (with an R-E-D prepared car) was a real fillip, as was David Llewellyn's Circuit of Ireland win.

The 6R4 was quick, but its rivals were even quicker. For example, at its peak the quattro was pumping out 600bhp. But FISA was becoming increasingly concerned over escalating power and increasing use of expensive composite materials. These were certainly factors, but it was the tragic accidents in Portugal and Corsica that brought Group B to its knees. During the 1986 Port Wine

Right: Torque directed to ultra-fat rear wheels could be varied between 55, 65 and 75 per cent to suit the event by changing the step gears.

Rally in Portugal, a Ford RS200 left the road, killing three and injuring dozens. In fairness, this was an accident that had been waiting to happen and should not be attributed to Group B. In many European countries, spectators play 'dare', jumping out of the way at the last possible moment. On this occasion the RS200 crested a brow only to find that the road was filled with spectators. Swerving to avoid them, it veered into the crowd.

Following this accident, every works team withdrew. Then on May 2, 1986, during the Tour de Corse, Henri Toivonen's Delta S4 left the road hitting trees and rocks while sliding down the hillside. Toivonen, a sublimely gifted driver, and his navigator, Sergio Cresto, were killed. Group B and the proposed Group S were instantly cancelled. FISA instigated an international Group B ban, taking effect from December 31, 1986. Ford and Audi withdrew immediately; the other works teams decided to see the season out.

Taking stock

Even before these tragedies, and despite winning the 1986 British National Rally Championship, 1986 Scottish Rally Championship and 1986 National Tarmac Rally Championship, Austin-Rover had become increasingly disillusioned. This, plus spiralling costs and the fact that only 50 Clubman cars had sold, meant the company was considering withdrawing. FISA then announced its plans for the 1987 WRC. Only Group A and Group N production-based cars with a maximum of 300bhp were permitted. The winds of change were blowing and the outlook, certainly as far as the 6R4 was concerned, was bleak.

In Britain, the authorities, 6R4 owners and Austin-Rover Motorsport had no rallying outlet for the 6R4. Mercifully, a stay of execution was granted. If power was reduced, the 6R4 could compete on British national rallies. A ceiling of 300bhp was imposed. Quick to respond, Austin-Rover Motorsport updated the cars to Clubman 300 specification. These were advertised for a paltry £16,000. Even greater discounts were available if you bulk-bought.

This put Austin-Rover Motorsport into a win-win situation – for a while. Within 10 months all had sold. Gates of Harlow bought 40 to convert into road cars. However, as the 6R4 was not type-approved, the registration process was rather involved. In any case it wasn't a good street car due to excessive cabin noise and heat. Nonetheless, Gates offered a bespoke conversion service, fitting leather seats, carpets, electric windows... anything the customer wanted!

Unfortunately, just when the dark cloud that had hung so ominously over Austin-Rover Motorsport was about to reveal a silver lining, the firm was beset with even more problems. The cessation of the motorsport programme meant redundancies. More damaging were the cases of theft and fraud. Unable to cope with the embarrassment and loss of face, it closed in May 1987.

Feature car

John Manklow, of Goodman Racing Engines (a much-respected tuning and 6R4 specialist company), owns the stunning MG Metro 6R4 feature car. 'I've had it since 2002,' says John. 'It used to belong to Mike Nevin and I've serviced the car ever since he bought it. When I heard it was up for sale I decided to buy it to broaden my business. Most people know what I can do with 6R4 engines, but I can do much more!'

John has been involved with the iconic breed from 1985: 'I started work with Judd Engine Developments at 17, then moved to Cosworth. In 1985 I went to Austin-Rover Motorsport to work on 6R4 engines. I built Tony Pond's 1985 RAC engine and his 1986 Manx unit.'

John left in 1986, although he was contracted to rebuild and service the works/customer engines. This was when Peter Goodman joined as business partner. Peter semi-retired in 2000, although he still does some machining work for John.

Since owning the car, John has gone through it. He's rebuilt the suspension and adjusted it to the correct tolerances. The propshaft features his design of damper, which reduces the shock loading especially on dog-engagement boxes. The engine has come in for some

Manklow magic, too. It's a Clubman-spec 3-litre, now with 350bhp. John's added his own slide-throttle system, developed from the works set-up for extra power, torque and reliability. Motec ECU engine management is also fitted. The Stack digital dash is a huge aesthetic improvement and 100 per cent accurate.

John is inextricably involved with 6R4s, as he admits. 'I've never really moved away from them. I love building engines and developing the car. My goal is to build more to this standard and keep the 6R4 alive and kicking!'

Having seen this 6R4 in the flesh, and also been privileged to ride in it, we can vouch that it is exceptionally well prepared and the modifications work with fluidity, adding to what is already a brilliant package. The 6R4 is an icon of our times; long may it survive.

Thanks

Goodmans Racing Engines: 07710 847150
John Price Rallying: 01981 570307, www.johnpricerallying.co.uk
6R4.net: www.6r4.net
http://metro6r4onlinenews.website.orange.co.uk/
David Sims

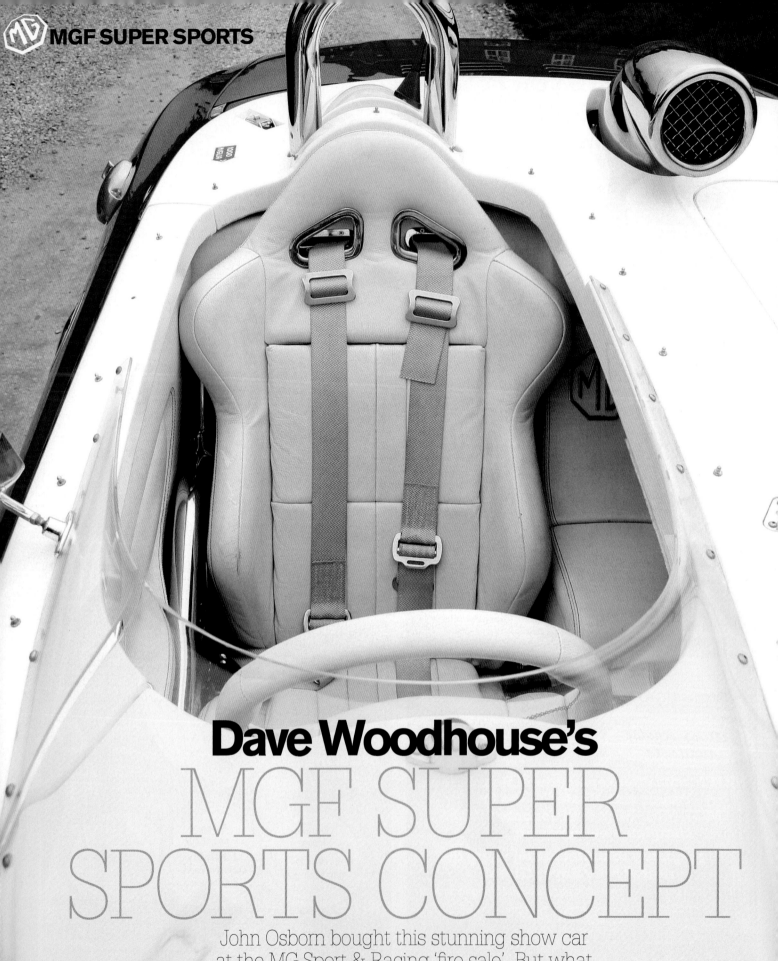

Dave Woodhouse's
MGF SUPER SPORTS CONCEPT

John Osborn bought this stunning show car
at the MG Sport & Racing 'fire sale'. But what
exactly is hidden under that beautiful skin?

Words Paul Wager Photography Richard Meadows

Above and left:
Super Sports is now registered for the road, although it has only 40 miles on the clock.

I once met 1980s Rover designer Roy Axe at the Gaydon museum – a venue which seemed entirely appropriate to chat to the man with an insider's knowledge of more than a few of the stillborn projects surrounding us. It was fascinating to hear how, with a tweak to a swage line here or a different wheelarch there, a concept could have been turned from an MG to a Healey to a Triumph in the blink of a marketing sub-committee's eye.

It is those concepts which have always made Gaydon my favourite car museum, but as I marvel at the glory of the SD1 estate or the Mini-based Midget replacement, I can't help wondering what's hiding away in the vaults. I know a man who's been in there, and he didn't speak for a week.

Just occasionally, though, the concept cars get out into the open and it takes something like the bankruptcy of a major auto manufacturer to let it happen. That was very much the case with John Osborn's MGF Super Sports concept, which was auctioned off at the MG Sport & Racing 'fire sale' several years ago when the receivers decided to maximise every last bit of revenue from the assets of the collapsed MG Rover.

Generally referred to as the Super Sports, this speedster MGF concept was also known as 'Rebel' inside Rover, and the early publicity shots show 'Little Bastard' graphics on the back in the style of James Dean's infamous Porsche Spyder. You might hear it referred to as the 'Mille Miglia' car, as well! Two models were built originally – one a road car and one more competition-orientated – as the result of a collaboration between the MG Motorsport team and the design workshops at Gaydon.

Described as a 'concept/development/show car' in the official auction catalogue, the speedster MGF was originally built very much as a runner, using a supercharged 1.8-litre K-Series rumoured to have been developed in conjunction with Janspeed and knocking out a handy 200bhp. The spec also saw uprated suspension and AP Racing brakes plus 17-inch wheels – essentially the kit used on MGF Cup racers – with the vehicle's dynamics apparently honed by MGF Cup racer and rallying legend Tony Pond, who is pictured driving the car at speed in period press shots.

The Super Sports began life as a sketch by Dave Woodhouse – one of MGF designer Gerry McGovern's team of stylists – under a brief to produce a concept to inject some of the glamour of '50s racers into the MG brand. Dave was influenced by the 'weekend racer' theme, explaining the James Dean connection, and Rover top brass were so keen on his idea that they wanted a finished show-standard car to unveil at the Geneva expo in 1998.

This involved turning Woodhouse's sketches into a running car in just 11 weeks, and to do the job Mayflower Vehicle Systems was brought in. At the same time, it was decided to use lightweight alloy bodywork on the car, which essentially involved replicating the standard MGF outer panels in aluminium. Some could be created simply by using the existing MGF press tools, while some required new fixing methods to be developed. The fresh panels were attached to the steel monocoque using rivets and a special glue to avoid the difficulty of trying to weld aluminium to steel and also to ensure that the adhesive formed a barrier between the two metals in order to negate reactive corrosion where the two meet. It is a clever solution to a tricky problem, and a similar system is now used on modern BMWs.

Woodhouse's work is at once quite extreme and really rather subtle. It's obvious at first ❯

Left and below:
Super Sports is a typical show car with glitz and glamour everywhere. Not all of it is real, though!

glance that the familiar MGF shape has been substantially altered, but just how much is apparent only when you look closer: only the doors and boot panel remain more or less standard, with the rear wings 40mm wider on each side and the front wings each 20-30mm wider. You don't have to be an MGF anorak either to notice the massive chromed air scoop or the Mini indicators.

According to documents of the time, the bumpers and speedster tonneau cover were moulded in carbon-fibre composite, but having taken a close look at the underside of the latter I can tell you with some certainty that it's nothing more exotic than fibreglass and duct tape. Equally underwhelming was my discovery that the rear diffuser is in fact made of MDF!

The inside is pretty much standard MGF fully trimmed in white Connolly leather, with every available surface covered in cow including the glovebox, dash and console. The plastic centre console, vent surrounds and instrument cowling are all now chromed, with a 'Super Sports' logo on the passenger airbag cover. One frankly bizarre touch is the old-school '70s-style 'bendy stalk' map-reading light screwed to the passenger door card.

After making its debut at the Geneva event, the Super Sports was displayed at various shows across the globe before being retired to a container in the famous 'Flight Sheds' area at Longbridge. 'It's been all round the world,' joked John, 'but it's still done only 40 miles.'

In both the front and rear boots there are special remote Hydragas unions to allow the suspension to be collapsed for shipping and then raised to driving height for display. Proof of the car's air miles status is present in the boot in the form of a handwritten note taped to the lid: scrawled in a corner of the instructions telling show staff how to adjust the Hydragas, is the legend 'Lou – MG Perth. Hi, April '99'. Interestingly, the instructions refer to the car as the 'MGF Rebel' rather than Super Sports.

Fast forward to 2006 and John Osborn had acquired something of an oddity. Undeniably an important part of MG history, it's a tricky thing to value and even trickier to enjoy. The Super Sports has next to zero underbody protection and as acquired couldn't even be registered, having just a Rover Special Projects 'SPL' number in place of a proper chassis number. Undeterred, John (as a former Rover sales director, a man who knows his way round the inside workings of the firm), took the 'SPL' number to the V5 department in Longbridge, who worked out the VIN from the approximate build date and issued a suitable plate and V55 certificate for the car. All of which explains why the Super Sports now wears an '06' number plate.

With the car at least registered, John was faced with the thorny question of what to do with it. The supercharger was removed soon after the MG left the show circuit (as were the gold wheels it wears in the original press shots) and it currently runs a standard (non-VVC) 1.8-litre K-Series engine, with 16-inch front wheels and 17-inch rears. It's a driver, but when you look closely at the details the nature of a show car begins to shine through. The starter button is a bell push from a Midland

Red bus, one of the filler caps is a fake, there's a radio aerial but no radio, and parts of the specially chromed dash are decidedly wobbly. Oh and there's that MDF rear valance, too.

It's an intriguing glimpse of what might have been though, and shows just what Rover was capable of even when stifled under BMW ownership – especially since a similar car was built at the same time but without the extreme speedster bodywork. Essentially a road model, this was finished in green and featured the revised panels and supercharged engine but with a standard screen and fully functioning roof. John also viewed this car at the auction but reported that it was well used and was even starting to look rusty in places.

After driving the car briefly round the factory after the sale, a spin at Stoneleigh during an MG show and then watching daughter Holly (a true MG Rover enthusiast and regular at www.mg-forum.org) piloting it up and down the drive for our photos, John had had as much use as he could from the Super Sport and admitted that to use it would be to spoil it. That explains why at the time of writing the car was due to be auctioned by Coys at Brands Hatch.

'I'd prefer to sell it to an MG enthusiast or specialist here in the UK so people can actually see it,' he said, but was resigned to the fact it would probably go to the USA or Japan. Not to China, though – Nanjing Automobile Corporation had been buying show-standard cars for a corporate museum back home, but with a whole production line on hand, it didn't need any MGF concepts just yet! **MG**

'After debuting in Geneva, the Super Sports was displayed at shows around the world'

Below: Seven decades separate two of MG's most impressive machines.

MG's Italian Job

The MG SV supercar was a truly international affair, and revived an Anglo-Italian link that went all the way back to the legendary K3 racers of the 1930s

Words: Andrew Roberts Photography: Matthew Howell

here could hardly be a more quintessentially British marque than MG, yet much of its most formative and successful history of sporting prowess has a marked Italian flavour. Arguably the most famous MG of all time, the immortal K3, made an indelible mark on motor-racing history by winning the Team Award and Class 1-2 on the 1933 Mille Miglia in its first season of competition. That same year the great Tazio Nuvolari won the RAC TT outright in another K3.

It is more than fitting therefore that MG's most recent foray into supercar territory should have been very much an Anglo-Italian venture. The MG XPower SV from MG Sport & Racing was just that. The design team was led by Peter Stevens, whose portfolio included Lotus, Lamborghini, BMW and McLaren in addition to MG Rover. The project was engineered by Giordano Casarini, who could count Ferrari, Maserati, de Tomaso and Qvale on his CV. The chassis and body were fabricated in the heartland of Italian supercars, while final completion was in a dedicated facility at Longbridge, Birmingham.

But surely the MG SV, whose hefty price ranged from £65,750 to £82,950 for the range-topping SV-R, was as far removed from high-volume MGs of the past and present as it was possible to get? Well, MG had been in bespoke territory before with the £795 K3 (around £36,000 in today's prices), of which just 33 examples were made. Handbuilding race cars beside mainstream Midgets was the way of things at Abingdon as far back as 1933.

How the MG SV project came about goes back to 2000, when the Rover Group was split from BMW and acquired by the Phoenix consortium. One of the earliest tasks for Deputy Chairman Nick Stephenson was an assessment of the MG brand and a subsequent product plan. The conclusion was that, in addition to offering a full model range, there should also be an MG 'ultra car' which would showcase the technical abilities of MG Rover.

This was very much a future project, but in a surprise move in 2001, MG Rover acquired the assets of the Italian subsidiary of the Qvale Automotive Group. Based in Modena, it manufactured the Mangusta sports car, a traditional front-engine/rear-wheel-drive design with a Ford V8. Initially shown as a concept in Geneva in 1996, the model was designed by Alejandro de Tomaso, with the rights being acquired by the San Francisco-based Qvale Automotive four years later.

Initial thoughts from MG were a reskinning of the car under the code name MG X80. A prototype styling exercise led to a major re-evaluation since it was considered insufficiently extreme. Essentially a completely new design was created, although certain elements of the Mangusta had to remain, since the model was already type-approved.

The outcome was a much more muscular and taut offering that literally oozed purposefulness and stopped Modena workers in their tracks when it was driven to the gates of Ferrari. But this was no mere styling exercise; it was a fully specified prototype whose performance astounded a test driver from the prancing horse in the surrounding hills. That this should have been the case was no surprise, given that Peter Stevens is much more than a design guru, having a specialist knowledge of aerodynamics and spending hours at the wind tunnel perfecting a prototype. Extensive testing at the Nado test track in Italy and at the old Nürburgring more than confirmed the car's aerodynamics and performance package.

The role of Chief Designer in a project like MG X80 is critical, and Giordano Casarini, who'd engineered the Mangusta, came on board. His intimate knowledge of the car was matched only by his abilities as a world-class chassis designer. Not only would the SV deliver ultimate performance, it would do so safely and predictably. It had to be as much at home in the Paris rush hour as being driven

Right: Total re-styling of the Mangusta resulted in an MG that looked both far more purposeful and aggressive.

Above, clockwise from top left:
Supercar was tractable enough for the daily grind; but it revelled in the freedom of the track; 3000 parts made up body that weighed 65kg; Peter Green shows K3 to Casarini.

to its max on the Nordschleife. Not for the SV-R the embarrassing overheating of lesser supercars awaiting their demo runs at the Goodwood Festival of Speed in 2003. It had, in the words of Nick Stephenson, to be 'a race car for the road'.

Such a formula was far from new to MG. The K3 was very much a similar supercar in 1933. Decades apart from its 21st Century successor it may have been, but both shared a common design philosophy, namely to be driven hard, far and fast, with ultimate handling and braking plus total reliability. Proving the point, the victorious Mille Miglia K3s were actually driven home from Italy to Abingdon after the race. The MG slogan 'Safety Fast!' was clearly no idle boast, and it continued to be the octagon's design mantra to the modern day.

A high-performance supercar is very much the sum of its parts and the MG SV drew on the proven expertise of companies who were the acknowledged leaders in their field. Chassis construction was by Vacari and Bosi – who also worked for Ferrari, Lamborghini, Jaguar, Rolls-Royce and Aston Martin – carbon-fibre was from the SP Group, the composite body was fabricated by Belco Avia and assembled by the OPAC Group. Engine development of the all-alloy Ford V8 4.6-litre and 5-litre was by Roush Industries and Sean Hyland respectively. Paint was by XK Engineering and Dupont, trim from Anderson & Ryan.

Peter Stevens and Giordano Casarini believed weight saving was free bhp. A maximum weight of 1450kg was the aim – ultimately the SV and SV-R would tip the scales at 1495kg and 1500kg respectively. By far the biggest contribution came from the adoption of carbon-fibre for the bodyshell. This was a major breakthrough, for the material is lightweight but immensely strong – a typical panel is as stiff as its steel counterpart but at just a quarter of the weight.

The raw material to make each body part was cut to specific dimensions using the CAD model at SP Group's Isle of Wight facility. Next, refrigerated packs, known as 'pizza boxes', containing the film and core were sent to Italy where each part was hand laid before being baked in an autoclave oven. The front wing with its distinctive cooling vanes was made up from no fewer than 90 precision-cut pieces of film and core material, while the complete composite SV bodyshell was made from 3000 parts using 32 different moulds. It weighed just 65kg.

Although the chassis of the SV was hugely strong, it had lost some 20 per cent in weight since its Mangusta days. Despite that, it retained the feature of an integral inner roof and FIA-specification rollcage, and met all European and US safety standards. The structure was actually stiffer, while the suspension geometry had been revised. Suspension was by long-arm double wishbones with coil springs and anti-roll bars front and rear. Spring rates had been stiffened and bump travel improved. Steering was power-assisted rack and pinion, while brakes specially developed by Brembo had four-pot floating calipers and Bosch ABS. Switchable traction control was fitted. The 18-inch OZ alloy wheels were shod with Michelin Pilot Sport tyres.

The engine and gearbox were both well proven components. For the SV the Ford V8 was used in its 4.6-litre form, with some 320bhp on tap. For the SV-R this was bored out to five litres and further modified to produce 385bhp. The Tremec five-speed manual gearbox was fitted, although a four-speed dual-mode Ford automatic could be specified for the SV-R if an owner chose.

The vision of the MG SV being painstakingly handbuilt was totally authentic, whether to rolling chassis stage in Italy or with final assembly and finishing in MG Sport & Racing's Longbridge facility, a clinically pristine area akin to a race shop. Here the cars were configured to meet individual purchasers' requirements in trim and finish, even including the owner's name etched on to the sill plates if desired. MG saw the production split as being 50/50 between the UK and the rest of the world – and limited manufacture, whether in SV or SV-R form, ensured its exclusivity.

What emerged from seeing the MG SV in build was how thoroughly developed and engineered the car was, and how MG Sport & Racing through the XPower brand clearly interpreted its role as the performance arm of the marque, in a similar manner to Mercedes-Benz and AMG. Experiencing the car at first hand merely served to reinforce this, as this ultimate MG was to prove immensely rewarding to drive and utterly competent, without any supercar foibles.

Our motorway dash to Donington Park was not merely a long-legged run to an ideal photo location, but demonstrated the high-speed stability, comfort and lack of cockpit noise of the SV-R. Headroom was immediately noticeable and the electrically adjustable Recaro seats were immensely comfortable and supportive. A four-point inertia harness was standard, which could be locked

> 'Stevens and Casarini were united in their view that weight saving was free bhp. A max weight of 1450kg was the aim'

for track use. No airbags were fitted.

Fittingly, Donington united the SV-R and K3 at the circuit where the 1933 model won its first race, straight out of the box, at the first-ever meeting at the Derbyshire road circuit. The Italian parallels were more than apparent, for Giordano Casarini made his acquaintance with the former Whitney Straight car, which had been taken to the Coppa Acerbo at Pescara the same year and won outright. Subsequently the vehicle was campaigned extensively by the brilliant Richard Seaman, later to drive for Mercedes-Benz. And it was no mere museum piece, for owner Peter Green raced this most famous car regularly, drove it on the road and had set National Class records with it at MIRA and Millbrook.

The performance and balance of the K3, equally at home on road or track, perfectly mirrored the handling philosophy of the MG SV-R's Chief Engineer. 'The centre of gravity is at hip level so you are at one with the car. With the front-mid engine (the Ford V8 is mounted behind the centre of the front axle) and rear-drive combination you know when you are reaching the limit and the car does not suddenly surprise you. There is a consistent steering response at all speeds; the driver's steering input is the same at 40mph as it is at 140mph.'

Whether at speed through the Craner Curves or being hustled along a rapid cross-country road, the MG SV-R impressed with its sure-footedness and utter predictability. The driver and car became one, the power was always controllable, the brakes were awesome and the clutch and gearbox decidedly driver-friendly. The massive torque available was a driver's dream and the entire SV-R experience was utterly addictive. For any of the doubters out there, the riposte was absolute. MG was very much in the supercar league with this Anglo-Italian creation that fused the best of both motoring cultures. Viva MG! ⑳

■ **Our thanks to MG Sport & Racing, Giordano Casarini, Peter Green and K3011, Nationwide Building Society (for 1933 currency conversion) and Donington Park.**

Above: Giordano Casarini, who engineered the Mangusta, at Donington's historic Starkey Bridge.

TECH SPEC

MG SV-R

Engine

5-litre all-aluminium V8, dohc, four valves per cylinder

Transmission

Five-speed Tremec manual or optional four-speed dual-mode Ford automatic. Rear-wheel-drive; electronic traction control; limited-slip differential

Suspension

Independent coil springs. Front and rear long-arm double wishbones with 25mm anti-roll bars

Brakes

Uprated Brembo discs with four-pot floating calipers and Bosch 5.7 ABS

Performance

0-60mph: 4.9secs
Top speed: 175mph
Power: 385bhp @ 6000rpm
Torque: 375lb ft @ 4750rpm

Weight

1500kg

Value

£82,950

Great British Marques: MG **151**

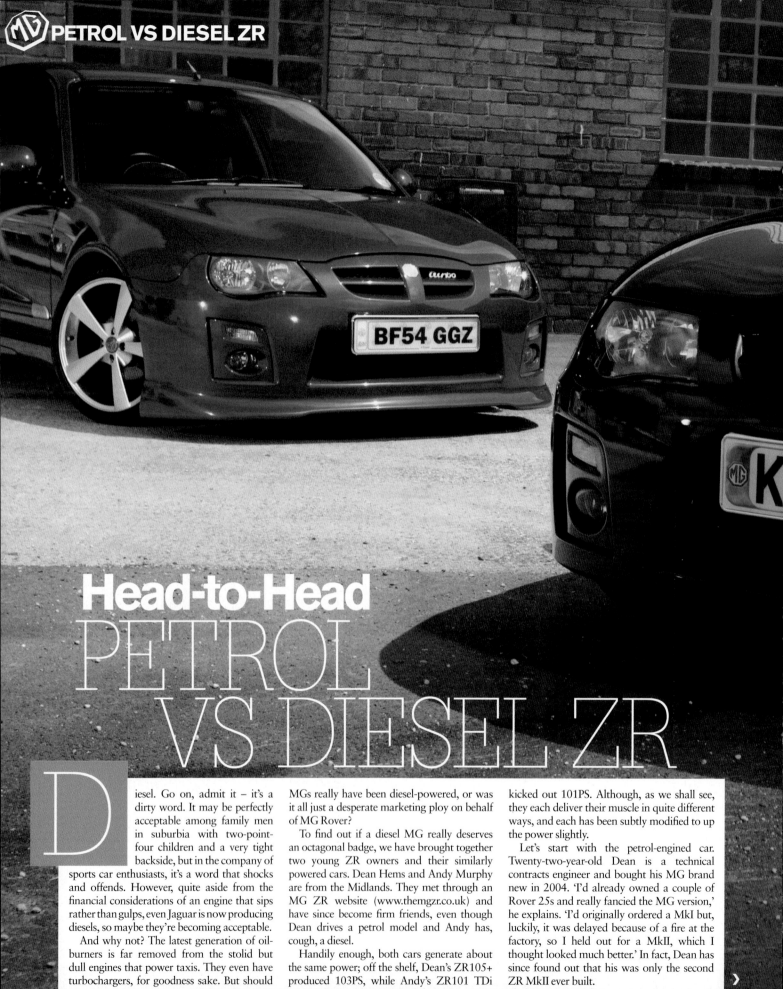

Head-to-Head
PETROL
VS DIESEL ZR

D iesel. Go on, admit it – it's a dirty word. It may be perfectly acceptable among family men in suburbia with two-point-four children and a very tight backside, but in the company of sports car enthusiasts, it's a word that shocks and offends. However, quite aside from the financial considerations of an engine that sips rather than gulps, even Jaguar is now producing diesels, so maybe they're becoming acceptable.

And why not? The latest generation of oil-burners is far removed from the stolid but dull engines that power taxis. They even have turbochargers, for goodness sake. But should

MGs really have been diesel-powered, or was it all just a desperate marketing ploy on behalf of MG Rover?

To find out if a diesel MG really deserves an octagonal badge, we have brought together two young ZR owners and their similarly powered cars. Dean Hems and Andy Murphy are from the Midlands. They met through an MG ZR website (www.themgzr.co.uk) and have since become firm friends, even though Dean drives a petrol model and Andy has, cough, a diesel.

Handily enough, both cars generate about the same power; off the shelf, Dean's ZR105+ produced 103PS, while Andy's ZR101 TDi

kicked out 101PS. Although, as we shall see, they each deliver their muscle in quite different ways, and each has been subtly modified to up the power slightly.

Let's start with the petrol-engined car. Twenty-two-year-old Dean is a technical contracts engineer and bought his MG brand new in 2004. 'I'd already owned a couple of Rover 25s and really fancied the MG version,' he explains. 'I'd originally ordered a MkI but, luckily, it was delayed because of a fire at the factory, so I held out for a MkII, which I thought looked much better.' In fact, Dean has since found out that his was only the second ZR MkII ever built.

When MG introduced oil-burners, it had the traditionalists spluttering real ale into their beards. However, with fuel prices reaching record levels, these days even the most performance-minded of us can be tempted by thoughts of 40mpg or more. But which ZR – petrol or diesel – is best to own, drive and modify?

Words: Philip Raby Photographs: Alisdair Cusick

Right from the start, he knew he wanted to make a few changes to his stealth-black MG while, at the same time, not going too over the top. Ultra LED lights were fitted at the rear and blue-tinted headlamps up front. The wheels were changed for ZS180 items, the windows were tinted and, when Dean hits the brakes, the word 'Stealth' (his online nickname) appears in the centre brakelight. Inside, he continued the black theme with black-ash trim from a Rover 25, while the sound system has been upgraded with the fitment of a JVC head unit.

It all looks the part but the really important changes occurred out of sight. 'I took the car along to XPower to have the firm's tuning kit fitted,' recalls Dean. 'This includes a BMC CDA induction system, a remap and an XPower twin-outlet backbox.'

These mods, he reckons, have upped the power to 123bhp, which he's satisfied with. 'The car is fast enough for me and yet remains economical. I don't know what it does to the gallon, but I get 250 miles from £30 of petrol, and I drive the car 30 miles there and back to work each day.' In our book, that equates to about 33mpg, which is pretty good going for a tuned engine driven by an enthusiastic 22-year-old owner!

So, with economy like that, who needs a diesel? Well, Andy Murphy reckons he does. 'I have a young son who lives on the other side of the country in Norfolk, more than 100 miles away, so I'm up and down there to visit him, which racks up the miles,' explains the 25-year-old courier driver.

Andy, like Dean, bought his ZR brand-new in 2004, just after the facelifted MkII version came out. 'I was working at an MG Rover dealer back then and had seen photos of the new ZR. I reckoned that it was one of the best-looking cars around. In fact, I still think it is,' he grins. 'It was my first new motor – I'd had a Metro before – and I was so excited, I was standing outside the showroom waiting for it to arrive!'

And when the Ignition Blue car finally did turn up, Andy knew he'd made the right choice. Like Dean, he wasted no time in making some changes. Unlike Dean, however, Andy hasn't been afraid to be daring. His ZR has been fitted with a Groundhog front splitter, rear spoiler extension and ZRX rear diffuser. The tail-lights have been changed for Afterburner body-coloured ones, the windows have a subtle tint

> 'MGs are all about having fun. It's no good having a great-looking car if it drives like an asthmatic snail!'

and he's fitted 17-inch Wolfrace wheels with AVO lowering springs. At the front, there is a neat 'turbo' badge tucked into the grille; well, after all, this is a turbocharged car.

Inside, the mods are less noticeable and are mainly limited to body-coloured trim panels and an uprated sound system. But, hang on, what's that boost gauge doing in place of one of the air vents? It's a hint that all is not standard in the ZR's engine room.

In fact, the motor is now producing around 127bhp, thanks in the main to a remap, something that diesel engines respond well to. He's also fitted an adjustable boost, so he can increase the amount of input the turbocharger gives. However, doing this can lead to engine detonation, especially when lifting off the throttle in a hurry. This is because the turbo is continuing to pressurise the air but the closed throttle prevents this air from entering the engine. Andy has got around this problem by fitting a dump valve between the turbocharger and the throttle body. This is a spring-loaded device that opens when the pressure gets too much, venting the excess pressure into the atmosphere. A sports induction kit and a custom-made exhaust system complete the performance upgrades.

But surely doing all this has buggered up the fuel economy? 'Er, yes it has,' admits Andy. 'When I got the car, it was doing as much as 52mpg, now it's down to 35-40mpg!' Never mind, they're still figures that make petrol users drool with envy, and better than Dean can manage with his ZR.

Let's not forget, though, that MGs are all about having fun, and it's no good having a great-looking car if it drives like an asthmatic snail!. So let's start by looking at the performance figures of the standard models – they're quite surprising.

We've already established that the two ZRs have comparable power, both before and after modification. The 0-60mph times for the standard cars are similar, too, coming in at 10.0 seconds for the smaller K-series petrol and – wait for it – 9.7 seconds for the diesel. However, where you really see a difference – on paper at least – is in the mid-range figures: 30-50mph in fourth gear takes a wheezy 10.8 seconds in the petrol car and just 6.3 seconds in the oil-burner, and while the former crawls from 50-70mph in 10.8 seconds, the diesel dashes there in 9.6 seconds. Finally, the ZR105 has a top speed of 111mph, which the ZR101 beats by 3mph.

>

'As my first new car, I was so excited I was standing outside the showroom waiting for it to arrive'

TECH SPEC	
ZR101 TDi	
Engine	2.0 L-series
Capacity	1994cc
Bore and stroke	84.5x89.0mm
Valves per cylinder	Two
Max power	101PS @ 4200rpm
0-60mph	9.7 seconds
Top speed	114mph
Combined economy	53.8mpg
Max torque	240Nm @ 2000rpm

TECH SPEC	
ZR105	
Engine	1.4 K-series
Capacity	1396cc
Bore and stroke	75.0x79.0mm
Valves per cylinder	Four
Max power	103PS @ 6000rpm
0-60mph	10.0 seconds
Top speed	111mph
Combined economy	41.3mpg
Max torque	123Nm @ 4500rpm

L-SERIES HISTORY

The 2-litre ZR diesel engine began life as an offshoot of the O-series powerplant which was, at one point, earmarked for use in the MGB – so there's a useful, if somewhat tenuous, MG connection.

In oil-burning form, the Longbridge-built unit was called PRIMA and appeared in, among others, the Maestro and Montego, where it gained a reputation for being tough and economical. During the 1990s, the engine was developed into the L-series and a five-cylinder variant was produced. By now, it was built by Land Rover at Solihull and used mainly in those cars.

When Rover and Land Rover went their separate ways, the latter kept hold of the five-cylinder engine, but passed ownership of the four-pot unit to Powertrain, which built MG Rover engines. And so the L-series found its way, first into the Rover 25 and then, by logical extension, into the MG ZR 101 TDi – the cause of so much spluttering into beards.

Gosh, so there's no denying that the diesel is the faster car across the board. Why? Because oil-burners tend to have more torque at fewer revs, so the gear ratios can be lower. The ZR101 with its extra capacity pumps out a beefy 240Nm of torque at just 2000rpm, while the ZR105 manages only 123Nm, at a heady 4500rpm. Maximum power, too, comes in a lot lower with the diesel at 4200rpm, while the petrol engine has to scream up to 6000rpm.

So that's the theory, but what do these modded cars feel like in practice? Seeing that Dean's has egg on its face after those performance figures, we'll start with that one. Any K-series-powered ZR is fun to drive and this is no exception. Its extra muscle is very apparent and it's a lively little car with an instantly responsive throttle. You do, however, have to rev the balls off it to enjoy the power – it only really begins to come alive when spinning over 4000rpm.

In Andy's car, on the other hand, you don't have this problem. Indeed, the motor runs out of puff at just 4500rpm, and you have to drive it in a quite different way, keeping the revs down so the engine can make the most of its power and torque. That extra torque means the diesel is an easier and more refined car to drive; more grown-up, if you like, and certainly a more relaxed motorway cruiser.

Despite being faster on paper, from standstill the diesel does feel sluggish to get going. However, once you're on the move, the extra mid-range power is very noticeable and there's no doubt that this is the faster car. And with that throaty exhaust system, it sounds surprisingly good, too; even better when you hear the dump valve opening when you release the throttle. In fact, you only really realise that you're in a diesel when the engine's ticking over. Once on the move, you can hardly tell it's an oil-burner and, in fact, it's quieter than the petrol-powered car because it's not revving as high.

There's no doubt that the diesel is the faster car (even Dean submits to this), and probably the better one, too, because it's more economical and less frantic. However, there's no getting away from the fact that the little K-series engine is more fun, simply because it's more responsive and you have to work the gears to keep it within the power band. And let's not forget that the ZR is a small car and, in our mind at least, one that should be zippy and fun to drive; it's not designed to be a refined cruiser. Diesels make more sense in larger vehicles, such as the ZT, where the better economy becomes more noticeable, too.

At the end of the day, though, both these MGs are great machines and a credit to their owners, who get a lot of pleasure out of them. And that, don't forget, is what MG motoring is all about. In all, we can confirm that there is nothing whatsoever wrong with owning a diesel-powered sports car.

W e hate to bring this up in case it re-opens old wounds, but do you remember the World Cup in Germany 2006? Well, are we alone in thinking that the beautiful game is now largely as dull as your average F1 race? You know, 87 minutes of tedium just to see three minutes of dramatic action. But the World Cup did have one adrenalin-inducing ace up its sleeve in the form of the infamous penalty shoot-out. All the drama and excitement of a whole tournament condensed into just a few moments of tension, causing spectators everywhere to leap out of armchairs, spill their beer and throw peanuts at the telly.

Wouldn't it be great if motor racing could come up with something similar – a heavyweight battle of raw power masking subtle finesse? Even better, why not make the track short and straight so that all the action takes place in front of the grandstand and you don't have to watch the telly to get the best view? Heck, if you could also make it cheap enough so that mere mortals could afford to take the family, then you'd be able to get a new generation of enthusiasts hooked on the sounds, the smells and the drama that go to make up a day at the races.

Of course, such a spectacle already exists. We are talking drag racing, and Chris Johnson is living proof that it does work. He went to his first race at Blackbushe airport as a schoolboy and liked what he saw. When a couple of friends bought a drag bike, he started going to meets with them. But when he decided to have a go himself, Chris opted for the added protection that comes with four wheels and a metal cage rather than straddling a two-wheeled rocket and lighting the blue touch paper. He bought an ex-Rob Turner chassis, built a small-block Chevy motor and a replica 1927 Ford Model T body and promptly won Best Newcomer for 1986.

This initial success was not immediately followed up though, numerous class changes meaning that his car became uncompetitive. So Chris built a new one, starting with an old-shape Rover 400, which was stripped, braced and sent to Webster Race Engineering in Bedford, just five miles from Santa Pod. John Webster designed and built a spaceframe chassis. Now using a 427ci Chevy, Chris won the National Championship in the Pro ET class with his new racer.

The next development came when the new MGs appeared in 2001. Chris works as a mechanic at Viking Garages in Southampton. At the time, it was an MG Rover dealer, so Chris ❯

The power and
THE GLORY

In one highly specialised branch of motorsport,
it is still possible to reach the top without spending
millions. Chris Johnson has done just that, and
he's done it in an MG ZS. Well, sort of...

Words: Simon Goldsworthy Photography: Dave Woodall

had plenty of opportunity to measure the internal dimensions of the new ZS. It was virtually identical to his old Rover 400 and he felt it was time to bring the car up to date, so a new ZS bodyshell was delivered straight from the factory and fitted to the old frame by Andy Robinson in Basingstoke.

This time, Chris was building to compete in the Super Comp class. While the ultimate Top Fuel class cars can accelerate from 0-100mph in less than a second and cover the quarter mile in under five seconds, Super Comp is still accessible to a privateer. It is based around an index time rather than a straight first-past-the-post fight. This sets a target time for the class – in Chris's case, 8.9000 seconds for the quarter mile. Competitors run in pairs, leaving the start line together and aiming to cross the finishing line first but – and here's the catch – they mustn't dip below that 8.9-second index or their run is discounted. So the object is to get as close to the index time as possible without going any faster, all the while staying ahead of your rival on the other side of the track!

It may sound a strange way to race, but the excitement levels remain at fever pitch and it is an excellent way of controlling competitors' costs. At a stroke it does away with all manner of

regulations, as you have a freer choice of engines, gearboxes and cars. Supercharging, turbos, nitrous oxide – Chris can choose how he manages to cross the line in 8.9 seconds.

In fact, he still uses his 427ci big-block Chevy bored out to 431ci. This may be an old truck block that's been around for decades, but it comes with four bolt mains as standard. The head and steel crank are stock, too, although the conrods and pistons are aftermarket items made for racing: the former by Manley and the latter by Ross. It's all pretty basic on the inside and, when put together with skill and care, will last a complete season – this is anything but a rich boy's class, and Chris has got to the top with a very understanding boss and modest support from within the trade.

That's not to underestimate the amount of skill and perseverance that it takes to succeed in this discipline. You need about 850-900bhp in a 2000lb car to achieve the required 8.9-second time and, despite its massive dimensions, the standard Chevy engine never got even close to this. Chris pushed his to around 580bhp breathing through a massive 1050cfm four-barrel carb, then topped it up with nitrous oxide. A total of 1.5lb of the stuff is fed in at various levels throughout the race, a good blast over the first 3.5 seconds to get the ZS moving and then adjusted down

electronically to get him to the line exactly on 8.9000 seconds and not a moment sooner.

Well, that's the theory, but Chris is still working on the programmable timer in an effort to get it spot on. It is all a matter of trial and error, and don't forget that he is working to 1/10,000th of a second, so even the most minute detail can have a major impact. One of the guys Chris races against has a weather station that sends information to a pager in his car, allowing him to punch data into his electronics, letting them to compensate for shifts in temperature and humidity.

Chris hasn't gone that far, working on the theory that if he keeps everything as simple as possible then there'll be less to break. But simple is, of course, a relative term. The gearbox, for example, is an auto item that he has redesigned to incorporate a manual shifter, using solenoids to activate the change at a set rpm. Initially these boxes were not strong enough to cope, until an aftermarket gear train made them man enough to take 2000bhp without self-destructing.

With precision so important in this class of drag racing, electronics play a big part in getting the time you want. Meetings are usually over two days, with practice and qualifying on Saturday. Chris would expect to get up to five qualifying passes, so long as the track remains dry (he can't

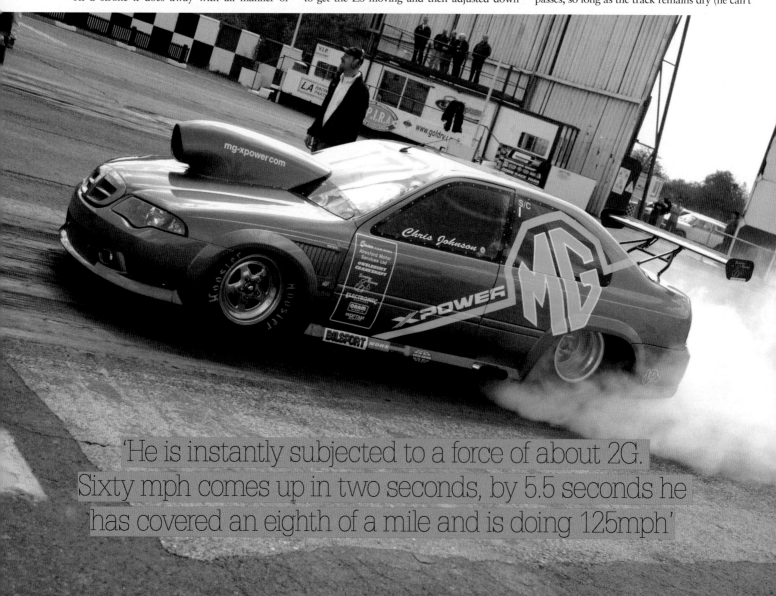

'He is instantly subjected to a force of about 2G. Sixty mph comes up in two seconds, by 5.5 seconds he has covered an eighth of a mile and is doing 125mph'

Left: It is fair to say that Chris Johnson's ZS is far from standard. But then, with a 0-60mph time of just two seconds, you'd expect it to be a little bit special underneath.

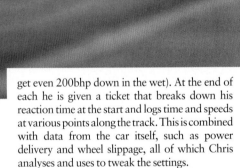

get even 200bhp down in the wet). At the end of each he is given a ticket that breaks down his reaction time at the start and logs time and speeds at various points along the track. This is combined with data from the car itself, such as power delivery and wheel slippage, all of which Chris analyses and uses to tweak the settings.

After qualifying, the person who comes closest to the magic 8.9000 seconds is in first position, while if you dip below this then you go to the bottom of the pile. On race day, the best of the qualifiers will race against the best of the lower-half qualifiers so if, for example, there is a 16-car field, number one will race number nine, number two will be up against number ten and so on. If you win your race, you go again in the next round. If you lose, it's the end of your weekend. Theoretically the two fastest qualifiers will face off against each other in the final, but of course, motorsport rarely runs according to theory.

In a run, Chris brings the ZS up to the start line and to a halt ('staged') when the first amber light at the top of the Christmas tree is illuminated. This brings on the second amber light. With the car still in first gear he pushes a button on the steering wheel to engage the reverse clutch pack to lock the transmission. When both cars are staged, the starter flips a switch that brings on a further four amber lights and, 0.4 seconds later, a single green light illuminates and the race is on.

By this point Chris already has his foot to the floor, although the revs are electronically limited to 5200rpm. He releases the button locking the transmission, almost instantly being subjected to a force of about 2G. Sixty mph comes up in two seconds, by 5.5 seconds the car has covered an eighth of a mile and is doing 125mph. Maximum revs are then matched to the gearing, bringing it over the line at 7500rpm, 155mph and – hopefully – 8.9 seconds. There is a parachute (all racers must have two forms of braking), but Wilwood calipers on the front and, incongruously, rear discs from a Citroën BX ('They were a nice fit,') are usually sufficient, although it does takes a further half mile to come to a stop.

If Chris has won his race, then he sticks around for the next heat. If he has come home second or has dipped below the 8.9-second barrier, then he can pack up and go home. As you'd expect from his track record, that doesn't happen too often. He came second in both the Avon Park and Santa Pod championships in 2005, just enough to make him National Champion. But Chris has his eyes on the European Championship, if he can find the finances. Despite the trophies, his biggest prize to date was just shy of £1000, and winning the British National was achieved using personal savings backed up by strong support both at work and at home. With a little extra help, there's no knowing where it will end. MG

USEFUL INFORMATION

How to get a piece of the action:
There are three dedicated drag-racing tracks in the UK, at Santa Pod in Bedfordshire, Shakespeare County Raceway (formerly Avon Park Raceway) near Stratford-upon-Avon and York Raceway. Considerable effort has been made to make the sport a family one, and typical entry costs for spectators are just £20 for the whole weekend, with each adult being able to bring in up to three kids free of charge. There are no restrictions for access to the pits, so you can get up close to watch engines being ripped apart and rebuilt between rounds. The big-glamour cars are the FIA ones, but no meeting will be lacking in excitement. If you want to try it out, contacts are:

Santa Pod
www.santapod.co.uk, 01234 782828
Typical events: What Ya Brung public test days, FIA European Finals, National Finals, Easter Thunderball, Flamer and Thunder fireworks special

Shakespeare County Raceway
www.shakespearecountyraceway.com, 01789 414119
Typical events: Public track days, Springspeed, Nostalgia Nationals, Hot Rod Drags

York Raceway
www.york-raceway.co.uk, 01422 843651
Typical events: Super Street Shootout, Ultimate Road Car Challenge

Back to the Salt

I t is just purest coincidence, really, that we should be getting together in London on this particular autumn evening to ponder the black art of land speed racing. None of us knew when we picked the date out of a hat that Richard Noble of supersonic Thrust SSC fame was going public even as we spoke with his next blockbuster assault on the ultimate in earth-bound velocity. The only thing on our collective minds tonight is maybe a small celebration of Jon and Daniel's safe return home from Bonneville, and a post-mortem of their second season on The Salt.

Still, when the conversation turns philosophical, and it inevitably does if chasing speed records is involved, Jon borders onto the clairvoyant. 'I can understand now, after we've gone through all this,' he says, 'why people keep going back again and again; it's addictive, it can become almost obsessive, and

when you're out there, you are wrapped up in it so completely that sometimes being there eventually becomes what's normal and real, and being back here is the unreal.'

I can understand far better now as well; the Bonneville Salt Flats, where Martyn Goddard and I first met Daniel Nash and Jonathan Suckling in September 2008, is one of the most Out There places on the planet. The bulk of any given year, Bonneville is simply a large shallow lake of briny liquid on a remote high plateau in the mountains of western Utah. For a few short weeks in late summer, however, the blazing high-desert sun bakes away enough water to turn it into a huge, perfectly level salt tablet suitable for driving wheeled vehicles at extremely high speeds. Provided, of course, you don't mind doing it under a heat lamp across what is effectively the salt-encrusted floor of a frying pan.

The two drivers and their MGs were already in the queue for the starting line on the five-mile Long Course when we found them, but that's not unusual.

Land speed racing holds a special place in the history of the MG name. Now, two amateur privateers carry on the MG tradition where the works left off

Report by Dale Drinnon Photos by Martyn Goddard.

There are no assigned starting times; you run when you think you're ready, and everyone from the fast and famous to the freshest-faced rookie waits together in the same tailback, under the same sun, with the same tension, often for hours at a stretch.

As the cars get closer to the front, last-minute preparations taper off but last-minute repairs get more frantic, until it's time to go or stand aside. This trip, it was Daniel and the ZT-T as the first MG off; there were nods all around and he squirmed among the tangle of roll cage tubing to be tamped in and strapped down. The engine fired with an open-piped V8 blast so brutal that even the seasoned for a moment recoiled in response; Daniel watched the dials and fidgets in anticipation of the starter's thumbs up.

Then the push vehicle nudged the racer gently off the line and when the launch speed was right, the driver found a gear and began to accelerate away, building momentum with the seamless inevitability of a steam locomotive. In

seconds he was gone from sight; there was no fanfare, no prize money at stake, very little media coverage, and virtually no audience save for the fellow competitors against whom, in truth, he wasn't really competing. There was only driver and car, disappearing into the shimmering heat devils that constantly danced on the blinding white horizon…

But of course the hard, dirty part is always getting there in the first place, and especially for this particular endeavour. Every great MG speed team of the past – Gardner, Moss, Hill, all the EX streamliners – they all ran with factory support. These last production-based MG-Rovers, the most advanced and complicated land speed cars in the marque's long history, originally came to the Salt with the staffing and funding of a modern automobile company with a point to prove. Now, though, they're being campaigned solely on the effort and resources of two independents, learning their craft as they go.

'It still seems a little bizarre to me that a couple of historic racers should wind ❯

up in such hi-tech machinery,' Daniel says. 'Both of us have always been fascinated with the idea of Bonneville, and we talked for ages about buying a car together, sharing the expenses and having a go. I think we just had something in mind more like a straightforward big-engine hot rod.'

That changed, almost accidentally, when MG-Rover folded and the motorsport assets came up for grabs in 2006. Of special interest was a land speed ZT estate designated the X-15, made on sub-contract by the legendary So-Cal Speed Shop in 2003. When it went unsold for six months, Daniel and Jon went along, you guessed it, 'just to have a look'. To make a long story short, EXF, the MGF built for Bonneville by the works in 1997, was parked beside it, and they went home with both.

The cars do make a handsome set, despite the fact they have not the slightest thing in common besides the Octagon. EXF is what Jon calls a boffin's car; starting from a plain MGF shell, Rover aerodynamicists trimmed the 0.37 drag coefficient to a mere 0.24, a quantum leap in aero terms. Then engineers installed a 1433cc K-series with a Garrett turbo and water-cooled Aston Martin intercooler, while the PR guys were making noises about how nearly standard everything was. EXF made 328bhp and went 217.4mph with American racer Terry Kilbourne, and if there's any genuinely standard bits of great consequence left, they're well hidden.

The ZT-T, on the other hand, while hardly being ordinary main dealer fare either, is a hot-rodder's car. A conventional front-engine/rear-drive platform, it's far closer to the old American 'cram in all the motor she'll hold and let's go' school of making speed. Power is from an electronically controlled 6-litre Ford pushrod V8 prepped by Roush Racing to a staggering 765 horses (without forced induction, mind), and the driveline would be at home in any first-class traditional racing or rod shop in the USA: Jerico five-speed box, Winters quick-change diff, Wilwood brakes, Morrison and Aldan suspension bits – and an extremely non-traditional Pi Research computerized data-logging system.

Like EXF, X-15 also broke the magic double-ton. Driven by Pat Kinne, another Bonneville veteran, it did 225.609mph, a true testament to the theory that enough horsepower can achieve anything, as basically the only aerodynamic help the big chunky wagon got was add-on spoilers and the windows rolled up (inspiring, no doubt, the press release claim that it was 'a virtually stock ZT-T').

Which was not to say that either car was capable of repeating those speeds as-purchased. Following EXF's Bonneville performance, MG-Rover modified it for an airport runway attempt on the world record for solo blind drivers by Brit ex-policeman Ken Moss (successfully, at 131mph). The audio guidance system installed for the run was subsequently removed, the steering and suspension mods were not, and after some publicity appearances, EXF was shoved into storage and forgotten.

The ZT-T had gone straight to the motor show circuit on return from the States, and then similarly into back-room limbo; both cars by 2006 were suffering from neglect and, more sadly, from downright abuse. Parts had gone missing. Lots of them. When Daniel finally got around to checking X-15's parachute, even that had been nicked and the bag re-packed with foam to cover the theft. The car had evidently also at some time been hoisted astride the tines of a fork lift, not very kind to components such as custom-fabricated exhausts.

There was no choice, given the team's experience level, but to enlist some expert help. And when word got around the tiny and incredibly interconnected world of land speed racing, an amazing number of people began stepping up to the crease to do their part. Alan Reid, a member of the Rover team that built EXF and who now works in Formula One, became available to take on its rebuild. 'Kiwi Steve' Davies, leader of So-Cal's labours on the ZT and currently owner of his own shop, agreed to bring the wagon back to spec, plus crew with the novices when they went to the salt. Sir Stirling Moss served as a consultant; so did Peter Stevens, former MG-Rover director of design and the creative force behind X-15.

Andy Green, holder of the outright World Land Speed Record with Thrust, did everything from speaking at the RAC fundraising dinner to giving driving lessons and tech advice, and was a Godsend. 'When you've got the world's fastest man telling you to move the spoiler,' as Daniel puts it, 'you think maybe you should move the spoiler.' John Wood, MD at MIRA, came forward with intelligence on a forgotten but invaluable stash of X-15 spares, then helped with wind tunnel time as well. Lloyd's Motor Club, where both drivers are members and Jonathan edits the club magazine, helped with critical sponsorship to pay for it all.

By summer 2007, the boys were ready to go, with X-15 at least. EXF would take longer because, as it happened, there was no record for which it stood a

Above: **Battery and dry sump; oil needs pre-heating before start-up.**

Above: **A surprising amount of the factory-fitted ZT interior was left in place.**

Above: **Five-mile Bonneville course reserved for vehicles capable of 200+mph.**

Above: **765bhp version of Ford V8 was to be offered in the MG SV.**

'With more aero tweaks and power tuned to 800bhp, it was getting consistent 225s'

practical chance. Rover in '97 had apparently never wanted anything other than 'the fastest production MG ever' on the anniversary of Moss's still-standing EX181 records, and adding an extra 400mm of rear bodywork to increase stability moved EXF forthwith from Production status to Streamliner. Returning it to the salt without unthinkable butchery would therefore take a touch more time and deliberation, whereas X-15 fitted neatly into an existing class.

'I wasn't terribly realistic, I'm afraid', Jon admits. 'I thought, I suppose, we'd just show up, hop in for a pass or two, and be handed a trophy…' Instead, it was like any other first season: qualify for licensing, learn the car, replace an engine (see previous comments on spares), gradually build speed, pay lots of dues. There was also the matter of learning to drive on a surface of such varying traction that fast road cars – and drivers – often struggle to reach three-quarters of their highest tarmac speed.

Still, the car was quick and had potential to be quicker. Were it not for engine computer problems – the programming used by Roush was so unusual even Roush couldn't access it any more, and it had to be cracked for power tuning by specialist Kris Valdez – the team might have reached the Gas (petrol) C-Production Coupé record of 225.995mph. As it was, they left the last of Bonneville's three annual events with a best of 223.5mph and high hopes for more in 2008.

They very nearly made it at Speed Week, the opening meet of 2008. With more aero tweaks and power now dyno-tuned to a whacking 800bhp, Daniel turned a 226.452mph, but unfortunately the repeat run necessary to establish a record couldn't be made until the following morning – a time when the cooler, denser air increases drag significantly.

A month later, at September's World of Speed where we met them, both drivers were consistently running in the mid-225s and a record seemed in the bag. Then, aero pressure started playing havoc on sections of bodywork, actually splitting the rear bumper skin and, on the last and most likely run of the event, the all-pervasive and all-corrosive salt seized the throttle linkage and Jon coasted to a frustrating on-course halt. That left just one more opportunity to make the record, but in October, the winter rains came early. The year-ending World Finals were cancelled, and the MG Land Speed Racing Team came home.

There's ample cause for optimism over our last round of post-season drinks, though. Both drivers are certain that with further tuning and tidying, there are records awaiting X-15 – it's just a matter of time. Daniel has also found a worthy goal for EXF, the last real works MG speed car and the first bio-ethanol Bonneville machine. There's a comparable petrol class record at 195mph, and considering EXF hit 197mph in shakedown runs this year, Daniel hopes to better it with ethanol on the 50th anniversary of MG's final streamliner records, set by the late, great Phil Hill.

But the red car is just so spine-tinglingly close to a big score you can taste it. 'It's right there, it's all within reach now,' Jon says as we adjourn into the street, 'it would be such a waste if the car didn't get to go that last tiny bit and grab it.' As always, of course, it will come down to money in the end, and in the end, that's usually the toughest challenge of all.

The TV news is on when I get home, and as I hang my coat, I can hear the headlines. 'Richard Noble will announce plans tomorrow for a £10million attempt to raise the world land speed record to 1000mph…' Once you've been Out There, it seems, the urge to go back is a mighty one indeed. Ⓜ

THANKS

Daniel and Jon (right) would like to thanks Hugh Coltharp of the Utah Salt Flats Racing Association, Don Lindsay of XPart, Brad Hanson of Flashback Auto, veteran racer Don Dicker, Kris Valdez of Dynamic Race Solutions, MG works driver Anthony Reid and Stephan Keating. For more info on land speed racing and the MG team, visit USFRA at www.saltflats.com, and www.landspeedracingmg.com.

THE £4000 QUE

Is it possible to choose the best MG roadster for under £4000, especially since very good MGFs are now down to that. We'll give it a go...

Words: Simon Goldsworthy Photographs: John Colley

I f you had £4000 to spend on an MG roadster, for many years the choice would have been limited to a Midget or MGB. But over the past three years prices for early MGFs have fallen to the point where they are competing head-on with the classic contenders. Of course, there's more to choosing between them than simple economics, with each car offering something very different in the way of MG appeal. We wanted to get all three cars together to assess their relative merits. After all, there's no better way to choose between them than a game of musical motoring chairs. And since the Midget was always something of an entry-level MG, it made sense to start with that.

Just looking at the Midget, it is hard not to smile. In some ways, that is down to its diminutive stature. But this mini sportster is a lot more than simply a baby that is trying to be a grown-up – the Midget is a perfectly-proportioned sports car in its own right. Many people have fond memories of the cars, too. A whole generation of schoolboys may have grown up with posters of Ferraris and Lamborghinis on their bedroom walls, but when they got that first pay packet or student grant, it was the Midget that got them eagerly scanning the classified ads. The cars were affordable, insurance steep but achievable and the cramped cabin something of a plus if the sporty exterior had helped you to pull a member of the opposite sex.

Nearly three decades after the end of Midget production, things haven't changed an awful lot. They are still ridiculously cheap, and careful shopping around could have you on the road in a reasonable 1500 for as little as a grand. The more popular chrome-bumpered cars will start closer to £2000 in a private sale, but only the most optimistic seller will ask more than £4000 for one of the best. The trick is to find one that has been properly maintained and repaired: as with any entry-level car, many owners struggle to invest the necessary cash in general upkeep once they've got the car on their drive.

Having said that, there are plenty of cracking cars out there and our car today illustrates the point beautifully. It is a round wheelarch model, perhaps the most desirable specification and one that was only produced from 1972-74.

Above and right:
A-series engine is a design classic; cabin is small but perfectly formed; twisty roads are the Midget's forté.

It is no disrespect to the later rubber-bumpered cars, which in their turn have many things to recommend them, but the delicate curve of the chrome bumper blades complements the body lines perfectly.

Getting into the cabin requires a bit of technique: stretch the left foot over the crossmember and deep into the footwell before sliding in bum-first. Once in, the ultra low seating position means there is plenty of headroom with the hood up. The screen is shallow, but so close to your face that forward vision is fine. The wheel is also very upright and close to your chest, a throwback to the 1958 Sprite origins of the design and one more ingredient in the recipe that makes a classic sports car.

Gripping this wheel, elbow room to the left is relatively generous but your right arm is pressed up against the door. It is a similar story down by the pedals, with any but the slimmest of driving shoes rubbing against the trim panel as you step on the throttle. The large speedo and rev counter are set ahead of the driver, the rest of the controls and gauges clear and easy to reach: a cabin this small creates its own ergonomics by default.

Out on the road, the Midget is everything you'd expect it to be. The low seating position, short wheelbase and light weight combine to give a bouncy ride that keeps you updated on the road surface passing so closely underneath but stops short of being so harsh that it jars. It feels faster than it is too: once on the move, you'd swear that the speedo is under-reading by a good 20mph which means you can have all the fun you want without endangering either yourself or other road users.

Even at modest speeds, on any but the smoothest road surfaces the standard suspension can make the car feel skittish through the bends. But it only takes a few curves to make you realise that this is the chassis feeding information back to the driver rather than the first sign of instability. It is an empowering characteristic after the sterile driving experience of so many modern cars, and one you soon learn to read and react to.

On faster roads, the Midget is not quite so in its element. A lack of any elbow support leaves no comfortable cruising position for your arms, and though the car is capable of 90mph, it feels happier at a rather more sedate 55-60mph. At those speeds, passing trucks on the motorway can make the Midget seem very small indeed. We are talking here, of course, of the standard Midget. Just about any aspect of the mechanical package can be modified to suit your needs, whether that be a period supercharger, the fitment of a five-speed gearbox or a full-on conversion to modern K-series power. But if it is the original design that lights your fire, then taking the pretty route from A to B is the way to keep that smile upon your face.

Getting out of the Midget and into the MGB can be a disconcerting experience. Designed in the same era and built at the same factory, you'd expect the overall package to be very similar. In many ways it is, on paper at least. The engine may be the bigger 1798cc B-series, but it powers through the same front engine/rear-wheel-drive layout. There is still a live rear axle hung off leaf springs, and seating is still strictly for two.

Seen on its own, the B looks compact and low and it is only when parked alongside the Midget that the difference becomes obvious. Yet the figures tell

'The bouncy ride keeps you updated on the road surface passing so closely underneath, but stops short of becoming so harsh that it jars'

the true story. The B is 5in wider than the Midget, it is 15in longer and the extra metal adds up to a significant gain of 630lb in weight. The cabin is still small enough to give that sports car cosiness, but now there is room for both your arms together with a padded cubby lid on the transmission tunnel where you can rest your left elbow between gear changes.

There's more legroom too, with enough seat travel for even the lankiest driver to get comfortable and still have headroom to spare. The screen is further away and more steeply raked than in the Midget, but the considerably deeper glass manages to keep the header rail away from most people's line of vision. The wheel is still upright and close, while the controls and heating vents are rather scattered around the fascia and central console.

Price-wise, the best MGBs will go beyond our budget with the Heritage re-shells costing around £12K for a professional build and finished ones available for around £5-6000 in distress sales at auction. Scruffy but sound GTs can be found for under £1000 on the road, although the Roadsters we are interested in today command double that in similar condition. Start moving towards £3000 and you should be able to find an excellent rubber-bumpered car, while another grand on top of that will net you a large selection of great chrome-bumper Bs for sale privately as well as a fair few from dealers.

The car we have brought along today backs these figures up perfectly. It is a chrome-bumper car that qualifies for the added perk of historic road tax by the skin of its teeth, being built on December 27 1972. The present owner had it insured for £3000, until a small fender-bender brought out the insurance assessor who suggested £4000-4500 was closer to the mark.

The running gear on this car is still pretty standard, and pulling away initially on the B roads it feels slower than the Midget. But this is a false impression brought about by the Midget having such an optimistic outlook: taking 1973 as an example, the B will dispatch the 0-60mph dash nearly two seconds faster than the Midget (13.7secs vs 15.5secs), cover a standing 1/4 mile more quickly (19.5secs vs 20.3secs) and carry on to a top speed of 100mph.

Yet with its extra weight, wider track and torquey motor, the B simply soaks up the bumps and bends with less drama. It still bounces around as befits a sports car of basically 1962 vintage, but less so than the Midget. There is none of the Midget's skitter when you hit a bump mid-corner, just the beginnings of a tail slide that is easily caught and corrected if your exuberance encourages you ❯

to carry too much speed into a curve.

On the highway, the difference is even more pronounced. The higher ultimate top speed may be an irrelevance on today's roads, but its importance lies in the B's ability to cruise comfortably at the legal limit. An overdrive gearbox helps immensely in this respect, bringing the revs down to around a non-intrusive 3500rpm at 70mph. The car feels more stable too, the extra weight helping it to resist buffeting from side winds and trucks better than its smaller brother.

And now we come to the strange part of this comparison. Reading to this point and comparing the B with the Midget, you could be forgiven for thinking the bigger car is relatively refined, almost modern in its ability to soak up both motorway miles and twisty back roads. Yet besides a modern interpretation of the MG sporting theme like the MGF, the B looks its age and the driving experience becomes altogether more archaic. In many ways it would be nice to have included an RV8 in this comparison as a bridge between the generations, but if you found one for £4000 then you'd need a broom to sweep it onto a trailer. So instead it is straight into a 1996 MGF supplied by MG specialist Hall's Garage in Lincolnshire. Some MGFs can now be had for less than £2000 but it's worth paying more for a really good onem and we're keen to see how the model compares with its classic forebears, whether if we had £4000 to spare we'd plump for old or new.

And that brings us straightaway up against that old conundrum: is the MGF a classic and so fair game to compare with the B and the Midget? To be totally honest, that's not a debate we care to enter because few of the protagonists are open to persuasion. Certainly MG themselves went to great lengths to project

> 'The higher top speed may be an irrelevance on today's roads, but its importance lies in the B's ability to cruise comfortably at the legal limit'

the MGF as a forward-looking design with the minimum of retro touches, but plenty of enthusiasts are happy to call it a classics in its own right and hopefully we can at least all compromise on the rather contradictory term of 'modern classic'. Certainly there is little similarity in the profiles, the mid-engine layout of the F partly dictating that car's low nose/high tail attitude, as well as the forward positioning of the cabin and the relatively long rear deck. It is light years away from the proportioning of both the B and the Midget, as is the quality of the panel fit and finish. Mind you, the F has so far had rather fewer winters to weather.

The screen is deep, but so steeply raked that once behind the wheel, taller

Above and right:
B-series motor is a
trusty slogger that
goes on for ever;
cabin can
accommodate all
sizes; MGB can
dispatch any kind
of road with ease.

drivers can feel they have to huddle down to see below the header rail. At least the frame is engineered to provide substantial rollover protection. The plastic dash curving away from the seating area is unashamedly modern, although there are nods to MG's heritage in the ivory faces to the instruments. There are some carryover items such as the Honda Civic stalks, but the cabin is certainly no parts-bin special. Overall it is a simple design, but none the worse for that.

That disappearing dash lends the cabin a far more spacious air than either of its rivals, but the feeling of being snugly enclosed is still there, thanks in part to the high and rising side profile. The mid-mounted engine does away with the need for a large central gearbox tunnel, but a substantial central box section is there instead to help give impressive torsional rigidity to the shell: you are less hemmed in than in the Midget, but the cabin is still divided into two clearly defined spaces.

The speedo is marked up to 150mph and the rev counter redlined at 6300rpm. We are not going to approach either of those extremes today, but are keen to see how it compares on the road to our two evergreens. Because the rain has started in earnest, that unfortunately means that the roof has to stay up. But at least it shows instantly how far designers have come in the suppression of wind noise: whereas the Midget and B were both so noisy by 30mph that they made the fitment of a radio virtually redundant, the wind whistles past the F's cabin in very subdued tones and there is a minimum of billowing from the fabric.

The K-series engine may have an almost identical bore and stroke to the old B-series motor, but it is a completely different animal that spins through the revs

at the slightest provocation. In standard 1.8i form it provides both more power (118bhp vs 79) and more torque (122lb.ft vs 94), while the technologically-advanced VVC boosts these figures further to 143bhp and 128lb.ft.

Our car today is the 1.8i variant, and the motor whirs away discretely a short distance behind us. The Honda-designed gearbox it drives through is connected to the gear lever via cables, a complicated system that works extremely well: there is the same narrow gate as in the B (only this time with five forward ratios and no overdrive switch), but you'd be hard pressed to detect the lack of a solid link between hand and cogs. Out on the road, the engine's wide band of mid-range torque and rapid throttle response allows overtaking manoeuvres to be dispatched with far less planning than in either the Midget or B.

The F is so quiet and refined that it can come as a shock to glance down and see just how much speed you are carrying through the bends. Fortunately the wide 205 tyres provide plenty of grip and give it up slowly to warn when you have gone a little too far. MG also designed in some understeer on the limit to help in this respect: they took their *Safety Fast!* heritage very seriously and the F is a car that drivers of all abilities can jump into and enjoy from the very beginning.

It has to be said that it is also very comfortable indeed. Some readers might have memories of getting sea-sick from BMC's Hydralastic suspension in the Sixties, but linking front and rear spheres together on the Hydragas-equipped F

> 'MG took their *Safety Fast!* heritage very seriously and the F is a car that drivers of all abilities can jump in and enjoy'

has tamed the system's tendency to pitch. MG also added conventional dampers to help deal with minor bumps, meaning the suspension is soft enough to cosset without becoming mushy.

So, does any of this get us any closer to deciding on the best way to spend £4000 on an MG sports car? The answer has to be both 'Yes' and 'No'. Each of the cars excels in different areas and it will be your intended use that largely determines the best car for you. The Midget is arguably the best looking of the bunch. It is cute without being cissy, sporting without being macho. It struggles

on motorways and the ride is bumpy, but as a fun car that can also be pressed into modest commuting, it's hard to beat.

The B is much more of an all-rounder. Faster than the Midget, it is perfectly capable of long-distance touring. On the twisty tarmac it feels the more assured of the two, but dampens out some of the seat-of-your-pants excitement generated by the smaller car. It is perfectly capable of daily use, but it takes a certain level of dedication to put up with the lack of creature comforts and the requirement for regular servicing.

In contrast, owning an MGF couldn't be easier – no grease nipples, 12,000 mile service intervals and the whole package was designed so that anybody could get in and feel at home. Not that the driving experience has been watered down to the lowest common denominator. The F still provides bags of feel, feedback and fun in a package that is safe and comfortable. A modern car in the best of classic MG traditions, as a fun car to use every day it is hard to beat. **MG**

Above: Sharp styling and a great mechanical package makes the F a superb daily driver: cabin is luxurious without being OTT.

■ Thanks to Martin Lauridsen for bringing along his MGB, to Lorraine Noble-Thompson for lending us the Midget and to Jim Leach for help with the shoot. The MGF was courtesy of Hall's Garage (01778 570286).

Modified Fs and

The tuning and style sides of the MGF and TF market are particularly strong at the moment: here are some of the UK's best examples

TFs

Right: Subtle badging doesn't do justice to the 205bhp power output.
Below right: It's a tight fit! In fact, the KV6 only fitted after extensive mods to bulkhead, fuel tank and subframe.
Left: Styling tweaks include Trophy spoilers and Trophy 160 wheels.

Chris Flanagan's V6 MGF

Experts said that it would be impossible to fit a V6 into an MGF but this car proved them wrong; the result is an MGF that will out-drag a Porsche Boxster, and yet looks virtually standard.

The engine in question is a 2.5-litre Rover KV6, as fitted to the more powerful MG ZS and ZT models. It's obviously significantly larger in physical size than the four-cylinder 1800 of the standard MGF, and it was always thought that it would be too large to fit the F's tiny engine bay.

In order to make the KV6 fit, owner Chris Flanagan cut away some of the front bulkhead to clear the front bank of cylinders and cut an access panel into the rear bulkhead to allow access to the rear bank's spark plugs. He also had to modify and strengthen the subframe and had a smaller fuel tank fabricated in alloy to fit around the modified bulkhead. The engine sump had to be reshaped to clear the subframe, but Chris was able to leave the standard MGF transmission and driveshafts in place, as they're known to be strong.

In such a tight space, engine bay temperatures were obviously going to be high, so Chris moved the oil cooler up front to keep oil temperatures down and added larger radiator fans to aid cooling.

With the wiring harness modified to match the KV6, and a remapped Siemens 2000 engine management system in place, Chris ran the car on a rolling road: it acheived 205bhp at 5500rpm and 260Nm of torque at 4000rpm. To enable the car to cope with the significant increase in performance, Chris modified the suspension and brakes, using lowered suspension knuckles, uprated dampers, poly bushes and AP Racing 304mm front discs and calipers . It's quite a machine!

Darren Brown's MGF

The modifications to Darren Brown's MGF are not particularly extensive or expensive, but they've resulted in a car that stands out from the crowd.

Following an accident that caused driveshaft and suspension failure, damaging a rear wheelarch in the process, Darren had the car resprayed in original silver but with Standox Crystal Rainbox added to the top layer, before the last coat of lacquer, to add extra sparkle. It's not even something that shows up in photographs but in the sunlight it's subtley different.

The original MGF bootlid has been replaced by a TF item with its built-in spoiler. At the front a Trophy bumper with lip spoiler has been added, with MGF foglights cleverly frenched in. Unusually, the rear lights have been left standard – and the car looks better for it.

Inside, the red leather seats are original but the rest of the interior is from a scrap MGF MkII, including the door panels, which have had red leather inserts added. The finishing touches are a red starter button in the centre console and puddle lighting in the doors.

When the engine suffered the inevitable head gasket failure, Darren had it rebuilt with a stage 2 cylinder head, and added a larger capacity radiator to aid cooling. Other mechanical modifications include Janspeed exhaust and manifold, Piper air filter, MGF Trophy throttle body, Mike Satur brakes and lowering knuckles.

'The modifications are not particularly extensive or expensive but the car stands out from the crowd'

Above: Extra trimming to complement the original Heritage red leather seats ads colour to the interior. Below: Red grilles are the least subtle part of an otherwise subtle exterior. Wheels are 16in MkII MGF.

On sign in background: RACE POSITIONS | 1ST CAR No. | 2ND CAR No. | 3RD CAR No. | 4TH CAR No. | LAPS COMPLETED | LAPS BEHIND LEADER | RACE | LAPS

Banner text: ENSIGN QUALITY BATTERIES · DUNLOP · LUCAS · MINT

Adrian Clifford's MGF

With its distinctive 'Good as Gold' colour scheme, Adrian's car is well-known on the club scene. Prompted by the 'horrible' non-original brown seats that were in the car when he bought it, he set about transforming the interior, sticking to a classic beige, cream and gold scheme to match the Sienna Gold exterior.

The black dashboard, centre console and door cards were replaced with lighter-coloured items sourced from scrapyards and specialists, and other parts added and colour-coded to match. A rare set of walnut trims from an MGF Abingdon was sourced, and then added to with a walnut steering wheel and gearlever surround, and the wooden MG dashboard logo, screen vents and door caps were custom-made for Adrian. Other extras include stainless pedals with MG logos and a mesh windstop.

For the exterior, the black hood was changed for a sleeker Sportster hood in beige and brown, with a heated glass rear window instead of the standard plastic window. A rear spoiler and front splitter were also added.

A set of 17in wheels improved the looks and allowed the fitment of 304mm discs and four-pot MG calipers. Power has been boosted by a Valeo 52mm throttle body, Fast Lane Tuning induction system, Blue Flame exhaust and a Piper 421 manifold. The gearshift has been fitted with one of Mike Satur's Slickshift IV kits – just another of the many extras that Adrian's car is loaded with.

**Above: Adrian drives his MGF all over Europe – but he only had to go as far as Goodwood for photoshoot.
Left: Interior is laden with extras and every item that could be painted gold, has been painted gold.**

Steve White's MG TF

Serial MGF and TF owner Steve White bought this TF new, making a point of ordering it in the distinctive pearlescent or 'flip' Biitersweet paint. He then added to the spec through MG Rover's Monogram programme, which allowed him to order a bespoke car.

The options he included were a green hood and green Alcantara seats. But he then added to them with chromed roll hoops and aluminium kick plates from Mike Satur, Lexus-style rear lights from XPart and a full sound system complete with a large subwoofer behind the passenger seat.

With his love of track days, it wasn't going to be long before Steve started to tune the TF. He handed the car to Marvin Humphries of Techspeed Motorsport, who boosted the 158bhp output of the VVC engine to 172bhp with the simple addition of a Janspeed 4-2-1 exhaust manifold and sports catalytic convertor, XPower exhaust system and an ITG induction kit. Marvin also swapped the brake pads for Mintex items.

Steve later returned the car to Marvin for suspension improvements, choosing 20mm lower springs, which not only improved the handling but also the ride – the TF suspension was notoriously hard-riding as standard. So, with just well-chosen bolt-on parts, this TF has been made faster, better handling and more distinctive. Result!

'With his love of track days, it wasn't going to be long before Steve White started to tune the TF'

Above: Steve used spare paint from a front bumper repair to colour-code the centre console. Below: The pearlescent 'Bitterweet' paint and the 20mm lowering springs make for a much more distinctive TF.

KAD's MGF

Love it or hate it, you can't deny that this MGF built by KAD is extremely distinctive.

It started with a Category D write-off, which KAD bought in with light damage to the front and smashed rear lights. Once repaired, it was fitted with a Carzone body kit from Poland, which KAD modified by cutting a much larger aperture in the front bumper.

But of course the change that everyone wants to know about is the Lamborghini-style door opening. This conversion was based around a universal kit bought in from America, and took a full five days to get right. The hinges are substantial, and the doors pull out in the conventional manner for the first six inches of movement before scissoring upwards. Gas struts assist the opening, but had to be carefully fitted to allow the outward and upward movements of the doors – KAD did so much work to the kit that they moved into supplying their own, tailor-made for the MGF.

The bodywork was painted in a flip colour and complemented with 17in Dare alloys, LED side repeaters, blue headlight bulbs and jewel rear lights.

The bright red of the interior was broken up by adding black sides to the red leather seats, chrome roll hoops were added, the instruments were fitted with a brushed aluminium surround and MGF Centre heater controls provided the finishing touch.

Above: Front is arguably the least successful part of the conversion but doors make up for it...
Below: Simple touches to the interior have made it look distinctive – especially with those doors!

Driving the new MG TF LE500

This is it, the moment MG enthusiasts have been waiting for since 2005 and the day that many thought would never come. I am sitting behind the wheel of a brand new MG sports car and about to hit the road for the very first time.

It creates a strange mixture of feelings. One is simple relief that despite a change of circumstances which has seen MG re-emerge under Chinese ownership, all the signs are that the marque's unique heritage is both recognised and respected in its new homeland. This is reflected in a UK retail network that is made up of former MG-Rover dealers and new appointees who display one thing in common – a love of MGs and an involvement in the marque that goes far beyond simple business economics. Their enthusiasm alone bodes well for a revitalised and reinvigorated octagon.

There is also some relief that the car I am sitting in is so recognisably a TF. There have been changes, but things have not been altered simply for the sake of change and the essential DNA is all there. This relief is, though, tempered by

a slight worry – motoring hacks up and down the country have delighted in pointing out that this is essentially a 14-year-old design and written it off as old hat before even giving it a go. Once we remove the rose-tinted spectacles that come with the territory of being so close to the brand, will we find the doom-mongers are correct or will our enthusiasm be tinged by a dash of disappointment?

Well, there is only one way to find out. So as I turn the key and bring the N-series motor behind my head instantly to life, I take a few moments to put the LE500 into its correct context. Yes, it is a brand new car, essentially built at a brand new factory in China and then assembled by hand at its former home of Longbridge. NAC-MG has never claimed that it is a new model. What the company has done is to put the TF back into production after a hiatus of over two years. This is likely to be a short-term measure to hold the fort and re-establish MG in the UK until a brand new sports car can take over the MG torch, in much the same way as the RV8 did in the run-up to the MGF. Therefore it has not been fundamentally re-engineered, but a pick-and-mix approach has

VX08 UTF

After two years of turmoil, upheaval and a massive dose of culture shock, MGs are back on sale in the UK. Selling all 500 LEs should be easy, but will the revived TF continue to deliver on this initial promise?

Words: Simon Goldsworthy Pictures: Mark Dixon

been taken from the previous TF range to provide the best combination of power, performance and handling.

As such the LE500 should have a character all of its own, but it would be wrong to expect it to feel radically different to what has gone before. That fact is emphasised as I look around the cabin. None of the controls has been moved or altered from the last TFs, and why should they have been? The layout is simple and the ergonomics good, so much so that even a newcomer to the model will soon feel comfortably at home.

The Piano Black detailing on these models set against the traditional Ash Grey dash sounds like a recipe for gloom, but in fact it only serves to lighten the grey and the overall effect is clean rather that oppressive. That is my view, though Adrian Clifford, PR Officer of the MGF Register who has accompanied me on this test, feels it is a little plain for his tastes – something that later production models may well address.

Although the controls are unchanged, the instrument binnacle is new. We do like the big, no-nonsense speedo and rev counter dead ahead, but are slightly

less convinced by the bar graph temperature gauge – when wearing sunglasses, this is not as instantly readable as we would like. Adrian has similar concerns about the other dials, feeling that the black-on-black formula can make information difficult to assimilate during a quick glance on the move. With fewer MGF/TF miles under my belt, I find them easier to adjust to though, and we agree to disagree on this point. We are both baffled though by those who have complained that the wheel obscures the instruments – we have a perfect view of them through a wheel that is unchanged in diameter at 13¾in.

And now it is time to put those instruments to work. As I manoeuvre my way off the Longbridge factory complex, the steering and clutch are very light. The gate on the gearshift is actually quite wide, occasionally fooling me into selecting third instead of first when setting off until I get used to it. It very soon becomes second nature though, as does the box's rather two-stage action from first into neutral and then on into second.

As I press on and out of town, the acceleration is impressive in the lower gears. Certainly with the engine up to temperature you can floor the throttle and send the rev needle spinning instantly around its dial. In first, 30mph comes up before the rev limiter cuts in at 7000rpm, second taking me on and up to the 60mph speed limit I am currently travelling in. All the while, the engine note remains unobtrusive in the background, arguably too quiet for many sports car enthusiasts who like to time their gearchanges by listening to the exhaust rather than by watching the rev counter. In this respect, NAC-MG is stymied by draconian regulations for vehicle certification, which restrict severely the noise that any new model can emit. I suspect a good few cars will find less socially frigid pipes stuffed under their tails within a few miles of the showroom.

Another production issue soon makes itself felt as I start to explore the higher gears. All the old TFs had a plastic throttle body, and this had a tendency to stick and stutter. The more performance-oriented models also had a VVC (Variable Valve Control) system that helped boost power from 135bhp to 160bhp, but all the extra oomph came in well up the rev range and was actually of limited use in normal driving – drive a 135 and a 160 back-to-back on the road and only the most committed of drivers would be able to tell the difference. The new TF comes with an aluminium throttle body as standard, which does keep the response crisp and sharp. But this is only the same 48mm as the previous plastic unit, whereas many owners of the older cars chose to upgrade

to a 52mm unit. I find that the smaller throttle body combined with a soft-breathing production manifold means that the engine can get bogged down a bit if I floor the throttle in the mid-range revs of the taller gears.

I do have to be fair to the LE500 though, and point out that any vehicle is a compromise. NAC-MG has opted for an engine in TF135 state of tune rather than the more asthmatic 120 or insurance-worrying 160, not least because it was the best-seller in the MG-Rover days. As such, it offers a great compromise between performance, reliability and running costs, and will more than match the expectations of most customers. Yes, there is scope for further tuning in the design and no doubt NAC-MG will offer more power in due course but, for now, if it is lairy that you want, then you will have to carry out the odd tweak or two.

If that sounds as though I am making apologies for performance that is below par, then you can take that thought and bin it. If you want to hustle, you simply hold the gears on the TF and make them work for a living. If, on the other hand, you want a more relaxed ride, then there is enough torque and power to register some very fast point-to-point times on both back roads and motorways. The biggest problem is keeping your speed under control – with such a quiet exhaust and the optimistic 160mph speedo zeroed at six o'clock, 60mph comes up with the needle pointing at nine o'clock, just where you'd expect 30mph to be!

Right: The new TF is a civilised sports car with power and handling that comfortably exceed what most drivers will use on the road.

This obsession we all have with speed and numbers is, though, in danger of making us overlook some of the car's other virtues, chief of which is the suspension. When MG-Rover first went from Hydragas suspension on the F to coil springs on the TF, it gave a very firm ride. This may have appealed to the most committed of sporting drivers, but proved to be rather too harsh for the vast majority of people who actually bought the things to use every day. MG-R responded by offering a number of option packs, of which the Comfort Pack proved the most successful.

NAC-MG has taken this Comfort Pack as its starting point and tweaked it to provide a superb compromise between ride and handling. It claims the overall

'It offers a great compromise between performance, reliability and running costs'

effect is to retain 90 per cent of the comfort but with a little more feel, and it's got the compromise spot on. There is little body roll and the lateral grip is impressive, but there is no harshness over uneven surfaces for either driver or passenger.

The steering that had been so light in the car park has firmed up a great deal as I get up to speed though, the variable assistance of the electric PAS being almost dialled out by this point. It remains light, however, thanks in part to the car's mid-engine configuration, something that will take fans of old-style MGs a while to get used to but which will be par for the course for anyone who drives a modern. Certainly I like the balance, and use it to good effect in a largely vain attempt to get at least a chirp of protest out of the Goodyear Eagle tyres. Those tyres also failed to register any protest when I make full use of the AP four-pot front brakes, the ABS unobtrusively translating my panic push into a controlled halt. The stoppers are lifted straight from the previous TF160, so should be more than man enough for repeated hard use in this LE500.

When I finally get a chance to cruise at 70mph (the gearing is unaltered from the previous TF, so this equates to a leisurely 3000rpm in fifth), I can pay less attention to the mechanical side and a little more attention to the rest of my surroundings. This starts with the pleasant realisation that the windscreen's header rail is not in my line of vision. The seats are no different to those in ❯

MG-R's TF and they are on the same mountings, so I am not quite clear on how this has happened, but later measurements against Adrian's MGF prove quite clearly that I am sitting two inches lower in the LE500 than I ever did before. Whether this will be common to all LEs I don't know, but if you have dismissed a TF in the past because you couldn't get a clear view, it might be worth taking a test drive in the new car to see if it works for you, too.

Rearward vision is not quite so perfect in the mirror, thanks to a windstop that runs right through my eyeline. Obviously the way you view this will depend on your height and body shape, but I find it more comfortable with the windstop down and although the buffeting increases like this, it is never intrusive. This problem's been caused in part by the desire to fit a shallow windstop that can be folded up or down without fouling the hood, and that hood is well worth a mention. With a glass rear screen (heated in case you prefer to make the most of the occasional winter sun instead of fitting the hardtop), it is simplicity itself to raise and lower with no danger of damaging or cracking a fragile plastic window.

As I pull back into Longbridge and surrender the keys, I am left

**Above: Interior holds few surprises for existing owners; ergonomics are very good.
Below: Natural balance is complemented by a suspension that is both capable and comfortable.**

'It delivers a sporting ride without requiring the driver to work hard for their thrills'

to reflect on the new car and what it offers. As expected, it is not radically different to the last of the MG-Rover TFs, and that is surely no bad thing. It is a very easy model to get in and just drive, delivering a sporting ride without requiring the driver to work hard for their thrills. If you do want to push it harder, there is plenty of power in reserve, although its hard edge always remains softened by the compromises necessary to create a one-size-fits-all offering.

Is that the right approach for NAC-MG to take? Without doubt, I think it is. Longbridge needs volume production to make it viable, and that starts here with the reintroduction of the TF. The LE500 and the TF135 promise the kind of comfort and reliability that make them quite capable of being used as daily drivers and attracting new members to the MG fold, but still manage to deliver the kind of driving fun that has endeared MG sports cars to generations of enthusiasts.

Is it better than the Mazda MX-5 it will inevitably be compared to? Not better, just different. Perhaps the Mazda is the more polished of the two (an air-con unit on the TF that hangs down into the passenger's footwell, for example, hints that money was always limited as the model was developed by MG-R), but in terms of ride and handling I reckon the MG edges it. And if NAC-MG has got both the engineering changes and the quality control right as early indications suggest, the car will finally be able to shake off a reputation for fragility, too.

Does it signal a bright future for MG in the UK? I think it does. I am not worried that the basic design dates from the 1990s – it was good in the first place and anyone who says it is outdated today either has not driven one, or does their driving on the closed confines of a race track. Besides, as I mentioned earlier, it is largely a holding operation until an all-new design hits the showrooms, probably in 2010, and this is a job it does extremely well. It is well screwed together, lavishly equipped and has had virtually all of the previous model's shortcomings redressed. Most importantly, it retains the combination of fun and practicality that is so essential to any MG. In short, I am impressed!

WHAT'S
stopping you?

If you like the idea of getting out on the track but are worried about taking the plunge, here is what you need to know

Words: Dave Livingstone Photography: Dave Woodall, Norman Law

With congested roads and speed cameras around every corner, it's no wonder people are flocking to track days to enjoy driving their MG. A race circuit has no caravans or traffic jams, and nothing coming in the opposite direction.

Just you, your car and a few like-minded enthusiasts on a challenging length of twisting tarmac. So why aren't you out there enjoying yourself? Perhaps you think it's risky – all those motors racing around and potential collision damage everywhere? Well, thankfully that's far from true. Track days are in no way, shape or form a competitive event. For that sort of driving, get a motorsport licence and compete in a speed or race championship. On a track day, organisers take a dim view of any participants racing each other or timing their laps. This is a fun event about driving quickly, but with due care and consideration for those around you.

How are track days organised?
There are always two things to do before you are let near the tarmac. First, you must sign on, where your driving licence is checked and you are asked to sign an indemnity form. Second, you must attend a driver briefing. This explains the track day rules and safety procedures, covering things like flag signals and overtaking rules. It also tells you how the day is organised and any circuit-specific information.

Typically, track days are organised into one of two formats: sessions or open pit lanes. In both cases, only a limited number of cars are allowed on the circuit at any given time. In a sessioned track day, all the participants are divided into three or four large groups, so usually you'll be with people with similar performance vehicles and with similar levels of experience. Each group will go out, one by one, for a session of usually between 15 and 30 minutes. Then you'll all return to the pits together and the next group will go out. This is a good, sociable format as it allows everyone in the same session to get together and compare driving notes.

An open pit lane has no sessions. You can go out whenever you like, and stay out for as long as you like. The marshals will allow only a certain number of cars on the track at any given time, so you may have to queue to get back on. This format is good fun, but remember: the longer you stay out on the circuit, the hotter your tyres get, the more wear your brakes receive and the more of a roasting your engine is given – so don't plan on spending the entire day out there!

Would I fit in? Would my car fit in?
OK, so track days are safe and now you know how they work, ❯

CAR PREPARATION

Checks are pretty much as for any road car:
- Tyre pressures and condition
- Wheel nuts
- Brake pad and disc condition
- All fluid levels and condition – water, oil, brake and clutch
- Indicator lights
- Battery connections
- Throttle return springs
- Seatbelt condition

'Passengers are free on any MGoT track day. The club encourages spectators to come along, hire a helmet and grab the odd passenger lap'

but will you fit in? Surely, there'll be all manner of especially prepared track day cars with drivers all decked out in racing overalls and driving boots?

Again, this definitely need not be the case. Choose a track day organised by a car club and things will be very familiar. Prices are keen as they are non-profit making, and people bring the same vehicles they would take to the local natter or club run. The MG community is no exception, and a branch of the MG Car Club called MGs on Track (MGoT) organises around one track day per month. All MG variants are welcome – and you don't need to be an MGCC member to join in the fun, though the prices are slightly more favourable if you are.

At MGoT track days you will find a mix of everyday cars and everyday motorists. Most people are not terribly experienced track drivers and the majority pilot fairly standard MGs, ranging from the odd T-series through to the latest Z car via everything in between.

What do I need to do to give it a try?

So, track days are safe, well organised and you can join in club days alongside like-minded MG enthusiasts. So, are you tempted yet? Or are you worried about other obstacles that might get in

your way, such as vehicle preparation, special clothing and insurance?

In actual fact, apart from a roadworthy car the only major requirement is a suitable crash helmet. However, if you don't have your own these can often be hired on the day for around £15. If you do possess one, then it does need to conform to a suitable standard (see above). Most circuits will require you to cover arms and legs, even in summer, but you do not need race overalls, boots, gloves or anything else. Indeed, on a club event you'll be the exception if you wear them!

Preparing your car for a track day is not as daunting as you may think. The engine is going to be used hard (you don't need me to tell you this), so check that all the vital fluids are topped up, but not beyond their maximums – having too much is sometimes just as bad as having too little. Check the condition of the oil and, if it looks dirty, consider changing it either before the track day or immediately afterwards. If you are aware of your car suffering from severe oil leaks, you'd be advised to get these attended to: circuits take a dim view of oil (or indeed any fluid other than rain) on the track.

Safety factors are again not difficult to predict, so ensure that your belts are in good condition

and your seat is securely and properly fastened to the floor pan. Check the condition of your brakes – you are going to be using these hard, so if you don't know when the fluid was last changed, then replacing it now would be a good idea. Likewise, inspect the brake surfaces and pads. If you are unsure how to do this, get your local mechanic or garage to check things out for you.

Tyres are the most vital interface between you and the road surface, so look at the tread, the rubber walls (make sure that they have no bulges or blisters) and pressures. For track days, you may need to add a little extra air (your handbook may give some useful hints on tyre pressures for prolonged fast running, but these are guides only, so get some expert advice and experiment on the track as necessary).

Beyond this, it is a question of having a car in good condition, paying particular attention, of course, to the suspension. Inevitably older MGs will need that little bit more care and attention, but apart from that, have fun as most of what we are talking about here is common sense.

Despite all the obvious preparation there is still the possibility of damage – will I be insured?

Many standard road-going insurance policies will specifically exclude track days, but check your policy's small print. If there is no exclusion clause, then it is possible to insist that your insurance company accept a claim from a track day incident – we've seen it happen – though you will need to be very persistent.

It's better, of course, if you have one of the enlightened insurers who allow track day cover, either as part of the normal policy or as an add-on. In the latter category, for an additional fee,

Peter Best will add cover for track days to its normal Abingdon policies. In the former category, free of charge, Heritage covers track days for all MG Car Club members. Other specialist policies are out there – AON, for example, covers up to five track days a year, free of charge, with its 'Everyday Roadster' policy. There may very well be others, so ask around. However, your excess will inevitably go up for the duration of the track day, to around the £1000 level.

If you do find that your current insurer won't cover you and it's not the right time of year to look for a more enlightened provider, then you can always resort to one-off cover. It is quite expensive, but there are companies that will insure your car just for the one track day. Competition Car Insurance (www.competition-car-insurance.co.uk) and MOtorSport Race&Rally Insurance Services (www.moris.co.uk) are two that come to mind. MORIS will cover you for more than one day a year. Again, expect a large excess.

The alternative is to take the risk. It's not as bad as it sounds and many people do this for all the reasons outlined earlier: no oncoming traffic, no junctions or distractions, rules that are well laid out and policed by marshals, with anyone driving discourteously or dangerously being black-flagged and taken off the track. Remember, club days are attended by fellow enthusiasts, who are just as protective of their car as you are.

How do I begin once on track?
Most track days begin with what are called 'sighting laps'. These are low-speed laps behind a pace car that takes the correct lines through the bends. Everyone sedately follows the pace car and learns where each bend is, checking out things such as where the marshal posts are as you go around.

Instruction is often available at a modest fee

(between £10 and £25 on MGoT days) from ARDS (Association of Racing Drivers Schools) instructors. They will accompany you in your car and give guidance on the correct lines and your driving technique. This is invaluable, not only for the novice track driver, but also anyone interested in cracking that corner they never quite get right.

So what does it cost?
Costs vary according to the circuit, the time of year and the day of the week. Famous circuits like Silverstone and Brands Hatch are more expensive than Croft and Anglesey. Hiring the Grand Prix circuit at Silverstone is almost three times as expensive on a summer weekend as it is on a winter weekday. Take a look at the MGoT calendar and you'll see prices vary from around £125 to £150. Check similar circuits, at similar times of year, with commercial track day organisers and you'll find that MGoT prices are very cheap – that is the big advantage of club days. Even so, don't expect MGoT to run a cheap day at Silverstone GP in the summer.

Passengers are free on any MGoT day. The club encourages spectators to come along, hire a helmet and grab the odd passenger lap. Second drivers, sharing one car's track time, are also nominally charged (typically £15 – again these are MGoT prices).

Any other questions?
So, have you run out of questions? Assuming you want to enjoy driving your car to the full and that track days sound the right place to do it, then we have covered pretty much everything we can think you might need to know. All that you need to do now is book yourself a place and join in the fun. If you do have any other questions, just contact MGoT on 01235 555552 or visit its website at www.mgs-on-track.com. **MG**

MGS OF THE SILVER SCREEN!

Screenplay
A B ROBERTS

Cinematography
MARCUS DIXONI

In association with
DRIVEPAST.COM

For any MG enthusiast, the crucial automotive moment in the 1978 classic film *Sweeney 2* comes in the first reel. It even manages to overshadow all the subsequent adventures of Regan and Carter in their Ford Granada MkII 2.8iS. True, that bank manager's lovingly restored black MG YB saloon is on screen for a sum total of only 32 seconds before the blaggers in their blue oval press fleet Granada GL estate take over, but it is more than enough to add that vital extra degree of distinction to an already interesting film.

Sweeney 2 is a prime example of how an MG's on-screen appearance can be little more than a cameo and still add extra merit to the narrative of a film or television programme made virtually anywhere in the world. Many C aficionados have in their DVD collection a particular 1969 'Tara King' era episode of *The Avengers* entitled Killer just to see a cameo from an MGC Roadster reg BWM 300G. As this particular show also features the C's saloon cousin, the Austin 3-Litre, BLMC's PR department was clearly pulling out all the stops – and at least the C's involvement with Steed & Co was happier than the MGB's was with *The New Avengers* some six years later.

As that show's producers, Albert Fennell and Brian Clemens, were keen to uphold a thoroughly British image for the new programme, they sought a local automotive supplier. It was also felt that the production team's needs would be logically served by one company who could supply all necessary vehicles for on and off-screen use and so, thanks to British Leyland, Miss Purdey was issued with an MGB Roadster. Unfortunately, when Clemens took delivery of the MG prior to the shoot he was totally unable to put it into reverse gear. The reason was simple, as he subsequently discovered that the gearknob fitted to the B was actually from an Austin – in which the reverse gear was in an entirely different position.

Of course, not all attempts to reinforce the MG message on the screen were quite so disastrous. The 1964 American racing epic *Redline 7000*, if it is now remembered at all, was famed for its GP racing, but the more intriguing footage is out of the paddocks with a very young James Caan at the wheel of his BMC PR fleet MG 1100. Indeed, the Octagon-badged ADO16 made many sterling contributions to British cinema, be it the duo-tone four-door 1100 driven by scientists Ian Hendry and Alan Badel in the cult 1963 sci-fi epic *Children of the Damned*, or the 1300 two-door that terrorised all of England in *Monty Python's And Now For Something Completely Different – The Killer Cars*. Incidentally, the first Python film ends with a MkIII MGB in 'The Upper Class Twit of The Year Competition'. Another fine example of Octagon product placement is in the 1967 crime classic *Robbery*, where a B Roadster is but one of a whole fleet of BMC products used by the train robbers. Slightly less well recalled is the Austin-badged Sprite driven by Richard O'Callaghan in *Carry On at Your Convenience*, but compared to the Morris Marina that BL issued to poor Sid James in the same film, it is a veritable classic.

However, not every brand new MG (or Austin-Healey) on the screen is there for PR purposes a la Britt Ekland's B Roadster in *The Man With The Golden Gun* – the Lancashire Constabulary MGA Traffic Cars that appear in the 1961 classic *Whistle Down The Wind* and the first series of Z-Cars are the genuine article. Meanwhile, aficionados of truly bad horror films may recall a 1967 offering entitled *Night of the Big Heat*, in which fried eggs from Mars rather unsportingly blow up a MkI Ford Consul, a Triumph Renown and a Humber Hawk, but leave a Sprite unscathed. The reason is simple – the car belongs to the film's young leading lady Jane Merrow. As the film opens with her heading towards a remote town where both Peter Cushing and Christopher Lee have taken up residence, she obviously will need a decent car in which to flee before the final reel. This is not always a cunning plan, as is clearly demonstrated by the fact that Robert Powell's brand new orange B Roadster in 1972's *Asylum* does not save him from the standard Amicus horror film fate involving Geoffrey Blaydon and a good deal of ketchup. An even more ghastly moment for all loyal B owners is the 1980 film version of *Rising Damp*, in which Mr Rigsby attempts to impress Miss Jones by ❯

A MARTHON PRODUCTION   A FILMGROUP PRESENTATION

"DATE BAIT"

starring
GARY CLARK   MARLO RYAN   RICHARD GERING

PRODUCED AND DIRECTED BY O'DALE IRELAND · ORIGINAL STORY BY O'DALE IRELAND, ROBERT SLAVEN
AND ETHELMAE PAGE · SCREENPLAY BY ROBERT SLAVEN, ETHELMAE PAGE
Hear "DATE BAIT BABY" as sung by REGGIE PERKINS · Music and Lyrics by JOHN NEEL and OSCAR NICHOLS · Distributed by RAYNOTE RECORDS

TOO YOUNG TO KNOW - TOO WILD TO CARE - TOO EAGER TO SAY "I WILL!"

AT SIXTEEN...a girl learns about love...ONE WAY OR THE OTHER!

Above: *Date Bait* – beware any film in which a TF gives the most convincing performance.

displaying the acceleration of his second-hand B. The fact that it is then overtaken by a bicycle does not assist Rigsby's courtship one iota but it is a screen moment that always seems to go down well with Triumph owners…

For those connoisseurs of MG appearances in the truly obscure, there is always the cult 1965 pop musical *Gonks Go Beat*, where an early B Roadster joins a Mustang convertible and several other sports cars to race across the sands. In 1968's *The Curse of the Crimson Altar*, the square-jawed B-film leading man Mark Eden combs his hair forwards and drives a B Roadster in his joint attempts to both look hip and to defeat evil in the form of Christopher Lee and a green-painted Barbara Steele. Even more forgotten is the 1963 Hammer epic *Paranoiac*, which was launched with the slogan 'Beware The Eyes That Paralyse'. This subtle drama starred a young Oliver Reed, who was highly imaginatively cast as a deranged upper-class landowner whose main hobby is raving around his country estate and causing PB Midgets to drive off cliff fronts. At the end of the decade this scenario was repeated in *That Smashing Bird I Used To Know*, in which Dennis Waterman and companion drive their Sprite off another cliff in order to escape from the dire screenplay. Happily the TD in the 1963 lorry-driving B-film *The Hi-Jackers* escapes this dreadful fate, with the bonus that it is piloted by one Anthony Booth – Tony Blair's future father-in-law.

In fact, the most overlooked MG by film and television producers is the Magnette Farina, but a MkIII may be glimpsed in the Bahamas scenes of the 1962 Cary Grant vehicle *That Touch of Mink* and another MkIII provides a red herring in the excellent 1961 British crime drama *Jigsaw*. Six years later, it was the world's most down-at-heel ZB Magnette that played a major part in one of the greatest John Le Carre film adaptations ever shot – 1966's *The*

> 'In *That Smashing Bird I Used To Know*, Dennis Waterman and companion drive their Sprite off a cliff to escape from the dire screenplay'

Deadly Affair. As James Mason's depressed middle-aged spy chases the suspect's £60 Magnette in his black Austin A55 Cambridge Farina through a seedy London, it is proof – if further proof were needed – that the MG does not have to be the latest model to contribute to the drama. After all, 1967 also saw *Two For The Road*, the only film to combine Audrey Hepburn with a TD. True, she is seen entering the car by stepping on the running board, and says: 'You never should have bought an MG, you should have bought a tractor', but even though the TD is swapped for a Herald 1200 Convertible later in the narrative, the character of Joanna Wallace is played by Hepburn so naturally we forgive her.

The other major sources of great MG celluloid moments are racing films and post-war Hollywood movies of almost any genre. The 1956 Rank motor sport drama *Checkpoint* may well be populated with tweed-jacketed types who are over-prone to saying 'Gosh' on every conceivable occasion, but the racing footage is 100 per cent authentic, shot in full colour and allows for brief ▶

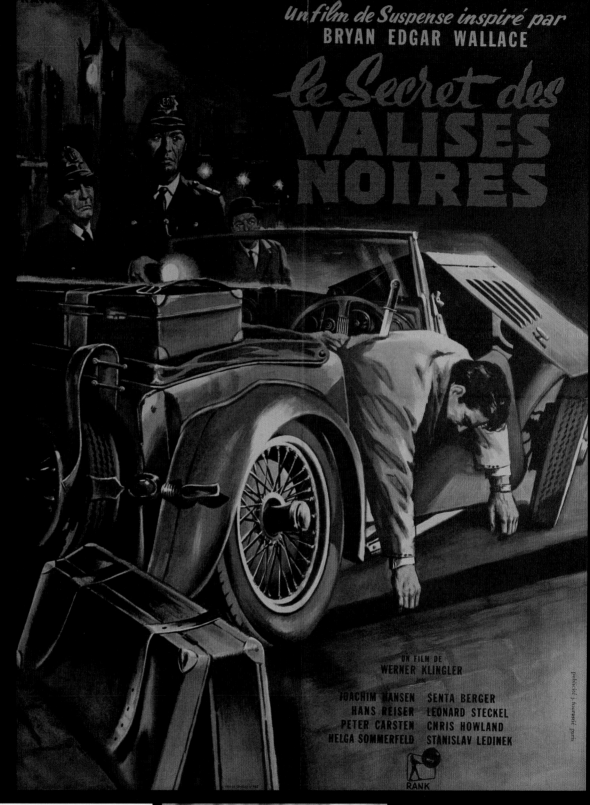

Un film de Suspense inspiré par
BRYAN EDGAR WALLACE

le Secret des
VALISES
NOIRES

UN FILM DE
WERNER KLINGLER
AVEC

JOACHIM HANSEN   SENTA BERGER
HANS REISER   LEONARD STECKEL
PETER CARSTEN   CHRIS HOWLAND
HELGA SOMMERFELD   STANISLAV LEDINEK

publicité j. tourassé. paris

RANK

Above: A long-lost West German
Edgar Wallace 'Krimmimovie', where
the crime appears to be 'severe neglect
of an MG'.
Left: A very young Russell Crowe in
the 1966-set Australian comedy
Spotswood.
Far left: Mickey Rooney's TD in 1954's
Drive a Crooked Road.

LA MERVEILLEUSE
ANGLAISE
(THE FAST LADY)
COULEURS
JULIE CHRISTIE
dans son premier film GA1..!
VISA DE CENSURE · 2455

Above: Leslie Phillips uses his red MGA 1600 to good effect in *The Fast Lady*.

drive-on roles for some very early MGAs. Similarly thrilling moments occur in *The Green Helmet*, which also features Wales doubling for Scilly and Sid James as an Australian F1 engineer. But it is US track films that often contain the finest scenes. The 1954 movie *Drive a Crooked Road* may not be particularly well recalled but it does star Mickey Rooney as a TD-owning track racer who becomes involved with crime, while TC-driving hip teens appear in a 1957 drama entitled *Eighteen & Anxious*.

T-series also appear in the cult classics *The Fast & The Furious* and *Speed Crazy*, plus a high-profile role in Stanley Kubrick's *The Killing*. All of this is rather a contrast to the MG image in British films of the same era, which is best exemplified by Kenneth More at the wheel of his TC in the 1956 domestic comedy *Raising a Riot*. However, the most notable T appearance in a US movie has the MG wearing a cunning disguise. *The Devil's Hairpin*, from 1957, may be one of the rare films where a parrot out-acts all of the human stars, but Cornel Wilde's racing car is none other than a seriously re-bodied 1951 MG TC.

Three decades on with *Ferris Bueller's Day Off*, the 'Ferrari 250GT' that was apparently destroyed on screen boasts rather more modest antecedents – Abingdon, Cowley and Longbridge to be precise. Yes, underneath the sleek red lines lurks a hybrid of MGB – that boot lid should have been a slight giveaway – plus an engine from a 5-litre V8 Ford Mustang. A company called Modena which built a small number of such replicas, including the four used in *Ferris Bueller's Day Off*, apparently constructed them with a specification that included leather trim, a five-speed gearbox, PAS, air-conditioning plus the added attraction of Ferrari allegedly suing the firm for the unauthorised use of its name. Modena went bankrupt but ironically the surviving replicas now sell for very large sums – $50,000 was the recent asking price of one example.

An even more notable MG role in an American film is in one of the most sensitive dramas of 1965 – Russ Meyer's *Faster Pussycat! Kill! Kill!*. This tells the moving tale of three karate-chopping homicidal lesbian go-go dancers who prowl the desert in a Porsche 356, a Triumph TR3 and an MGA. Even better, a preppie twit in his new MGB Roadster attempts to race Varla, the gang's awesome leader, and is promptly karate-chopped to death for daring to compete against a Porsche and for wearing the most appalling plaid check trousers.

Of all films and television programmes, the genre that causes automotive enthusiasts most pain is 'historical drama'. Inevitably anachronisms will abound, from the TC that makes strange Second World War appearances in the *The Battle of Britain* and *Eye of the Needle*, to the bizarre vision of 1960s England that is *Heartbeat*. But although pointing out such details often leads to family disputes and MG fans being banned from many a living room (or cinema), it is nearly impossible not to comment on such details.

In fact, the chief problem with MG spotting is that it is a very difficult habit to cease, from the orange MGA in *Animal House*, Leslie Phillips's red MGA 1600 in *The Fast Lady* or the MGA 1600 chased by a Lancia Aurelia Spider in *Il Sorpasso*. But that is overlooking Nigel Greene's powder blue B Roadster in *The Ipcress File*, the MGB GT in *An American Werewolf in London*, the green TD in the 1968 Elvis vehicle *Speedway*, Nannette Newman's MkII Sprite in *The Wrong Arm of the Law*, Michael Caine's B Roadster in *Sleuth*, Daniel Massey's TF in *The Entertainer*, Michael Dennison's PB Midget in *Landfall...*

■ **All of the fine posters used to illustrate this feature – and countless others besides – may be purchased from www.drivepast.com, the world's leading purveyor of original car-related film posters and prints. Proprietor Paul Vesey can be contacted on 01452 790672 or via email at paul@drivepast.com.**

Making history

The Heritage MGB bodyshells have now been available for longer than the MGB itself was in production! This is how they're made...

Words: David Lillywhite

We take the British Motor Heritage bodyshells for granted now; after all, it was back in 1988 when they were first introduced. But we shouldn't, because where else could you buy an all-new, rust-free, rust-proofed body for just a few thousand pounds – not a small amount, but nothing on the cost of having a rotten shell professionally restored?

Sure, you can piece together all the parts for, say, an E-type; BMW Mobile Tradition has made much of being able to build an all-new 2002 (at a price); remanufactured MG T-series body tubs are still available; and there are various glassfibre Lotus bodies still hanging around. But the MGB, Midget, Triumph TR6 and Mini shells from BMH are still unique in the market for their price, quality and availability.

In the early days of the BMH shells, there were question marks over quality, mainly because shells were provided without doors, bonnet and boot fitted, and many of us DIYers weren't skilled enough to get them to line up. Now, with panels fitted, the gaps genuinely are as good as – and usually better than – those you'd have seen when new MGBs were coming off the production line.

With MGB bodyshells produced only in small batches now, we were keen to witness the production line in action, to see how the shells are made and the amount of work that goes into them. It's fascinating stuff, as we reveal here.

For more information on buying a bodyshell direct from BMH, or having a complete car built up, call 01993 707200 or visit www.bmh-ltd.com.

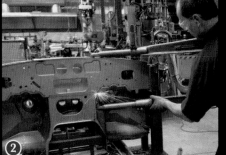
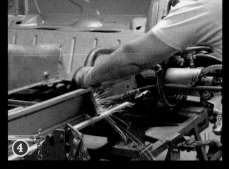

'Where else could you buy an all-new, rust-free body for just a few thousand pounds – not a small amount but nothing on the cost of having a rotten shell restored?'

1: The work at British Motor Heritage starts at the front, fixing chassis legs and crossmember into the jig. Most panels used are produced on the original factory dies. The jigs at BMH are also the same as those used at the factory, although originally several such jigs would have been mounted on a carousel on the production line.

2: Next on are the pedal box assembly and bulkhead, followed by the front 'valance' panels (inner wings) and the bonnet landing panel. The 'valance' term is an Americanism, stemming from the formation of Pressed Steel alongside US company the Budd Corporation in 1926. Many Pressed Steel drawings refer to wings as 'fenders'. The assembly is then moved from the jig into the 'turnover', which allows it to be tilted to weld in the gearbox tunnel and finish other welds.

3: Then, on a different jig, the rear-end underframe is built up as a separate assembly. It consists of back chassis legs, boot floor, the over-battery floor and the heel board (the step up behind the front seats). The inner rear wheelarches are added, too. For GT bodyshells, a false floor support is also included at this point.

4: It's the stuff of legend how complicated MGB sills are to repair. They're not much better to make in the first place, particularly as this is the stage at which the two assemblies (from the previous steps) are married together: first the inner sills, followed by the bracing pieces being welded here. Then the castle rails, along the base of the sills, are welded in, and finally the centre sills (or membranes). Then the floors are made up, with the relevant captive nuts and splash plates included.

❯

BMH BODYSHELLS

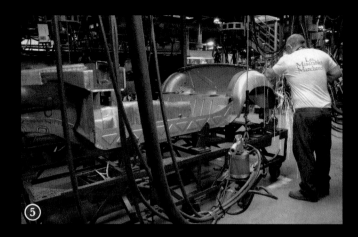

'Front wings are made up from ten separate pieces, the result of cost-cutting when tooling was first specified prior to the 1962 launch of the MGB'

5: Here the bodyshell is really taking shape. The outer sections of the rear inner wheelarches are shown in place, and the next stage is to attach the back skin assembly – that's the rear wings and the rear deck, pre-assembled and fitted as one piece.

6: With the shell now moved into the turnover once again, it's easier to spot weld the bottom sections of the rear wings and the sills into position. However, there are still various areas that require extra work, so the shell is moved into a welding bay where it is MIG welded anywhere that the spot welder cannot reach, where seam welding is needed for strength or where a seam needs to be sealed for cosmetic reasons. In the factory, these areas would have originally been gas welded or, if strength was not an issue, brazed. You can see some of these MIG welds on the front inner wings in picture 7 in particular.

7: The GT shells go through the same process as the Roadster shells initially. Then, extra sections are bolted on to the jig, to hold the window frames of the rear wings, the front screen surround and the roof into position. The rear wings are then attached, followed by the screen surround, then the roof. This is the trickiest part of the build, particularly ensuring that the tailgate aperture is absolutely square.

8: Back to the Roadster, and on goes the box section under the scuttle, followed by the scuttle. Note the build sheet attached – there are 12 possible derivatives of the Roadster shell and nine of the GT shell. A popular option is chrome bumper externals on rubber bumper underpinnings, for the wider engine bay and tunnel. Three-synchro' spec needs the supply of an original transmission tunnel, while RV8 mods can be specified, as can seam-welding for a competition car.

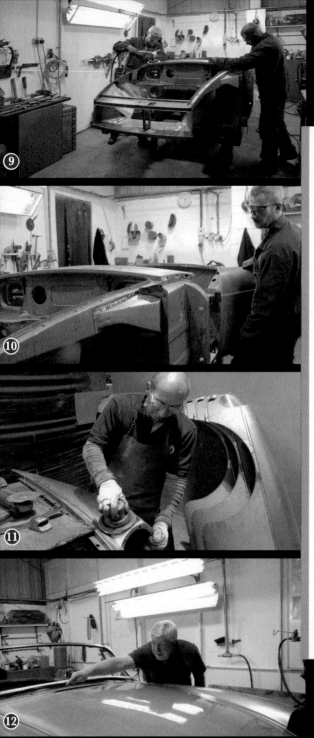

9: The amount of work needed on each shell is an eye-opener – in period, it would have been similar. Skilled craftsmen run light body files over all external panelwork, highlighting imperfections that are then dressed down with panelbeating hammers and sanders. The work starts with the scuttle, seen here, even before other panels are attached.

10: Doors are next. This is where the early shells (and even factory cars) used to show up any defects, with alignment difficulties and sometimes unsightly gaps around the lower trailing corner. Panel fit is now at RV8 levels, which is pretty good – we looked over a number of completed shells and were impressed with the accuracy of fit.

11: Front wings are made up from ten separate pieces, the result of cost-cutting when tooling was first specified before the 1962 launch of the MGB. This made many jobs far more labour-intensive, with the wings the most labour-intensive of the lot. Once assembled, several welded seams have to be dressed back and ground smooth.

12: Once all outer panels are fitted, aligned and checked for imperfections, the windscreen is trial fitted. Again, given the shape and rigidity of the screen surround, there's no room for inaccuracy. By this point, it's taken about 33 hours to produce a Roadster shell, and an extra 10 hours for a GT version.

13: The bodyshells are electrophoretically treated to improve their rust resistance (it also helps that they're built from zinc-plated steel rather than the plain mild steel that the originals were produced in). The 'e-coat' is applied off-site; a cathode is attached to the body to attract the paint. Customers can now buy shells like this, or with the top coat of their choice already applied. BMH will also build up a complete car from a shell – but that's a whole new story. **MG**

Ex-Works – or is it?

These cars are the real deal, but former BMC Competitions Department manager, Peter Browning raises some controversial issues relating to the many claims that surround ex-works cars.

There is today unprecedented interest in ex-works cars and none more so than those that were entered by the BMC Competitions Department at Abingdon. Just about all of the 70 works Minis from the 1960s and 1970s have been resurrected in some form and there are many more replicas running around, some proudly wearing a valued competitions registration number.

Many works MGBs are also around and a number of big Healeys have survived. The recent 50th anniversary celebrations of the MGA have brought renewed interest in these ex-works race and rally cars too. There are also enthusiasts who have tracked down the rarer ex-works BMC and later BL models like the Triumph 2.5s, 1800s and even Austin Maxis. We also have at least two examples of restored former BMC transporters.

There is a cynical view that this interest in ex-works cars is all about money and certainly many of the cars without their cherished competition registration numbers are probably not worth much more than a tidy example of the model. As an example, there have recently been two astronomical price tags on ex-works cars. A works Austin-Healey 100S, advertised as having taken part at Le Mans and the Mille Miglia in the 1950s, was recently on offer at an astounding £395,000. Remarkable when there is some doubt as to whether it was this or the sister car which actually raced at Le Mans!

The highest price paid for an ex-works Mini recently topped the £100,000 mark for a car which even the owner and the auctioneers admitted was a replica built upon an entirely new bodyshell. That hasn't stopped this from raising the stakes for all the genuine ex-works Minis to a whole new level.

Owners would justify their enthusiasm for ex-works cars as a challenge to not only restore a classic car, but also have the added pride of preserving and driving a genuine piece of motor sporting heritage – a sentiment that one totally understands and applauds.

However, there is concern at the growing number of so called ex-works cars running around with the all important competition number plate possibly being the only original part of the car. It seems perfectly acceptable today to build a replica for which there is often dubious previous history of ownership, which nevertheless is then used to support an application to the DVLA for the vital missing competition registration number. Once DVLA approval is given, any question of the car's authenticity seems to be forgotten. These cars then take their place in the competitions hall of fame for all time.

Tracing the competition history of a works car is not always straightforward and my scepticism about the claims of so many of the cars is based on first hand experiences of what went on at Abingdon when cars were first disposed of to private owners. Firstly, it is true to say that most of the cars were generally knackered otherwise they would not have been sold off. Any car for example

Above: The two prototype MGC GTS cars, the last works MGs to be built which competed at Sebring, the Nürburgring and the Targa Florio, are a fine example of genuine ex-works cars with proven provenance and beautifully restored.

that had done a rough event like the Liège, RAC Rally or Acropolis would almost certainly have been pensioned off because it needed a new chassis/bodyshell since under body damage would have been severe.

The most likely history of a works car, when it was no longer practical to rebuild it after an event, would be that it would join the fleet of recce or practice cars and would thus end its days at Abingdon thrashed to an inch of its life. Recce and practicing could be as tough as the event itself, there would be no service crews to fettle the cars and a mechanic once joked that he doubted whether a certain crew actually ever found the bonnet catch to check the oil level. So when the cars came up for disposal, they were generally pretty tired examples, they were sold 'as seen' and while some of them continued to motor on merrily, there were others that hardly made it to the factory gates.

Most of the cars were sold to a fairly exclusive circle of successful private owners who were racing or rallying their own cars. So, the next scenario in the life of an ex-works car would be that it would be used in competition by the new owner, who would have been encouraged to do so by Abingdon with perhaps some spares from time to time and certainly technical help if required. These cars were built for competition, not as museum pieces, and were sold to active private owners for that purpose.

It would be true to say at this point that nobody in those days would have had any idea that 40 or 50 years on, their £50 'wreck' from Abingdon (the going price for a used Mini) could have been worth £100,000.

Along the way it would not be unreasonable to suppose that most already well used ex-works cars had an equally tough time in the hands of their new owners. In many instances the cars were used as spares, the original body may have been destroyed and the competition parts transferred to a replacement body. There is certainly evidence that many of the cars were involved in accidents which again led to the provision of a total or part new bodyshell. Certainly I suggest that the original power units would have expired in time and many other mechanical components would have needed replacement. So very early on in the life of an ex-works car we see that there is a strong possibility that the car may not be as totally original as could be claimed today. These changes would not have been documented because at the time they were not significant.

Having said that, there are a few cases where an ex-works car survived its first period of private ownership in good shape and through a series of subsequent sympathetic owners exists today pretty well as it left the works. Such a car in my book represents the genuine, very rare and highly valued ex-works car.

Above: Mini-Cooper DJB 93B. A replica of this Mini-Cooper recently sold at auction for a record £100,000.

But even before the car was handed over to the new owner, the unseen goings on within the Competitions Department may well have contradicted the 'official' documented competitions history of the car. Firstly, cars going abroad for events had to have a Carnet de Passage which was a very detailed customs document that included body and engine number, registration number, colour and many other identification details. These had to be filled in and the required number of copies prepared for customs well before the event.

Often between the time when the forms were submitted and the relevant car was prepared for the event, there may have been a problem necessitating, for instance, a change of engine or possibly the substitution of a totally different car. With little time available to have a new Carnet issued, the easy solution of course was to swap registration details, body and engine number onto a replacement car. Thus we now have a situation when two cars, both of which may have had a previous competition record, now have totally new histories and identities! So 40 years on it may well be that the records claiming that a certain car was driven in a certain event may not actually be true.

Another example of how the Competitions Department caused confusion was when a motoring magazine asked to do a road test on a car immediately after it had won a very rough rally. The winning car was so badly knocked about that it was decided we could not sensibly let them test a car that was virtually wrecked. So in a panic the car was changed to an identical team car which had retired on the first day of the event and was therefore in very good shape. The swap was instantly achieved by exchanging the bonnet, boot and doors which effectively swapped the competition numbers, rally plates and registration numbers. The magazine was highly impressed with how well the car had stood up to this car breaking event. History does not reveal whether the two cars were eventually reunited with their genuine identities.

Top prize for total confusion goes to one works Mini which had five totally different identities in its four year life at Abingdon. It started life as a Group 1 car for the 1966 Monte, Flowers and Tulip rallies. It was then converted to Group 2 for the 1966 RAC and 1967 Circuit of Ireland. Written off on the

'One works Mini had five totally different identities in its four year life at Abingdon'

1967 London Rally it was rebuilt with a lightweight body and 970cc engine for the 1967 Marathon de la Route at the Nürburgring and in this form it was sold to a private owner. Still wearing the original number plate, its fourth bodyshell was fitted with a Group 6 engine for the 1967 Tour de Corse. Finally a Mark II body shell was fitted for its last event, the 1968 Shell 4000 Rally in Canada. Along the way the original Group 1 body was passed on to the Pressed Steel Apprentices at Cowley and later 'escaped' to find a home with a rallycross competitor and then a Welsh rallying enthusiast. The final Shell 4000 Rally car was reputedly sold for £55,000.

So here we have Competitions creating five totally different cars, all carrying the same registration and each earning its own little piece of competition history through a total of nine events. I do hold my hand up and admit that I have contributed in no small measure to assisting those who are determined to produce an ex-works Mini and who may not have a totally authentic car to work on. In my *Works Minis* book I published the body, engine number and registration details of all the 70 cars built along with their complete competition history. I even listed the names of the first private owners. Armed with this vital information, a copy of the original build sheets for the car (which are available) and copies of the very detailed reference photos of the cars, you have all you need to start work. It was relevant that most of the competition parts were available from the Special Tuning Department at Abingdon identical to the specification of the works cars. Replacement chassis/body and engine plates are freely available with no questions asked.

The situation with ex-works MGBs is less complicated for only 14 cars were

Right: Two MGB GTs were built for Sebring, one of which passed to the US importers after one race (later sold to a private owner) while this car returned to the UK after a later race. Both now wear the same registration number but the chances of them meeting up are fortunately slim.
Below: Final phase of a works car's life at Abingdon was to be relegated to a punishing time on the fleet of practice and recce cars. Three Minis pause on a Monte Carlo Rally recce – but probably not to check the oil levels!

Left: Mini-Cooper GRX 5D. One of the five works Minis that carried the same registration number through four years and some nine events – this is Paddy Hopkirk winning the 1967 Circuit of Ireland.

built, 11 MGBs, one MGB GT and a pair of MGC GTS cars. However, the problem with tracing the authenticity of MGBs is that many of the works cars ended up running at Sebring and after the race these were handed over to the US importers as a 'thank you' for the support programme at the race track and handling the shipment of the cars and local transportation costs. It also saved the cost of shipping them back to the UK. These MGs tended to be sold on to dealers and then run by private owners across the States. There was at the time understandably little interest in works heritage and, as the cars were often not very competitive for US national and club racing, they were extensively modified and the works competition identity often lost. Only in more recent years has the value and interest of ex-works MGs been realised and some of these cars have now come to light. In some cases one has to say that their authenticity has to be questioned on the basis that their history through the years across the USA has not been well documented.

The major controversy over most ex-work cars is the issue of the original works registration number which of course sets the seal on the value of the car. People do go to enormous lengths to try and prove the authenticity of their vehicles. Today the procedure is that the DVLA have appointed selected organisations to verify the claims which have to be presented with supporting documentation and photographs. The MGCC handles applications for submission to the DVLA for MGs. While in the past the DVLA enquiries may not have been too diligent and some cars may have slipped through the net, they do now have a more experienced and efficient department handling applications.

In some cases the DVLA enquires have led to cars being examined and former Abingdon works mechanics have been involved. It does not take a works mechanic more than a few minutes to spot whether a bodyshell has the works tell-tale features. One of the most definitive pieces of evidence is the special wiring of the cars, which was done by a resident Lucas mechanic at the factory. Special wire was used for the wiring looms which did not run in conventional routes and which used special connectors (which have not been available for some years).

Tracing the authenticity of pre-war cars is more difficult and often equally contentious. Here we are talking about cars which could be up to 70 years old and any car that has survived an active competition career with the original chassis and body would be remarkable. Pre-war competition cars tend not to be referred to as 'works' cars but more likely described as a Mille Miglia K3 or Le Mans C-type indicating that they took part in that specific event (although not necessarily entered as a works car). Proving the provenance of these cars is a minefield when sale prices for a genuine example of a rare model can be more than the value of your house.

My personal view (and I am no pre-war expert) is that the chassis is the 'backbone' of the car and as such has to be as near to original as possible to justify any claim – and there seems to be enough documentation of chassis numbers around to get this right.

In summary there is a general view that in order to claim the valued competition registration number, the car must surely have the original basic body/chassis. This should be identified with the original body/chassis plate, not a fake replacement. Ideally there should be a continuous record of ownership ex-Abingdon.

The purpose of this article is not to discredit those who own genuine ex-works cars which have full and undisputed documentation to prove the car's provenance. Indeed I hope that my comments may help to protect the value of these cars. What I have tried to explain is how the activities of the Competitions Department at Abingdon, and subsequently the exploits of later owners, have made it very difficult and sometimes impossible to correctly confirm the authenticity of a car's provenance and competition history. If I have been critical of the replicas, it is only that I do not believe that a totally re-bodied car built a year or so ago should today bear the registration number of a long lost famous competition car. I do however have tremendous admiration for the workmanship, the attention to detail and the time that has gone into the building of these cars.

But, how often have we seen today's inconspicuous replica appear as tomorrow's star ex-works exhibit at auction?

A sad tale

Peter Sharp has a passion for black and white British movies, and also for MGs. Unfortunately he discovered that the two don't always combine to give a happy ending... Words: Peter Sharp

After reading *MGs in the Movies* (see pages 190-194), I came across an MG playing a central role in an old British comedy recently issued on DVD by Odeon Entertainments. The film is called *It's a Grand Life*, and it stars Frank Randle and Diana Dors.

If these names mean nothing to you, you are far too young and probably drive an MG TF or a ZS; look them up on the net. You'll find that Diana Dors was an English sex bomb in the 1950s and '60s, a British answer to Jayne Mansfield, if not quite to Marilyn Monroe or Brigitte Bardot. Frank Randle is largely forgotten now, but was a hugely popular comedian and comic actor in the 1930s, '40s and early 1950s, especially in the north of England. This irreverent, anarchic character was considered low and vulgar by the posh southern middle-classes, but always sold out Blackpool summer shows and pantomimes. His touring revue 'Randle's Scandals' filled theatres to capacity all over the country for years.

It's probably true that the films Randle made were no patch on his stage performances, but they give some idea of why he was so well loved. *It's a Grand Life* was his last film and follows the formula of most of them, made cheaply and quickly by the Mancunian Film Corporation. The plot, such as it is, concerns a young women's army corporal played by Diana Dors and a wicked

sergeant major trying to have his evil way with her. To this end he tries persuasion, threats and blackmail while Randle and his bunch of mismatched ne'er-do-well squaddies try to thwart him.

'What's all this got to do with MGs?' I hear you cry. Well, one of the sergeant's ploys is to invite Corporal Diana on a drive out to a country pub in 'my new sports car, I had a bit of luck on the horses'. The camera pans away to an MG; a 1934 four-seat MG NB with Edinburgh registration WS 6231.

Randle and his pals are asked by Diana's boyfriend to try and make sure the date doesn't go ahead and we cut to a close up scene of the car, with the sergeant and Corporal Diana sitting in it. The sergeant can't start it and in trying to do so, pulls the steering wheel off. He then attempts to start the car with the starting handle (though why he should want to when the steering wheel has fallen off is not explained). This doesn't work; luckily for him, because no-one has told him how to crank-start a car without breaking your thumb.

Frank Randle and his chums now enter stage left and offer to help, obviously with the intention of ruining his evening (though again, why this is necessary when the car will not start anyway and has no steering wheel, is another of those great comedy mysteries). They proceed to jump all over the car in the pretence of knowing what they are doing (and haven't we all met someone like that at one time or another?) until, with the bonnet open, a lighted cigarette is

Above: MG NB goes up in flames, apparently as a mere special effect – but in fact it actually did catch light, accidentally.

Facing page:

Above: .

dropped onto the engine and the car appears to burst into flames. End of scene.

I said 'appears' because it is obviously an effect. The flames come from the far side of the MG and are caused by rags or paper on the ground, away from the car. Or so I thought until I was given a book called *Hooray for Jollywood*, a fascinating history of the Mancunian Film Corporation.

The car was prepared for the film by the studio handyman Arthur Mackleston. He spent a lot of time and effort getting it running and looking good; one can see in the film that all five wire wheels have been cleaned and painted, the chrome work has been polished and the car is spotless. As a reward for his hard work, Arthur was promised that he could keep the car after the film, something he set his heart on. He knew that the script called for the car to be on fire but as Arthur says in the book: 'I remember Bud Kelly the studio manager saying to me 'don't worry Arthur, it will look like it's on fire but it won't be really'. However, some bloody fool had put petrol over it and it really did go up in flames, so I never got it.'

So a 1934 four-door MG NB in running order that would have been cherished forever by someone who really appreciated it was unceremoniously cremated for the sake of a two minute comedy sequence. Just adds to the endless list of 'if onlys' we classic car lovers carry around with us, doesn't it? **MG**

Above:
Mancunian Film Studio staff try to extinguish WS 6231 (note the steering wheel on the ground next to the car).
Right: Frank Randle (second from right) and his pals offer to fix the car.

■ **Thanks to Philip Martin Williams for permission to reproduce Arthur Mackleston's memoir and for supplying the picture of WS 6231 being extinguished. Hooray for Jollywood - The Life of John E. Blakeley & The Mancunian Film Corporation by Philip Martin Williams & David L. Williams is available from the authors at £12.99 (phone 0161 343 3928 for details) or can be ordered through bookshops at £15.99. Wired to the Moon: Frank Randle - A Life, the biography of Frank Randle by the same authors is also available with price and ordering details as above.**
■ **It's a Grand Life, starring Frank Randle and Diana Dors is available on DVD for £8.99 by Odeon Entertainment in their Best of British collection.**

HOW TO BUY...

MG Y-TYPE

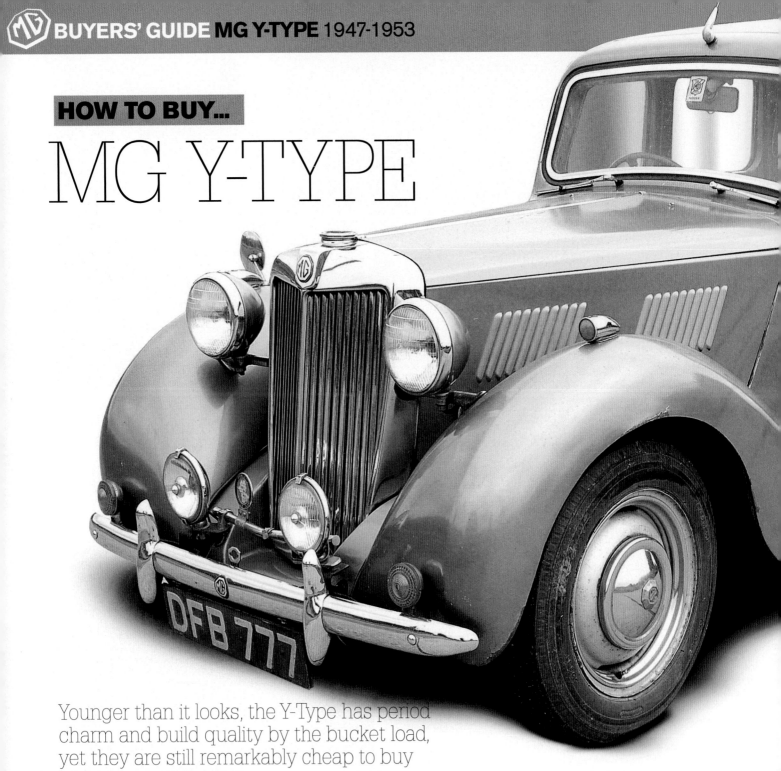

Younger than it looks, the Y-Type has period charm and build quality by the bucket load, yet they are still remarkably cheap to buy

Words and photography: Russ Smith

What you might consider to be the ZR of its day, MG's Y-Type would probably have had a much longer and happier life had it not been for a set of badly timed hostilities. That in effect meant the One and a Quarter Litre sports saloon was seven years old before it even turned a wheel.

Styled by Gerald Palmer around the Morris Eight Series E body and chassis, a prototype was built in 1939 with plans to launch the new Y-Type at the 1940 Earl's Court Motor Show. Palmer's design gave the car more sweeping wings than the Morris, with a longer bonnet and MG's traditional upright grille. He played another tradition card by reverting to separate headlamps when the trend followed by the Series E was to set them into the wings.

There was progress underneath, however, with Alec Issigonis-designed independent front suspension and rack and pinion steering that was still very much a rarity on British cars. The engine was also Morris based – this time from the Ten M – but stretched to 1250cc and first used in the very short-lived pre-war MG TB of 1939. For the Y-Type (it wasn't called the YA until the YB replaced it) the engine used a single carburettor and milder camshaft, but its 46bhp was considered lively enough at the time. In its class only the 1389cc Rover Ten put out any more power, and that 2bhp was sat on rather heavily by the Rover's extra 4cwt.

All that, along with an extra helping of wood and leather, plus a steel sunroof and built-in jacking system, made sure the YA was still well received when it appeared in 1947. It might not have enjoyed much straight-line speed, but the well mannered handling and lively, direct steering were the envy of most rivals apart from the Jowett Javelin. Despite a rather stout price at the time of £671 11s 8d including purchase tax, the car sold well enough.

It was joined the following year by a four-seater tourer, the YT. This got the full twin-carb and hot camshaft TC engine with its extra 8bhp, but sadly MG exported all but three of the 891 that were built by the time the model was discontinued in 1950.

The following year a very mild facelift and some mechanical improvements (though sadly not including more power) gave us the YB. Distinguished by deeper rear wings to cover the inch-smaller 15in wheels, the YB also got a front anti-roll bar, heavy-duty rear dampers, a stronger rear axle and much improved twin-leading-shoe front brakes.

So definitely a better car, but the rest of the world was advancing fast and only 1301 YBs (compared to 6144 YAs) were sold before the Y-Type was replaced by the Magnette in 1953.

Left: **Separate headlamps and rear-hinged doors are a big part of the Y-Type's pre-war appeal.**

Left: **You won't find a rust-free original car, so carefully assess the quality of any previous repairs.**

▨ The following checks all need making so you at least know what you are getting into, and can avoid a car that's bad in an area that you don't want to get involved with. But your findings must be tempered by the fact that you aren't going to find a lot of Y-Types to choose from. There are rarely more than a couple for sale thanks to rarity and owners tending to hang onto them, which should tell you something in itself.

▨ **As the last Y-Type was built over 55 years ago, you'll struggle to find any that have escaped being restored to some extent, possibly several times. A car's history file should tell when any major work was carried out, but only your eyes and fingers can decide the quality of what was done. Bear in mind that full replacement panels for these cars are all but non-existent, although NTG Motor Services do carry a good range of repair panels for the areas most commonly affected by rust. As ever with partial panels, though, fitting requires some degree of skill. Despite being based on them, the only panels shared with Morris Eights are the doors.**

▨ For most people, a good body is going to be the highest priority. Rather than list all rot spots, it's easier to advise looking at the lower six inches of every panel on the car. Also check for bubbling where the rear wings bolt to the body, the base of the bootlid and at the bottom of the spare wheel compartment. The chassis tends to be pretty robust, and oil escaping from the engine (we'll come to that) keeps the front half well protected. Do check the rear, though, especially around spring mounts and below the spare wheel well.

▨ YA bumpers differ from those used on the YB and YT, but neither type is available new. NTG's solution is to use the rear bumper of a TD and replacement irons. The bumper is slightly longer, but can be used either at the front or the back and only concours judges will spot the fact that it is not original.

TRIM

The value of a Y-Type is greatly affected by the condition of its leather seats. Work on the basis that a retrim of these will cost in the region of £1500, though if you've bought right, you should recoup a large chunk of that outlay when you come to sell the car. By the same token, expect to pay more for an example that's already had the job done.

There's plenty of wood in there, too, which must also be evaluated. Faded or cracked lacquer is quite straightforward to refurbish, but if there's any water damage or lifting and peeling veneer, you quickly get into hundreds of pounds – and a lot more if it's all bad and you need specialist help.

The rest of the interior coverings are quite basic and easy to replace, but do be wary of a headlining that is damp or stained around the sunroof aperture. This means water's getting in (question for how long?) and can usually be traced to blocked, split or perished drain tubes, which are not easily accessible. There has long been a problem with cracked steering wheels, but these have recently been reproduced, so scruffy ones can at least be replaced – albeit at a cost of £178.

Right: **The front screen opens and the steering column is telescopically adjustable.**

'Well mannered handling and lively steering were the envy of rivals'

Left: Flashing indicators on upright and imposing nose are later additions. Below: Rear is more flowing. Over-riders were an option on the YB and are dear.

ENGINE

As pointed out in the introduction, The Y-Type uses detuned TC/TD engines, so parts supply is not a problem. Keeping oil in them can be, though – it can leak from the crank seals, rocker cover gaskets and side plates, so expect that issue to some extent. What's of concern is just how much is escaping. A recently cleaned sump is a bad sign as someone may be hiding something, so try and see where the car is usually parked.

Blue smoke from the exhaust is normal on cold start-up, but the engine shouldn't smoke once it's warmed up. Oil pressure when hot should stay above 40psi at 30mph and 10psi at idle. It may well be much higher than this, but anything below those lower limits means engine work is needed. That is also indicated by smoke coming out of the engine breather pipe that runs down behind the distributor. None of it signifies the end of the world, but you should budget on spending in the region of £1500 on a motor rebuild.

Gearboxes should be pretty quiet, except in first and reverse, and shouldn't leak oil. Go up and down the box a few times to see if there's much synchro wear, and lift off in each gear to work out if the lever jumps out. Rear axles may whine at higher speeds, which is often accompanied by a buzzing from the gearlever. However, if this noise is there without any axle whine, it suggests worn box bearings.

Left: Engines may leak a little oil, but this should not be a flood. Rebuilds cost more than for A or B-series motors.

BRAKES/SUSPENSION

The suspension system is very much like that still found decades later on the MGB, with wishbones at the front using the lever arm dampers as the top link, and a live axle on leaf springs at the rear, so there's nothing to fear there. Make sure the trunnions look like they've been greased regularly – you want to see muck, not rust – and on the YB inspect the lower spring pans for cracks where the anti-roll bar attaches to them.

Steering should feel direct and responsive. Radial tyres will make the steering feel heavier, but the trade-off is much better grip and none of the cornering squeal you get from crossplies. Many owners stick to those, however, not least because the fatter radial won't fit in the YA's spare wheel slot below the bootlid. This was enlarged on the YB, but you can still need to deflate the tyre to squeeze it in. Using a crossply simply as a spare is not an acceptable alternative.

Make sure the brakes pull the car up well with no veering to either side, and with no squeals or pulsing in the pedal. It's not a big problem on YBs as these use the same system as the TD so parts availability is good. On YAs, the rear wheel cylinder is the same as a front one on a TC, but the YA's front cylinder is unique and prices reflect this.

MODIFICATIONS

It is quite likely that you've already figured out that the Y-Type's lack of power is easily cured by bringing the engine up to the T-series specification it was detuned from in the first place. After all, MG did this itself with the YT. You'll need the twin carbs of course, but to make it work properly and add every one of the missing 8bhp you'll also need to fit a TC-spec camshaft, freely available from specialists.

That would also be a good point to install one of the spin-off oil filter conversions that are available, for much improved filtration. Engine stress can also be reduced (and cruising speeds raised a little) by fitting a taller 4.875:1 ratio rear axle, as used on the TF. The other option, which also goes well with increased power, is the Sierra five-speed conversion offered by NTG. It's £1128 – and you need to provide the gearbox on top of that – but that's not a great deal more than rebuilding an original box.

'The Y-Type's lack of power is easily cured by bringing it up to T-series spec'

Capable and pleasant to drive, Y-Types were designed for a pre-motorway era.

DRIVING

You should expect good handling and roadholding from these sports saloons, with direct steering that should feel more modern than you'd expect from the somewhat conservative lines. 'Modern' is something of a relative term here, so perhaps 'more MGB than MGF' would be more accurate.

There's not a great deal of urge from the engine, but if you find it too slow, there's either a fault with the motor or you really should be looking at a newer model. The brakes are all good for a car of this age, though definitely better on the YB, but with no servo and over a ton to bring to a halt, both need a firm push on the pedal to make them work.

These are cars better suited to A- and B-road use rather than motorway journeys, and on that point the long-stroke engine design means they don't appreciate cruising at more than 55mph for any length of time. To do so is to invite accelerated wear to the bores and piston rings, so get used to the idea of planning journeys for entertainment and scenery rather than slog.

'Considering what they offer, £6500 represents something of a bargain'

COST

You might expect the improved and rarer YB to be more expensive than the YA, but in fact both saloon versions can be bought equally cheaply. Considering what they offer, the £6000-£6500 you can realistically expect to pay privately for a good Y-Type represents something of a bargain. Even well prepped and guaranteed dealer cars rarely top £7250. It should be a safe investment too, as those prices really only have one way to go.

Tired but still usable examples tend to fall into the £2750-£3000 range, and if you really want a challenging retirement project, they can be had for around £1500. Make sure that what you are buying is as complete as possible because it's a small jump from project to parts car, and low value means bad ones are still more likely to be broken than restored.

There's not the same sort of choice if you're looking for a YT. Most of those that are in the UK are in good condition. Depending on exactly how

Above: YAs sat on 16in wheels, YBs on 16in versions. Both, of course, wore crossply tyres.

good, they range in price from £10,000 to £15,000. Aside from money you also need much patience to wait for one to come onto the market. But whichever variant you want, visit the excellent www.mgytypes.org for both more information and invaluable contacts. MG

Above: The rear number plate panel is removable for access to the spare wheel.

YA/YB SPECIFICATIONS

Engine	1250cc, 4-cyl, OHV
Power	46bhp @ 4800rpm
Torque	59lb/ft @ 2400rpm
Top speed	71mph
0-60mph	28.2secs
Fuel consumption	30mpg
Gearbox	Four-speed manual

Above: Unusual dash uses octagonal clocks. Handle in middle is to open up the windscreen.

USEFUL TO KNOW

- Most mechanical parts are common to the TC and TD, ensuring a healthy supply of parts from their network of specialists
- NTG Motor Services, Ipswich, 01473 406031, www.ntgservices.co.uk
- www.mgytypes.org
- MG Octagon Car Club, Staffs, 01889 574666, www.mgoctagoncarclub.com
- Brown & Gammons, Herts, 01462 490049, www.ukmgparts.com
- J&L Spares Ltd, Lancs, 01706 644210, www.jlspares.com
- IC Woolstenholmes Ltd, Lincs, 01778 347347, www.woolies-trim.co.uk
- Thanks to Brian Cox for providing the car

HOW TO BUY...

MGA

Possibly the prettiest of all MGs, with the purest of Fifties driving experiences, the MGA still makes sense today. But what should you be looking for?

Words and photography: Russ Smith

The sight of a full-bodied MG sports car might have upset a bunch of moustached and scarf-wearing traditionalists when it first appeared, but Syd Enever's sleek design soon became the world's best-selling sports car. And it still looks the part today – never mind that the modernity hides a separate chassis and wooden floorboards.

Famously delayed for a few years while BMC poured its sports car budget into the Austin-Healey project, the MGA was finally launched in September 1955. Under the bonnet was the well established B-series engine, wearing twin carburettors for the first time. Add those sleek lines and, even in this early form, the MGA was only a modest down-gradient away from the magic 100mph mark.

Higher compression added 4bhp in 1956 to make that 100mph a real possibility even without the aid of gravity, but the mark was well and truly surpassed two years later when engineers tried a taste of the exotic on the B-series. With fine sporting

intentions, and perhaps a little envious of what Jaguar had to play with, they created an alloy twin-cam head for the engine, which itself was bored out a little to give a 1588cc capacity. With more development this could have been really something – properly sorted ones today are a joy to drive with their revvy 108bhp – but they were rushed into production for owners to discover their high oil consumption and fondness for melting pistons. Warranty claims for MGA Twin-Cams were horrendous, their reputation shot through the floor, and production ceased after just over 2000 examples had been built.

On the plus side, regular MGAs also got the larger capacity for 1959, becoming MGA 1600s, and the last 395 Twin-Cam chassis – with their disc brakes and centre-lock wheels – were also fitted with either this or the new 1622cc version of the engine, and badged as the MGA De Luxe. This has always been a rather sought-after version by those in the know.

Finally we got the MGA 1600 MkII, with the

1622cc engine and a higher final-drive ratio. These cars are easily distinguished by their inset grille bars and horizontal rather than vertical rear light units.

MGAs have always been popular with tuners, and many have been tweaked or improved in some way. Don't be surprised to find an early MGB three-bearing engine under the bonnet – in fact, be quietly pleased. Only the concours-competing originality freaks get at all hung up about mechanical improvements, and non-original running gear should do no harm to a car's value these days unless it lays claim to those highest of standards.

In its seven years of production, less than six per cent of the 100,000-plus MGAs built were sold to UK buyers. However, thankfully many have been repatriated over the years since, largely from America where 80 per cent of them went, so you'll find plenty for sale here now. Cars converted from left- to right-hand drive should hold no fear, as it's a simple job that merely requires an exchange steering rack plus a new dashboard and pedals.

Left: Fit and finish of panels is crucial, as a minor problem in one place can become huge elsewhere.

INITIAL CHECKS

Left: Add up any repairs – rear lamp is £20, the indicator £16, but the plinth they sit on costs £80.

> 'Less than 6 per cent of the 100,000-plus MGAs produced were sold in the UK, but many have been repatriated since'

TRIM

Even a poor interior shouldn't be a deal-breaker. All parts are available at reasonable cost, and if the price is right it might be to your advantage to redo the interior. All MGAs originally came with leather seat facings, but you may find some with vinyl now as seat upholstery kits are sold in this material for £250. Mind

you, it's only £300 for leather, so do consider the motives for such cost-cutting. Trim panel kits for the rest of the interior come out at a surprisingly affordable £168 for a Roadster, or £380 for the Coupé. Do watch that the gauges are original and haven't been swapped for MGB items.

Right: New seat covers are not exorbitant at around £300 for leather and just £250 for vinyl.

■ Body condition in all respects is the be all and end all of buying a good MGA. Though replacement panels are available, these cars were largely hand-built and any new panel will require adjustment to fit a particular car with any sort of ease. Then there are the complications added by doors, bonnet and bootlid being aluminium panels fitted to steel frames – with the odd bit of wood thrown in for support.

■ **Any repairs that require disturbing the body-to-chassis mountings make things even worse, as MGAs are notoriously hard to realign on the chassis – a little bit out in one place magnifies to a lot somewhere else. Even professionals can spend days taking the body on and off before it all lines up just right, which gets very expensive if you're paying for it and frustratingly time-consuming if you try and do it yourself.**

■ For that reason, the alignment of panels is a big clue to what a car is like and may have been through. You shouldn't expect perfect panel gaps – there's always likely to be some discrepancy, and was from the factory – but really poor fit spells problems which will be expensive to rectify.

■ **The most important places to inspect for rust (and repairs) are the sills and door posts, closely followed by the flanges where the front wings bolt on. Boot floors and the steel door frames are also common rot spots, and of course you need to look for bubbling anywhere that steel and aluminium meet.**

■ As mentioned above panels are available, but expect a front wing to be £633, front valance £188, bonnet £600, and the shroud panel that surrounds the bonnet and runs from front bumper to windscreen nearly £800. At least the bumpers are not too expensive, at £88 front, £70 rear.

■ **Chassis are tough and quite resistant to rust, but watch for ripples from accident damage which can easily misalign the whole frame. You can also expect to find some corrosion in bits that run off the chassis like floorboard supports and battery boxes. The area below the A-post between the inner sill and chassis rail is prone to filling with mud – at least on those examples that are still used on less-than-sunny days – so have a good dig around here, too.**

›

Left: Bonnet, surround is a big panel that rusts along the wing joints.
Below: Rear shroud also corrodes, and repairs here are no easier.

'No rev-counter drive on the back of a 1500 or 1600 means you are probably looking at a saloon engine'

ENGINE

BMC's B-series engine is tough, and it's easy to rebuild if it wears out too, so again its condition isn't a great worry. However, if you want to make sure you get a bit of use out of it, look for 50-60psi hot oil pressure at 3000rpm, listen for rumbles and make sure there's not a lot of oil weeping from the bellhousing area, which spells a leaky rear crank seal.

Of slightly more concern is establishing what the engine actually is, as many have been swapped over the years, and not always for the MGB upgrade. Lack of a rev-counter drive on the back of the camshaft on a 1500 or 1600 means you are probably looking at a saloon engine that's had twin carbs bolted to it. As the MGA engines had different cams, head and pistons, anything else will do the job but be short of the expected horsepower output.

Pay extra attention to Twin-Cam engines. Most of the original problems have been eradicated by experience and all are likely to have been rebuilt at least once by now, but you want to know when and by whom. They aren't as robust as regular B-series lumps, some parts cannot be replaced, and that next rebuild could cost £5000 – or about four times the cost of doing the single-cam engine.

Left: B-series is a tough old lump. The odd rattle or drop of oil is not unusual. If it runs poorly, check the carbs for tune and wear.

Above: What's in there now? On the left side of the motor just above the engine mount bracket you'll find the capacity cast into the block.

Above: Affordable chrome trim is available – the radiator grille and surround for example costs £150 from specialists such as the MGOC.

MODIFICATIONS

Engines benefit from at the very least electronic ignition and a sports coil, perhaps even a freer-flowing tubular exhaust manifold. Brakes can be vastly improved by fitting the MGB's larger calipers using adaptor plates sold by Moss. To balance things out, you can also get competition linings for the rear drums, but don't get fancy ideas about swapping to the rear discs used on Twin-Cams unless you have a magic wand to source the parts.

That B-series gearbox has always been the weak link in the chain, yet can be invisibly replaced by a Ford Sierra five-speed using Hi-Gear Engineering's conversion kit. This comes with everything from a new propshaft and bellhousing down to the smallest nut and bolt, and costs £852. Just add your own gearbox.

It's widely agreed that fitting a ¾in front anti-roll bar does wonders for handling and reduces the MGA's tendency to lift the inner rear wheel during hard cornering. A suitable bolt-on kit is available from Moss. Add a pair of one-inch lower, slightly stiffer front springs and drop the rear to match on lowering blocks. At the rear a telescopic damper conversion is preferred to uprated lever arms. You can get kits with Spax or Konis. Don't be tempted to supplement this with an anti-roll bar, even in conjunction with a stiffer one on the front, as it only aggravates wheel lift and oversteer problems.

BRAKES/SUSPENSION

All consumable brake parts are freely available, even for the Twin-Cam, so no worries there. The MoT man will have checked the suspension for you, but do be a bit wary of stiff steering. It might be down to lack of use if a car's been standing for any great length of time, but it could also be due to DIY kingpin or trunnion replacement by the inexperienced.

Those parts should really be replaced as matched sets, lapped in to suit each other, but in reality that doesn't always happen and disappointingly heavy steering is the result. If this is the case, negotiate a discount based on new kingpin sets being just under £200 a side, plus fitting.

Right: Despite its delicate lines, the MGA is a traditional sports car and real fun to drive.

DRIVING

More than anything else, it's the driving position that gives the MGA's age away. You sit low on a rather flat seat, with legs outstretched and the wheel relatively close to your chest. However, we mean none of that as a criticism, in fact quite the opposite. This is real classic motoring, with icing, cherries and a good sprinkling of hundreds and thousands.

The MGA does exactly what you want of a classic sports car. There's just enough power to have fun, just enough room in the cockpit, and just the right amount of wind in your hair with the top down. Add a surprisingly comfortable ride and direct steering, and it becomes crystal clear that MGAs are valued for a lot more than their good looks.

OK, it all starts to sound noisy and harsh once you get near 80mph, and the brakes – whether drum or disc – are only adequate, but none of it is to the sort of extent to cause serious complaint. It's part of the deal with a car such as this, and if you cannot live with such 1950s realities, try the cosy modernity of an MGF instead. The Twin-Cam does all the above but with the addition of enough extra power to put it in another league entirely. Infectiously fast, if you drive one you'll want one – so beware! If only those engines had been properly sorted, the history of MG might be very different. Imagine MGBs with that head and their extra 180cc...

COST

MGA Roadsters occupy that gap in the British sports car market between Austin Healeys and Triumph's TR3/TR4 gang. Expect to pay £14,000 to £16,000 for the best 1500 or 1600, an extra thousand for a De Luxe. Projects start at about £5000, and you can get something useable for £8750 upwards, but make sure that anything priced under £10,000 isn't about to become your winter restoration project.

Twin-Cams are another thing altogether, with top prices now in the £20,000-£22,500 area. You might find a project for £7500, but there'll be little worth gambling on for under £15,000. Big bills await the unfortunate, and you want to see history of them being paid already!

Coupés come cheaper, even though they are weatherproof and better equipped. It makes them a good choice for historic rallying, where you'll find plenty already competing. Pay from £11,000 to £12,500 for top examples, though you might get something a bit scruffy to rally for as little as £6500. Project cars can be as low as half that, but you have to weigh up the cost and complexity of restoration. **MG**

Above: Classic wire wheels are popular, but we reckon that these steel rims look even better.

USEFUL TO KNOW

- Bob West Classic Sports Cars, W Yorks, 01977 703828, www.bobwestclassiccars.co.uk
- Abingdon Parts 4 MG & Triumph, W Mids, 0121 543 1617, www.mg-tr-parts.co.uk
- MGOC Spares, Cambs, 01954 230928, www.mgocspares.co.uk
- Moss Europe, London, 020 8867 2020, www.moss-europe.co.uk
- Brown & Gammons, Herts, 01462 490049, www.ukmgparts.com
- SC Parts, W Sussex, 01293 847201, www.scparts.co.uk
- Halls Garage, Lincs. 01778 570286, www.hallsgarage.co.uk
- P.J.M Motors, Shropshire, 01630 652873, www.pjm-motors.co.uk
- Hi-Gear Engineering, Derbys, 01332 514503, www.hi-gearengineering.co.uk
- Hoyle Engineering, Surrey, 020 8393 2555, www.hoyle-engineering.co.uk
- www.mgaguru.com.
- Thanks to: Steve at Halls Garage for providing the car in our pictures.

'The MGA does exactly what you want of a classic sports car'

SPECIFICATIONS

	MGA 1500	MGA Twin-Cam	MGA 1600	MGA 1600 MkII
Engine	1489cc, 4-cyl, OHV	1588cc, 4-cyl, DOHC	1588cc, 4-cyl, OHV	1622cc, 4-cyl, OHV
Power	72bhp @ 5500rpm	108bhp @ 6700rpm	80bhp @ 5600rpm	90bhp @ 5500rpm
Torque	77lb/ft @ 3500rpm	105lb/ft @ 4500rpm	87lb/ft @ 3800rpm	97lb/ft @ 4000rpm
Top speed	98mph	113mph	100mph	102mph
0-60mph	15.7secs	9.1secs	14.2secs	13.7secs
Fuel cons.	28mpg	22mpg	24mpg	22mpg
Gearbox	Four-speed manual	Four-speed manual	Four-speed manual	Four-speed manual

Right: Round rear wheelarch Midgets are generally considered the prettiest.

HOW TO BUY...

MG MIDGET MK I-III

MG's miniature roadster maintained the marque's lightweight tradition for 18 years. Here we'll be focusing on the pre-rubber bumper A-series versions

Words and photography: Russ Smith

For decades the Midget has provided entry-level access to the delights of MG sports cars; in fact, to classic sports cars in general. There is an extremely good reason why they always pop up in magazine features on the top ten starter classics – cheap to buy, cheap to get bits for, easy to drive and relatively easy to work on.

Only now is the MGF starting to challenge its first sporty MG status, and that arguably scores only two out of four on those points I just made. The flip side is that being so cheap and popular with less experienced owners means Midgets are not always as well looked after or repaired as you might hope, so finding the right one takes more than an average amount of care and legwork. But that's what we're here to help you with!

You will certainly have plenty of choice, as nearly 233,000 MkI-III Midgets were manufactured between 1961 and 1974. This guide also of course includes the near-identical Austin-Healey Sprite, but for simplicity's sake, we will keep referring to them as Midgets. But first, before you can figure out which Midget is right for you, we need to outline the main differences between the various eras of Midget Mks I-III.

The Frogeye's replacement was launched in 1961, May for the Austin-Healey, June for the MG. These were basic cars, with clip-on side windows, a pack-away hood, no exterior door handles or locks, and the earlier model's 948cc engine, quarter-elliptic rear springs and drum brakes. Thankfully the specification went up to 1098cc and front discs from September 1962.

The MkII brought civilisation in March 1964, thanks to new doors with wind-up windows, external handles and quarter-lights, larger main bearings to prolong engine life, and semi-elliptic rear springs to improve the ride.

That was also a fairly short-lived car. In October 1966 the MkIII was announced, although none would be released to buyers until the New Year. The rear of the cockpit was revised so the Midget could now have a permanently attached folding hood (to the relief of many), but the big change was the tougher and much more powerful 1275cc engine.

A facelift in October '69 brought slimmer bumpers and eight-hole Rostyle wheels, along with a black grille and sills. At the end of 1970 the Healey name was dropped, and for the next six months you could buy an Austin Sprite. After that, all the cars were MG Midgets.

A further facelift came in October 1971 (January '72 in the UK) with the prettier styling of rounded rear wheelarches and the more familiar design of four-spoke Rostyles. Known now as 'RWA' Midgets, they are the most popular version and ran until October '74, the dawn of the rubber bumper and a return to square-profile rear arches.

'Finding the right one takes more than an average amount of care and legwork'

INITIAL CHECKS

◼ Given the wide availability and low cost of all the mechanical parts, it will come as no surprise that your main focus when buying a Midget must be on the condition of the body. That doesn't mean you should run scared from a car with a bit of rust, as long as you don't mind waving a MIG welding torch about a bit, as panels are freely available and not that expensive. What you don't want to do is overpay for such a car that's hiding its issues behind shiny paint and filler.

◼ **The worst problems are always the ones you can't see easily, so be prepared to check behind the sills, and where they end in the wheelarches and join the door pillars. Pay particular attention to the rear end of the sills where they join a triangular closing panel. The telltale line of rust here that spells major troubles beneath is easily disguised. Also peel back and prod beneath the carpeted area behind the seats.**

◼ Another 'iceberg' rust point is the bottom of the A-post just ahead of the door – any rust here means an involved repair. Wriggle your way into the front footwell area and check the floor where the throttle pedal mounts. Rot is common here. It's one of the easier areas to repair, though, so more of a negotiation point than a worry.

◼ **Panel fit is another important indication of a Midget's quality and value. The more you're paying, the better you should expect, as rectification of anything will not be easy, which is why it hasn't been done before sale. As with most cars, it pays to use the old trick of standing back about five metres and looking down each side of the body for imperfections, especially if it's painted one of those hide-all colours like yellow, white or red.**

◼ The smartest buy is a Midget that someone else has properly restored not too long ago – preferably with an album of photos to prove it – and preserved with rustproofer. That will almost certainly have cost them several thousand pounds more than is being asked. Pie in the sky? There are loads claiming to be such cars in the classifieds – you just need to select a right one from them. If that restoration happened to include a Heritage shell (though unsurprisingly that's rare) then you've hit the jackpot!

TRIM

For once we have the pleasure of saying that there's no need to worry about the condition of the interior. Well, as long as it's a MkIII Midget you're looking at. Everything is available, and at very reasonable prices. There really is no excuse for a scruffy Midget interior when you can buy a set of new vinyl seat covers for £170, a complete cockpit trim panel kit for £160 and a carpet set for £85. The situation is nearly as good for earlier cars, though the prices are up to 50 per cent higher due to economies of scale.

Even new hoods are refreshingly cheap to buy. Reckon on about £150 for a MkIII top to original equipment specification. Mind you, fitting it is probably a day's work, and if you are keen to have a perfect wrinkle-free finish, it's a job best entrusted to specialist hands. The pack-away hoods of earlier cars cost nearer £200, depending on spec, but you don't have the same fitting issues. They also left the factory with a touch of Nora Batty's stockings about them, so the odd bag or wrinkle is to be expected.

Right: Standard interior trim is cheap; options for upgrades/personalisation are plentiful.

Above left: A thicker front anti-roll bar can improve the handling.
Left: Rear leaf springs are already stiff – uprated ones are overkill.

ENGINE

Relax, it's an A-series! Obviously you should listen for knocks and rumbles from within to make sure it's not going to spoil your immediate enjoyment of the car, but rattles from tappets and timing chains are normal and unlikely to lead to breakage. When they do wear out, these are simple motors to work on, ideal for a first engine rebuild, which can be completed quite cheaply. Alternatively, a complete reconditioned engine, converted to unleaded, can be had for under £900.

It's not unusual to find the MkIII's 1275 unit in earlier cars. Many people upgrade rather than rebuild an original unit, and it doesn't harm the value at all. Nor does a bit of tuning gear. You'll often find Midgets with aftermarket air filters and tubular exhaust manifolds – they appeal to folk who like to tinker and tweak.

Gearboxes aren't particularly robust, but £450 for a reconditioned unit isn't the end of the world. Remember there's no synchro on first, and all units tend to whine a bit, especially in lower ratios. Just make sure it doesn't jump out of any gear, particularly on the over-run. That and markedly worn synchromesh on second gear are the definitive signs that the time has come for a rebuild.

Right: Minor tuning gear such as K&N air filters are common on Midgets, as are 1275cc engines.

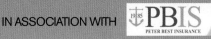
'Rattles from tappets and timing chains are normal and unlikely to lead to breakage'

Left: Standing well back and looking along each flank will give the best indication of a body's condition, and if the paint's hiding anything.

MODIFICATIONS

Midgets are popular for tuning and there are plenty of specialists to help you do it. Dropping in a 1.4-litre K-series engine has become quite the thing to do, but you will have to pay around £1800 for the fitting kit, plus source an engine and Sierra five-speed gearbox.

To be honest, the car is so light that a bit of mild tuning for the 1275 engine will be enough for most. You can also put the Sierra box behind the A-series engine for less noise, more relaxed cruising and better mpg.

Brakes really need no more than a set of EBC GreenStuff pads to sharpen them up, but there's plenty to be done with the suspension. One inch lower 330lb springs are cheap and effective, and can be matched by lowering blocks at the rear. Don't fit uprated rear springs, though – most people find that the standard ones are more than stiff enough.

Polyurethane bushes tighten things up nicely, and are especially recommended for anti-roll bar mounts and rear springs. And while we are mentioning the anti-roll bar, uprating to a 5/8-inch-thick one at the front improves the handling. Smaller steering wheels add a bit of weight to the steering, but if you go too far they can make a car feel too twitchy for comfortable road use.

BRAKES/SUSPENSION

There really isn't much to check or worry about with the suspension. Nothing's expensive if it does need doing. However, the front kingpins and trunnions do require regular greasing – say twice a year for a car in normal use – and it's worth a glance at the grease nipples to get some idea of whether or not this regime has been kept up.

The brakes are also simple. With front discs on all but the very earliest of MkIs, they didn't change and should feel adequate (though never startling) for the Midget's size. If you're not impressed, or the car pulls to one side under braking, expect to spend a bit of money. As ever, calipers can get sticky on models that haven't been used much, and at the other end of the scale, on very hard-driven examples, you can get glazing of the pads and discs that reduces efficiency. Either way, they're not expensive and are easy to work on.

DRIVING

The key to how the aptly named Midget drives is all down to weight, or rather the lack of it. With around 675lb less than an MGB to haul around, a Midget always feels lively. It can even keep pace with a B up to 50mph, or along a twisting road where the smaller car's poise and eagerness to change direction give it an advantage.

Put the top and your foot down and you get an amazing impression of speed in a Midget. You won't be going fast at all, of course, but that's all part of the car's magic – you can drive the pants off it without posing too much threat to our speed limits. Every trip's a guilt-free one.

The back end can feel a little skittish on bumpy or tight corners, and the steering can actually seem too light and sensitive until you get used to it. The gearchange is so right that you soon notice it only when baulked by the non-synchro first gear. Most owners learn to smooth this out by flicking the lever back into second before going up into first.

All you have to find out is whether you are of the right size and agility to enjoy all this. Anyone over six feet tall is likely to struggle, not so much with the space once settled in the cockpit, but with getting in and out. It's a bit like putting on a wetsuit, so try that aspect before you worry about the condition of a car.

COST

A concours-standard car might run as high as £7000, but you can easily find something to be very proud of for under £5000, probably nearer £4000. Half that – around £2000 – will get you something to smoke around in and improve as you go, but expect to be welding it up one winter in the not-too-distant future.

There's no real price difference between the different Marks, as the rarity of MkIs and IIs is balanced out by the greater usability and popularity of those with the 1275 engine, especially RWA cars. Perhaps you might be able to get a square-arched MkIII for a few hundred less, but it's not enough for the various price guides to make a distinction.

You can pick up project cars for around £1000, sometimes less, but by the time you've added a van load of panels, some trim and a respray, you're almost certain to be on the wrong side of £5000 – though undoubtedly proud of your achievement. If all else fails, there is the safety net of brand new Heritage body shells, for post-'66 cars anyway. The £4500 cost of a new shell (unpainted) is roughly the same as the price of a good restored or original MkI-III Midget, but can make a lot of sense if you are into a particular car for the long haul.

Right: MkIII hoods are easier to use than the erect-a-tent versions fitted to earlier cars.

SPECIFICATIONS

	Midget MkI	Midget MkII	Midget MkIII
Engine	948cc, 4-cyl, OHV	1098cc, 4-cyl, OHV	1275cc, 4-cyl, OHV
Power	46bhp @ 5500rpm	56bhp @ 5750rpm	65bhp @ 6000rpm
Torque	53lb/ft @ 3000rpm	62lb/ft @ 3250rpm	72lb/ft @ 3000rpm
Top speed	86mph	90mph	95mph
0-60mph	20.2secs	17.2secs	14.6secs
Fuel cons.	34mpg	30mpg	29mpg
Gearbox	Four-speed manual	Four-speed manual	Four-speed manual

USEFUL TO KNOW

■ Mike Authers Classics, Oxfordshire, 01235 834664, www.mgmidgets.com
■ MGOC Spares, Cambs, 01954 230928, www.mgocspares.co.uk
■ Moss Europe, London, 020 8867 2020, www.moss-europe.co.uk
■ Brown & Gammons, Herts, 01462 490049, www.ukmgparts.com
■ Halls Garage, Lincs. 01778 570286, www.hallsgarage.co.uk
■ Frontline Spridget, Bath, 01225 852777, www.mgcars.org.uk/frontline
■ Peter May Eng., W Mids, 01384 422424, www.petermayengineering.co.uk
■ Magic Midget, Wilts, 01225 704257, www.magicmidget.co.uk
■ Oselli Ltd, Oxon, 01993 849610, www.oselli.com
■ www.mgcars.org.uk/midgetspriteclub/index.html

HOW TO BUY...
MGB

Practical, fun to drive and unmatched parts availability are just some of the reasons for the MGB's great success. But which one's for you, and how do you spot a good example?

Words and photography: Russ Smith

The MGB needs little introduction here: it's the best-selling MG by a country mile or two. And with a lifespan that evolved over 18 years encompassing both Roadster and GT coupé bodies, there are plenty of different versions to appeal to different tastes and wallets – even if superficially the design changed little from first to last.

It was the Roadster that came first, three years before Pininfarina styled the GT's coupé back. Worldwide, the Roadster reflected the hunger for British sports cars and outsold the GT by more then three-to-one. Partly this was because 40 years ago the GT was the premium product, with prices set over 15 per cent higher than Roadsters. In fact, in 1968 the difference between a BGT and an MGC Roadster amounted to no more than a pocket of loose change. How quickly our perceptions shift – we can't ever remember Roadsters costing less than

GTs secondhand. That might be because in the damper UK market, the GT actually outsold the Roadster – you have to remember that 75 per cent of all MGBs went to America – by around 15,000 cars.

That's one choice you have to make, and with GTs now significantly cheaper than Roadsters it's a decision that may be made for you. Then there are the various evolutionary changes the cars went through. The most significant of these came in September 1974 with the raised ride height and rubber bumpers. These are often criticised, but claims involving poorer handling apply only until June 1976 when a stiffer front anti-roll bar was fitted along with a rear anti-roll bar (there had actually been none at all on rubber-bumper Roadsters until this point). So these later Bs are fine in this respect, and you just have to balance those subjective looks against the lower values.

As is so often the case, the early cars are the most coveted. In many ways they are more basic, but many enthusiasts prefer their purity, particularly with leather seats and wire wheels, plus a bonus point if it's Iris Blue.

MkIIs came along in December 1967 and offered an all-synchromesh gearbox (there was previously none on first and reverse) and an alternator. Then from 1970 there was a simpler-to-use hood, Ambla seats, a matt black grille and the option of Rostyle wheels.

In August 1972 the MkIII brought with it another new interior – with nylon seats for the GT – and a plastic grille in an aluminium surround, while Rostyles were now standard.

Taste went out of the window with the stripey nylon seats in rubber-bumper cars, but the Roadster hood did get a zip-out rear window in 1976. The last MGB was a Roadster built on October 22, 1980.

Panel availability is unrivalled, but fitting is costly – body condition is paramount.

TRIM

There's little to actually worry about inside the car as everything can be replaced to original style and standard. What does affect your decision to buy a particular car is whether its price has or can be adjusted to take account of what needs replacing.

And the sums involved can soon add up. A new set of leather seat covers (for pre-1970 Bs) is around £365, though for later vinyl or vinyl/cloth combinations

this drops to £150 or so. Those earlier seats can also be recovered in vinyl instead of leather, which loses you originality points but does save you £200. Added to this, for all of them you should really also budget another £30 per seat to replace the foam and diaphragm at the same time.

From 1973 GTs got brushed nylon seat facings, usually in navy blue, but from 1977 all MGB seats received the

infamous 'deckchair' pattern brushed nylon. All are prone to going baggy with age, though otherwise looking OK. It's up to you whether you can live with it or not.

Carpets are also worth haggling over. Top-quality new sets are £185 for Roadsters and £274 for GTs. You can probably halve those figures for low-grade replacements, but we wouldn't do that if you plan to keep the car for any length of time.

INITIAL CHECKS

■ Unsurprisingly, the MGB's greatest weakness has always been rust. If you are buying a B with the intention of reshelling it, purchase an example that is otherwise as good and complete as possible.

■ **There are more than enough MGBs out there for you to be fussy about choosing a car with a straight body and good panel fit. We'd value this above any other aspect, so buy the best you can afford in this respect, even if it means making improvements in other areas.**

■ Replacing sills properly is expensive, so make sure that there aren't cover sills or blended-in patches that will be covering all sorts of horrors. Then reach up into the back of the front wheelarches. There's a box section here that collects mud and, if rusted, is tricky (and therefore expensive) to repair.

■ **Are the floorpans rusty or patched? Proper floorpan replacement is an involved job. Inspect the mounting points for the rear springs as problems are common here.**

■ Look in the battery compartments behind the seats (under the rear ones in GTs). Any well used car is likely to show signs of corrosion in here. Repairs are straightforward enough, but made awkward by their location.

■ **On GTs with sunroofs, check for signs of leakage. A damaged Roadster hood may be unsightly, but new ones to original spec are just £166, and even a showy mohair one can be had for little over £300.**

Right: Interior trim supply is excellent. Many cars have been upgraded from vinyl to leather.

BRAKES/SUSPENSION

Mostly there's only wear and tear to worry about, and nothing is that is expensive to replace. You could almost trust that a fresh MoT means the tester will have covered all the issues you're likely to be concerned about. However, if you're looking at a car with servo-assisted brakes (that's post-'73 as standard, up to three years earlier as an option) and the brakes don't feel good, it's probable that the servo seals have gone. Reckon on £150 for a new one.

It's worth jacking up the front of the car to rock the wheels, holding them top and bottom. Any play means you need new kingpins – about £50 and a few hours' work each side. Also probe the lower wishbone spring pans for rot where the spring sits, as you can't always see problems that are developing. If left, the spring can punch through.

If the rear arch lip is below the top of the tyre, the suspension has either been lowered, or you're in need of new rear springs – although that's less than £100 the pair.

Right: Boot is shallow but adequate; luggage rack is popular touring addition.

Left: Black bumpers look best against the bright colours such as yellow and orange.

ENGINE

The fairly agricultural B-series engine is tough and long-lived, but all will need rebuilding at some point. First signs of this are puffs of smoke, particularly when you reapply the throttle after backing off, or low oil pressure. When hot, this should read between 15-25psi at idle and 50-65psi above 3000rpm. Below that probably means bearing wear, and at least a worn-out oil pump. Either way, the engine will be coming out soon.

Regard the past fitting of an unleaded head as a bonus, as otherwise the car will need an additive in the petrol at every fill-up to prevent valve seat recession. All these engines tend to leak a bit of oil, particularly from front and rear crank seals, so don't be too dismayed at this unless you see drips on the tarmac after stopping somewhere for a minute or two. They also always sound a bit 'tappety' (a light clattering from the top of the engine) even when properly adjusted. Be concerned only if there's an uneven louder tick at idle that suggest something is badly worn or a valve has burnt out.

Both types of manual box can suffer from weak synchromesh and jumping out of gear on the over-run. Check the car in all ratios for this as it means a rebuild. Also ensure that the overdrive engages and disengages smoothly and without hesitation.

Right: Roadster has a shallower screen than GT; test drive both if this could be an issue for you.

Right: B-series engine is tough as nails. Rebuilt units can be picked up for as little as £875.

'Having evolved over 18 years, there are versions to appeal to different tastes and wallets'

MODIFICATIONS

You can buy MGB tuning bits all day, so we'll concentrate on those that we believe provide genuine improvement and good value.

If you do nothing else to the engine it's worth adding electronic ignition such as an Aldon Ignitor, along with K&N filters and a three-branch exhaust manifold. This will make the most of whatever power you have, and aid reliability. As will a Kenlowe or similar fan, even on the electric fan-equipped rubber-bumper cars – their units aren't that efficient.

The simple route to better brakes is Powerstop's X25 upgrade. This uses EBC Greenstuff pads that are, as the name suggests, 25 per cent bigger than standard pads but fit the standard calipers. They are just £38.11 for a set. If your brake hoses are starting to age, fit Aeroquip stainless items. You'll get a firmer pedal feel and they last for ages. A set of three for the car shouldn't cost much over £40.

Ignore all those fancy telescopic damper conversions. Most experts agree that 30 per cent uprated lever arms do just as good a job and can be had for as little as £130 for all four. A thicker – ¾in – front anti-roll bar is good value, as is a set of polyurethane suspension bushes. Polybush does a whole-car set for around £85.

If you have a B with Rostyles, a switch to the Minilite-style alloys used on the car in our photos will reduce unsprung weight to improve both ride and handling.

AYR 289T

›

Right: A stock MGB is an easy delight to drive, plus there are endless tuning options.

SPECIFICATIONS

MGB

Engine	1798cc, 4-cyl, OHV
Power	95bhp @ 5400rpm
Torque	110lb/ft @ 3000rpm
Top speed	106mph
0-60mph	12.9secs
Fuel cons.	26mpg
Gearbox	Four-speed manual (some + O/D)

DRIVING

Good low-down torque means a B nips off the line smartly and has plenty of mid-range urge that makes it a relaxing car to drive. You don't need to use the gearbox as much as with many contemporary sports cars, but when you do the short, precise change is always a pleasure.

However, low gearing means that the optional overdrive is almost a must these days. We wouldn't buy a B without it, but rubber-bumper cars have it as standard, and many earlier ones that didn't have it fitted at the factory have since been converted,

so that's not being too restrictive.

Brakes are just about a match for the car's pace, and likewise the suspension is competent rather than exciting. It's user-friendly and forgiving, though; from the driver's seat an MGB always feels tidy and safe, with neutral handling that errs towards understeer if you start to push on too hard. The steering has a 'manly' heaviness, especially at parking speeds, that is only made worse by the common addition of an aftermarket steering wheel, but it always feels precise and free of play.

> 'An MGB nips off the line smartly and has plenty of mid-range urge that makes it a relaxing car to drive'

Above: An MGB's steering is good but 'manly'; don't go too small on the aftermarket steering wheel, particularly if the car also has wider tyres.

COST

The big split is between Roadsters and GTs. Whichever version you go for, and in whatever condition, expect to pay roughly double for the privilege of having a soft-top. Aside from that, the simple rule is that prices rise as you go back in time. That's partly due to people preferring the purity of early versions, though survivor numbers also weigh heavily on the values. Few people thought of preserving the seemingly endless supply of MGBs until they went out of production, so time and rust already had taken their toll. Put simply, the older an MGB you want, the fewer there are left to choose from.

Bought privately, early Roadsters can fetch as much as £9250, equivalent MkIIs reach about £1000 less, and for MkIIIs you can knock off another £1000. Rubber-bumper Roadsters make it to only £5750. Halve those amounts for average examples, and expect to pay from £1000-£2000 for a project, with MkIs at the top of that range. Good cars from dealers, or anything with a replacement Heritage shell, can fetch significantly more, but each will have to be judged on its merits.

Even the nicest privately sold MkI GTs are worth only around £5000, going down to £3250 for a similar-condition rubber-bumper GT.

USEFUL TO KNOW

- Abingdon Parts 4 MG & Triumph, Wolverhampton, 0121 544 4444, www.mg-tr-parts.co.uk
- Beech Hill Garage, Berks, 0118 988 4774, www.beechhillgarage.com
- Brown & Gammons, 01462 490049, www.ukmgparts.com
- Croydon Classics, Surrey, 08000 556155, www.croydonclassics.com
- Former Glory, London, 020 8991 1963, www.former-glory.com
- Hall's Garage, Lincs, 01778 570286, www.hallsgarage.co.uk
- MGB Hive, Cambs, 01945 700500, www.mgbhive.co.uk
- MGOC Spares, Cambs, 01954 230928, www.mgocspares.co.uk
- Midland Sports & Classics 01905 621331, www.MGPartsUK.com
- Moto-Build Ltd, Surrey, 01784 477477, www.moto-build.co.uk
- Moss Europe, 020 8867 2020, www.moss-europe.co.uk
- Rimmer Bros, Lincoln, 01522 563344, www.rimmerbros.co.uk
- SC Parts Group Ltd, 01293 847204, www.scparts.co.uk
- Sussex Classic Car Parts, W Sussex, 01403 711551, www.sussexclassiccar.co.uk
- Thanks to: Steve at Hall's Garage for advice and the loan of the car in our photos.

HOW TO BUY...

MG MONTEGO

The Montego might not be the sexiest car ever to wear an MG badge, but for some time it was at least the fastest. Let's don those red braces and investigate

Words and photography: Russ Smith

Once Austin-Rover had reintroduced the MG badge and given the Metro and Maestro red seatbelts, it was inevitable that the Montego would come in for similar treatment. But those readers wincing in anticipation of a cheap jibe here can relax. Whatever you think of Montegos as a whole, the factory actually made a pretty good job of the MG version. And, yes, the Turbo variant really was the fastest-ever MG for a while, although by only 2mph over the BGT V8. This does give it some genuine notoriety though.

Launched in April 1984, the Montego was built on a Maestro floorpan stretched by two inches to increase rear passenger legroom. With the addition of its capacious boot, the Montego finished up 16 inches longer than the Maestro, but still managed to share at least half its panels.

The MG Montego EFi, as the sporty version was christened, used Austin-Rover's Lucas fuel-injected top-of-the-range version of the firm's O-series engine (based on the B-series but with an overhead-cam

aluminium cylinder head). It was bolted to a new Honda five-speed gearbox in place of the VW unit found in the Maestro. The Montego got the Maestro's steering, suspension and brakes, though the front discs were upgraded to ventilated status.

To distract buyers from the reality that 115bhp wasn't that sporty, the MG Montego got front and rear spoilers plus red seatbelts and carpets. There were also optional alloy Dunlop TD safety wheels with special metric-sized low-profile tyres, but don't worry – many of these have been replaced with conventional rims and rubber by now.

In addition, early cars were treated to an even more complicated version of the LCD instrumentation, trip computer and talking dashboard that had seemed so *Tomorrow's World* on the more expensive Maestros. However, this thankfully barely saw 1984 out before Austin-Rover relented and brought back conventional instruments that worked. You are unlikely to find many survivors still fitted with it now.

After a year the thrusting Montego Turbo was

added to the MG range. This was a rather different beast to drive, as the Garrett AiResearch T3 turbocharger forced a significant 150bhp from the 2-litre O-series, though strangely it reverted from fuel injection to an SU carburettor for fuelling.

To cope with it, stiffer springs and anti-roll bars were added along with gas-filled dampers, and larger front discs and rear drums were employed. Lengthening the final gearing from 3.9:1 to 3.65:1 made good use of the extra power and gave the surprisingly aerodynamic Montego that top speed of 127mph. Just what the marketing department wanted, as adverts proudly trumpeted the 'Fastest Production MG Ever Made' mantra.

There were very few production changes before both cars were eventually dropped in 1991 to clear the air for the MG badge's return to more sporting purposes. However, the glaring red carpet did give way to a sober grey effort, which was matched by plainer seat coverings. The EFi tag went, too, to be replaced by more straight-talking MG Montego 2.0i badges.

'With a top speed of 127mph, adverts proudly trumpeted "the fastest MG ever made"'

Left: A new problem for MG owners to deal with is plastics that deteriorate with age.

INITIAL CHECKS

■ Around 42,000 MG Montegos were built, just 7276 of which were Turbos, but the biggest hurdle to ownership is not finding a good one, it's finding one at all. They are out there, but the survival rate has not been good, and owners of good ones tend to hang onto them. Your best bet is to join the various clubs and online support groups, then make it known you are looking. It's a surer way than waiting for something to pop up in the classifieds or on eBay.

■ **Inspecting the body for problems isn't hard. Though all Montegos are liable to rust with a vengeance, unusually it is mostly cosmetic. Apart from the rear ends of the sills and around the rear suspension 'domes' – an area that you must lift the carpet to inspect and which is particularly hard to repair – you don't get much structural corrosion. However, it does break out on wheelarches, doors, and around the windscreen and fuel filler. This is what has seen so many off: when they started to look scabby and weren't worth the cost of new panels and a paint job, they were scrapped.**

■ Unless you are lucky enough to find a mint, low-mileage example, or one owned from early on by a fanatic with access to Waxoyl, these areas should also be checked for the quality of the inevitable repairs to them.

■ **At least panel availability is still pretty good, as are prices, so apply a little DIY and you can make most repairs quite reasonably. Front wings are £48.75, rear arch repair panels £22.09, sills £18 a side, and front door skins £71.49 each. You can even buy a complete new bonnet for £110 if the common stonechip-induced nose rash has got too bad.**

■ Something we're less used to is deteriorating plastics, but that can be a problem with Montegos. The bumpers become brittle with age and often crack. When found, replacements can be expensive, and obviously breaker's yard stuff is likely to be just as bad. Plastic repair stuff is available now, and it's an idea to reinforce vulnerable areas from the inside with glassfibre matting. The plastic external door handles also break, but are fairly easy to replace.

TRIM

For the most part the interior trim is quite hardwearing and very comfortable. There are a few common faults, however. That bane of 1980s British motoring, the saggy headlining, is waiting to greet you. Jump for joy if it's already been replaced, for this is the only real answer, and negotiate heavily if you find it held up by drawing pins, untidy gluey patches or similar bodgery.

Rattling dashboards and carpets of approximate fit are to be considered normal. What you don't really want to see are cracks in the dashboard moulding of earlier cars, or the bends and tears that can happen to those in later Montegos. Switchgear is not of the highest quality, so check that for condition and function. Most parts can be sourced, with the Maestro & Montego Club's parts service being a useful first call, and autojumbles or Araldite will usually deal with the rest.

Most of all, check the notorious central locking. This often doesn't work on all doors, though you can often restore function by stripping down, cleaning and lubricating the locks and operating mechanisms.

Right: Clear, unfussy and of its era, Montego cabin is generally hard wearing.

Left: Viewed head-on, the Montego loses its distinctive styling...
Below left: ...but look at that airy and spacious passenger compartment.

'The O-series is a tough old lump, long-lasting even in Turbo form. Don't worry if it sounds clattery'

ENGINE

The O-series is a tough old lump, long-lasting even in Turbo form. Don't worry if it sounds a bit clattery at the top end – that's quite normal. There is a design weakness with these engines that means oil seeps from the head gasket near number four cylinder, though. You will find a fair bit of oil around the gearbox end of the motor, and possibly also on the bellhousing. This isn't a concern, but if you find oil escaping from lower down, around the bottom of the bellhousing, do worry – it's probably the rear crank seal. That's a big job to put right.

Poor running is often blamed on the ECU, but in most cases it's actually either a sensor or corrosion in the connector to the ECU, that can easily be cleaned off. Always try this for a cure first.

It's usually a struggle to get the injected models through the MoT emissions test. The adjustment is hard to get spot-on and many owners resort to one setting for regular use and another just for test days. At least you don't have to worry about the gearbox. It's as tough as you'd expect from Honda, with few reported problems. The Turbo's was beefed up to take the extra power so lasts just as well. Boxes are theoretically interchangeable, but the EFi's gearing is too short for the Turbo, and fitting an EFi with a Turbo box makes it sluggish.

Left: Engines can be clattery – re-shimming valve clearances requires a special tool and is often neglected.

Left: Red detailing both inside and out complemented comparatively discreet badging on the MG Montegos.

MODIFICATIONS

Moto-build Racing has always been the place for modified Montego stuff. It still retains stocks of some parts – especially suspension – and will happily build you a tuned engine. A set of one- or two-inch lower springs will cost you £105, with a matching set of gas-filled dampers going for £210. Add another £104 for an eight-piece polyurethane bush set and you have pretty much sewn up the handling. However, if you have a injected model, add the rear anti-roll bar and larger front one from the Turbo to your shopping list.

The same gearbox as the Montego's was also adopted by later Rover models, and those used in turbo versions of the 16-valve T-series engine came as standard with Torsen limited-slip diffs. They also have broadly similar ratios to the Montego. Another later MG-Rover product to source from is the MGF, whose wheels are a good fit on Montegos and come in a wide range of sizes. As for tyres on more standard rims, if you have 14-inchers the current recommendation is 185/60s, and for 15in wheels use 195/50s. Both are slightly wider and lower profile than original, but are close enough in diameter for speedo accuracy. And they can be picked up cheaply and easily.

Below: Metric-sized tyres are very expensive, but cheaper alternatives are available.

Above: In the 1980s everyone was fitting spoilers, but MG's Montego Turbo really was a performance star.

BRAKES/SUSPENSION

It's all very conventional in this department and easy to work on, so don't worry too much as long as the car steers and stops OK on your road test. If it does clonk over bumps, those are best viewed as mere negotiation points.

It is worth checking the CV joints, especially on the Turbo where they are under rather more strain. They are no more prone to wear than anything else, it's just a pig of a job that no one wants to do if they can help it.

One day cars with their original metric-sized alloys may be revered by originality freaks, but you'll find most Montegos without theirs now. This is largely because the tyres, though still widely available, are a lot more expensive to replace. So don't worry about originality in this area, as non-standard wheels are more practical.

›

Above: If you've dismissed the Montego as a driver's car, prepare to be surprised.

DRIVING

The rather surprising overall impression of the Montego is just how smooth it all feels. Not only is there a comfortable ride that makes it a good car for long journeys, but the steering and gearchange are pretty slick and it sweeps through bends in a manner befitting much more expensive sports saloons. If it doesn't feel like this, order will be restored once you replace the dampers and maybe a few suspension bushes. The finesse does start to slip away if you really push the handling, though less so on the Turbo model with its uprated suspension package.

Noise levels build up on the injected models at motorway speeds, but in general the engines are pretty quiet, and you can learn to ignore any chattering from the dashboard. The Turbo's taller gearing makes it an even better high-speed cruiser, but its real trick is scintillating acceleration, with a 0-60mph time that shames, for example, modern Saab 9-3s with 2-litre turbos.

Early Montego Turbos do suffer from quite startling torque steer under hard acceleration, yet this had largely been brought under control by the 1988 model year.

'The overall impression is just how smooth it feels'

Above: With enough power to rival the BGT V8, economy is not remarkable – as you might expect.

Above: Montego is a real MG sporting saloon in the finest of the manufacturer's traditions.

COST

As mentioned earlier, finding an MG Montego is the hard part; once you've cracked that, actually buying it is quite easy. For once, the rarity of a car is not reflected in the price. Even the very best concours Turbo shouldn't cost you more than £2500, even if it is really low mileage or was once owned by the Spice Girls. A more realistic figure to pay for a good Turbo is £1500. A fuel-injected Montego in similar condition might make £1200 on a good day, but be patient and you'll pay under £1000 for something nice.

Scruffy yet usable cars can still be found for as little as £250, no matter what engine is fitted, but you'll be lucky to find any real bargains at this price nowadays. Have a go, by all means, but check those rusty areas carefully to see how far they go and be clear that what you are buying will soon be either a donor car or something to invest much time and money in. Most MG Montegos, however, will fall somewhere in between those prices and conditions.

More than in most cases, it really does make sense to buy the best you can and look after it, safe in the knowledge that there will be even fewer left when their time comes to be recognised as cars worth making a fuss about. MG

SPECIFICATIONS

	Montego EFi	Montego Turbo
Engine	1994cc, 4-cyl, OHC	1994cc, 4-cyl, OHC
Power	115bhp @ 5500rpm	150bhp @ 5100rpm
Torque	134lb/ft @ 2800rpm	169lb/ft @ 3500rpm
Top speed	115mph	127mph
0-60mph	9.6secs	7.5secs
Fuel cons.	29mpg	23mpg
Gearbox	Five-spd manual	Five-spd manual

USEFUL TO KNOW

- Halls Garage, Lincs. 01778 570286, www.hallsgarage.co.uk
- www.triple-m.co.uk
- www.mgmgroup.org.uk
- www.maestro.org.uk
- www.mgcars.org.uk/mglong/html
- www.aronline.co.uk
- Moto-build Racing, Middlesex, 020 8893 4553, www.moto-build.com
- Beevers Auto Panels, 01226 780542, www.beeversautopanels.co.uk
- Sterling Automotive, 01323 438754, wwwsterlingautomotive.co.uk
- Thanks to: John Collier for providing the car for our photos

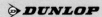

HOW TO BUY...
MG RV8

A true British sports car with performance to spare, the RV8 is a whole lot more than just a V8 MGB. Here we explore why – and how to buy a good one.

Words and photography: Russ Smith

After its sad but inevitable demise in 1980, nobody could ever have thought we'd see the MGB resurrecting its career. But then no one predicted the MX-5 either. That little gem was the catalyst for properly reviving the MG badge, which Rover set about doing in 1990 with what was to become the MGF. In the meantime, however, they needed something to revitalise the public's faith in the MG logo, which had been slightly tarnished by too much association with Austins and red seat belts.

By lucky coincidence the Heritage MGB shells had just been launched, and there was no shortage of Rover V8s around the factory. Add in a development time span of roughly a week's tea breaks, with a budget equating to about £27.50 in car manufacturing terms, and the RV8 was suddenly the only option worth looking at. It was ready for the 1992 British Motor Show.

Despite stonking performance from that four-litre V8, Autocar greeted the RV8 with the sort of enthusiasm usually reserved for the reappearance of last night's shepherd's pie at the breakfast table, via the microwave. 'Keeps the MG name alive – but achieves little else,' they said. The RV8's popularity and solid prices ever since only highlights just how wrong they were.

Admittedly the Chimaera-sized £26,000 price tag made things hard for the MG in the UK market, but Japan was still swimming in pre-banking crisis riches in the mid-Nineties and they loved the whole retro thing. In the end, 1583 of the 1982 MG RV8s built went to Japan, though how many are left there is anyone's guess as so many have since been re-imported to the UK or gone to other enthusiast-filled right-hand-drive markets like Australia.

Though it wholeheartedly resembles one, only about five percent of the RV8 is composed of MGB parts, and with all that wood, leather, aircon and fancy paint it's a far more luxurious proposition.

Oh and, get used to the idea of Pearlescent Woodcote Green. Despite a choice of ten colours in the brochure, that's the shade two-thirds of RV8s were painted in, with Pearlescent Oxford Blue a distant second with just over 250 examples. Only five people requested Old English White.

Japanese motoring habits, particularly in relation to cars bought almost as toys, mean that a great percentage of the RV8s being repatriated have covered little mileage, certainly by our standards. They are also usually nurtured by loving owners, and to a large degree that is what you are looking for evidence of when buying one today. Service history is important. Yes, it is likely to be largely in Japanese, but the more conscientious importers, like Classic & Sportscar Consultants, have this translated. That should also confirm that a car's claims of minimal mileage are completely genuine. Without that it's hard to trust any claims being made.

Left: **The WA body is steel over an ash frame, a wider version of the earlier SA.**

INITIAL CHECKS

■ This would normally be the point where I ramble on at length about all the areas where you should try and prod holes or spot filler and dodgy repairs. However, the MG RV8 bodies were electro-phoretically dipped and so far it seems to have worked – they appear to be almost rust-free. I say almost because there has to be a catch somewhere or it wouldn't be a proper British sports car. In this case the one place to look for rust is the windscreen frame. These bolt-on items were bought in by MG-Rover, were of poorer quality steel than the rest of the car and were fitted after the anti-rust treatment had taken place. Rot broke out so quickly that some were even replaced under warranty. To find one that was is a nice bonus as the replacements were filled with Waxoyl. New ones are now available in both steel and carbon-fibre, but the price is over £900 for either. Incentive enough to carefully check what's on the car. They normally go first across the bottom, so look for filler there.

■ **Check the hood condition – the originals weren't of the highest quality. New ones are £500-£600, and few fit correctly off the shelf. This may be because it has recently been discovered that there were actually two different frames used. The only way to guarantee a good fit is to have the new top made to fit the car by a good trimmer like Motobuild. They quote around £950 for the job.**

■ Panels to specifically check for damage are the vulnerable body-coloured bumpers. New front and rear ones are £405 and £468 respectively, plus fitting and painting, so at least make a strong bargaining point. The rear lights are also more crucial than you might think. Though styled on original MGB units, they are wider and unique to the RV8. They have been in short supply but are now available – at £205 each.

TRIM

The condition of the interior has an enormous affect on any given RV8's value. With burr elm veneer on the dashboard and door cappings, and stone beige leather everywhere else, retrimming will always be expensive. And while the leather may be Connolly, that comes in different grades, and the one used in the RV8 isn't the same as you'll find in Aston Martins and Bentleys.

Few cars are broken, so decent secondhand interiors that do come up for sale fetch big money – around £500 for a dashboard and up to £2500 for a complete interior. The message should be clear: buy a car with the best interior you can, then clean and feed the leather regularly so it's still good when you come to sell the car on.

The gear knob is covered in the same leather and this is always the first thing to look shabby. New ones are £50.

Another common problem is glove box lid fit, which is variable at best and tends to worsen with age.

Most RV8s were sold with air-conditioning, so check that's working and pay less if it's not. Other specifics to check are the fuel gauge, which can malfunction if a printed circuit board cracks, and the heater blower motor – they often suffer from failure of a resistor pack.

Right: **Interior is complex and expensive to restore, up to £8k for a full leather retrim.**

■ **A small but important point is that the bootlid should always be closed by one hand on the badge, otherwise the panel can distort.**

BRAKES/SUSPENSION

Apart from listening for knocks from worn bushes at the front, which are cheap enough to replace anyway, there's little to go wrong with the old-fashioned coil-and-wishbone front and leaf-sprung rear suspension.

On your test drive, brake hard and feel for any slight pulling to one side or the other. This is most likely to be due to a stuck slave cylinder in one of the rear drums. It's a well-documented problem and they need regular replacement, though at £30 each it's not so serious that it should put you off a purchase.

There are still low mileage Japanese imports coming home wearing their original tyres, and some sellers even make a virtue of the fact. However, at this age they will have age-hardened, be well down on grip and dangerous. Classic & Sportscar Consultants change them as a matter of course, and anyone else should, too.

> "The dear old Rover V8 is easily tuned, and there are many specialists to help you"

ENGINE

There really isn't a lot to worry about with the under-stressed V8, especially as it's unusual for an RV8 to have covered a serious amount of miles. As long as the oil has been changed regularly they'll go on well into six figures, so check that service history.

When starting the engine, turn on the ignition and wait for the fuel pump to stop buzzing. That tells you the system is primed and ready for the key to be turned all the way.

It's not uncommon for these cars to have an idling problem, but don't worry,

it's usually the stepper motor and can be cured with switch cleaner.

Get the engine properly hot to see if it overheats. This can happen if the cooling system isn't correctly bled after topping up or refilling, using the hex nut above the offside valve cover. If this is left then damage can occur, in which case you are likely to find evidence of oil and water mixing due to a blown head gasket. If there's no sign of that, bleeding the system should return things to normal. The other possibility is a leaking water pump. They are unique

to the RV8, but you can get replacements for £120 exchange.

By the way, it's very common for the original plastic hex nuts to round off, but brass ones are available for under a tenner.

Neither of the two gearboxes used are prone to give trouble, but the later Land Rover Discovery 'box is said to be a bit better, certainly in its gearshift, than the older SD1 unit. You can tell which unit is which by the position of reverse gear — next to first in the older cars, below fifth in later ones.

Right: Engine is unstressed; most problems are minor and don't require an engine strip.

Left: A hood will not be MGB-cheap to replace and should be tailored to each individual car.

Left: Bumpers are susceptible to accident damage and will set you back over £500 fitted.

MODIFICATIONS

The dear old Rover V8 is easily tuned, and there are many specialists ready to help you, even when you have 190bhp as a starting point. After all, the very same injected four-litre engine was used in TVRs in 240bhp/270lb.ft form. That's a difference you'd notice, though it would be wise to also fit one of the high efficiency radiators too, that are available from specialists.

The original fitment Lucas alternators fail with monotonous regularity, but you can swap it for the Magnetti-Marelli one used in V8 Land Rovers. One point to note is that some of these have their regulators set at too high a level. It's not a problem, but the ignition light will stay on until the throttle is blipped hard.

Polyurethane bushes are a good idea, especially as replacements for the wear-prone front wishbone and anti-roll bar rubbers. You can also get polyurethane replacements for the front bump stops, which crack and shouldn't be ignored.

The hardtops made by Krafthaus are a highly sought after accessory for RV8s, but you'll need to search long and hard for one, and have a well-stuffed wallet.

SPECIFICATIONS

MG RV8	
Engine	3948cc, V8, OHV
Power	190bhp @ 4750rpm
Torque	234lb.ft @ 3200rpm
Top speed	136mph
0-60mph	6.9secs
Fuel cons.	23mpg
Gearbox	5-spd manual

Above: The original leather used by MG is not the most durable, but usually modest mileages do at least keep wear and tear under control.

DRIVING

This isn't a car that suits inexperienced drivers; you need to respect its performance and capabilities, just like you would a Porsche 911. That V8 delivers its big whack of power everywhere from idle upwards, and you don't have the most sophisticated chassis to control it with. Much like a TVR though, that makes it great fun to drive, and despite the low technology it all feels very well resolved and behaves in a predictable manner.

Traction is good thanks to the anti-tramp bars and limited-slip diff, but it can get a bit fidgety over bumps. The vented front discs with four-pot calipers should feel strong and confidence inspiring, and it's certainly no problem that there are only drums at the back.

It's an easy car to get comfortable in, though tall drivers can find the top of the screen cuts across their sight line. You'll also notice that the steering wheel is offset a bit to the left, but it's something I'm told you soon get used to.

> "That V8 delivers its big whack of power everywhere, from idle upwards"

COST

RV8s have been known to change hands for as little as £6000, but at that level you'll be buying something with a rusty screen frame, poor interior and probably mechanical problems as well. Cars that have been allowed to get that tired are few and far between, and by the time you've put it right you might as well have bought a good one in the first place. Those can be had for somewhere between £9500 and £12,000, a fair variation to allow for condition, mileage and colour, and will almost certainly have done less than 50,000 miles. These prices have been steady for some time now, so it seems the RV8 has found its level.

Beyond that we get into the surprisingly well-populated domain of the immaculate and low mileage cars. Expect to pay £14,000-£15,000 for one of these, maybe a little more if the speedo hasn't reached 10,000, the car is in one of the more unusual colours or has rare extras. No modifications though – the market likes these standard.

USEFUL TO KNOW

- Classic & Sports Car Consultants Ltd, Bucks, 01494 434414, www.classic-sportscar.co.uk
- Clive Wheatley, Shropshire, 01746 710810, www.mgv8.homestead.com
- Brown & Gammons, Herts, 01462 490049, www.mgrv8parts.com
- Fisher Services, SE London, 020 8776 7695, www.fisher-services.co.uk
- MG Owners Club Spares, Cambs, 01954 230928, www.mgocspares.co.uk
- Rimmer Bros, Lincoln, 01522 563344, www.rimmerbros.co.uk
- Thanks to: Fred Jenns for imparting his vast knowledge of RV8s.

Above: Modifications are not generally popular in the RV8 market, and with original details this good it is easy to decide they are not necessary.

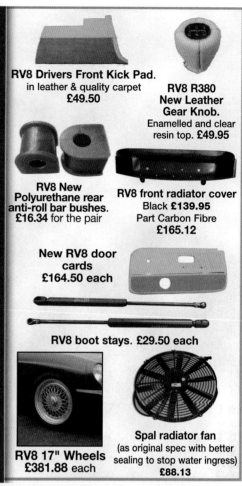

HOW TO BUY...

MG ZR

Whether you consider it a pukka MG or a badge-engineered
Rover, the ZR's fun factor has captured the imagination
of younger drivers. Here's how to pick a good one

Words and photography: Russ Smith

When MG-Rover bosses finally woke up to the value of the Octagon badge and applied it across their range rather than just to the MGF, the thought caused more than a few marque enthusiasts to shudder. Would it be just another cynical rebranding exercise that further devalued the MG name? However, this time the marketing and engineering departments got it right. The cars looked good, and enough had been done under the skin to justify their wearing of the MG badge.

The ZR was, of course, based on the six-year-old Rover 200, or 25 as it had been rechristened in 1999. To set it apart from the Rover, the MG got a new front bumper and grille, plus the tailgate spoiler from the rare and slightly incongruous Rover 25 GTi.

In the bad old days that would have been enough, but the real work on the ZR was done on the suspension to make it handle like an MG should. Compared to the 25 it got lower, stiffer springs and harder bushes, plus thicker anti-roll bars, uprated dampers and sharper steering – it's like reading a Demon Tweeks catalogue. And it worked. In fact, by 2004 the ZR was outselling the Rover.

All versions of the ZR got the same suspension, so they handle just as well as each other. The big difference between the models is under the bonnet, where you have a choice of three petrol and two diesel engines, as detailed in the specification table. Oil-burners may be all the rage in the new millennium, but don't get too excited: this is the old-tech and rather agricultural Perkins-based L-series turbodiesel, just a few small steps on from what you

might have found in a Maestro. However, if you must have a diesel, make sure it's the intercooled TD 115 and not the uninspiring rep-spec TD 100 version. You will have to look harder for one, though, as at the time of writing only one in 20 of the ZRs advertised for sale on *Auto Trader's* site had the diesel engine.

All the petrol engines do a good enough job, even the remarkably spirited base-level 1.4 K-series in the ZR 105 – which is just as well, as about three-quarters of ZRs are 105s. The ZR 120 and 160 both use the 1.8-litre K-series, the latter in screaming VVC form, lifted straight from the MGF. Which you choose depends on your driving habits, but the reality is that you won't feel much difference between the two 1.8s in normal driving – all the VVC's extra power comes in high up the rev range. The ZR 120 is also the only one to get the Stepspeed CVT automatic gearbox option.

'The cars looked good, and enough had been done under the skin to justify the MG badge'

Left: The ZR revived an MG saloon tradition and ended up out-selling the Rover that sired it.

INITIAL CHECKS

■ Hopefully the engine won't have been warmed up before you view the car, as you really want to hear it idling both from cold and once warm. It should be smooth – an uneven idle, if not caused by the inlet manifold gaskets, spells problems with either the ECU (expensive), or a sensor (cheap enough once you've found out which). Of course, you'll barter on the worst-case scenario.

■ **Wind noise is common from window and sunroof seals. The extent of this varies from car to car thanks to MG-Rover's patchy build quality, and can be near-impossible to eradicate.**

■ More serious is a whining from the gearbox, especially in fifth, though you should also be wary of a whine at idle that doesn't go away when the clutch pedal is depressed. Quite simply, either means the transmission is on the way out, and though nothing like as common as the head gasket problem detailed later, it's far from unknown on these cars. It's not the end of the world – we've even seen brand new units for sale on eBay for £250 – but the cost and time off the road do need to be taken into account. If the whine at idle does vanish when the clutch is operated, that's the input shaft bearings complaining, which can be replaced on their own.

■ **If you're looking at a ZR with ABS, check that for faults. Reluctor ring or sensor failure is quite common with these cars, and you need to budget £75-100 for repairs. Problems will show up as a pulsating in the pedal when braking gently at low speed, so try this out during your test drive.**

■ Check electric windows for smooth and complete operation. Any juddering means problems with the regulator. It happens enough to have made good secondhand regulators quite rare, and you can pay £150 to have a new one fitted. This, by the way, is far from the ZR's only electrical worry. Check that everything works, including the heating system and air-con where fitted, and leave the engine running to see that the cooling fan kicks in.

■ **A ZR that knocks over bumps, doesn't track straight or has uneven tyre wear needs new ball joints. They don't last particularly long, especially with the larger wheels and tyres. New joints are straightforward to fit, but genuine parts cost close on £70 a side. They will last longer than pattern parts, though.**

TRIM

There were two basic trim options, standard and ZR+. When new the latter cost £1875 extra, which got you electric front windows, mirrors and sunroof, remote central locking, better seats, a leather wheel and gear knob, plus front fog lights. Now, however, the price difference is almost negligible. The ZR 160 also got bigger brakes, air-con, part-leather seats (an option on lesser models), bigger alloys and sculpted sill finishers. Full leather seats were a £750 option on these, which put most buyers off, so jump for joy if you find one that has them. Once again, most of that £750 has vanished from the car's value.

All versions could be had with three or five doors, but in keeping with the ZR's sporty nature more people took the three-door option, especially for the 105.

Expect to hear a few rattles and squeaks from the interior during your test drive – that's just the way ZRs were put together, though later cars did get better. You can spend your free time trying to track down and eliminate them, but don't expect complete success.

Right: Higher-spec interiors were available and now they command little premium.

Left: Styling and performance distanced ZR from Rover parentage...
Below left: ...but spoiler was lifted from the Rover 25 GTi and suited ZR.

'The 60,000-mile mark is an expensive time for ZRs so a lot come up for sale just before then'

ENGINE

As these cars use the K-series engine, we're sure you can work out where the buying advice is heading first – towards the notorious head gasket problems. These motors have very little tolerance to overheating, largely because they were designed with low coolant capacity. Any drop in water level quickly leads to problems, so owners need to be paranoid about water leaks and the coolant level. A low-level warning indicator is a very useful aftermarket addition, not least for the added peace of mind it brings. The radiator should also be considered a 60,000-mile service item due to the inevitable furring up that takes place. If the car is at or past this mark and hasn't had a new radiator, check the engine very carefully and budget around £100 for a replacement rad.

Head gasket failure will show up as 'mayonnaise' on the dipstick or under the filler cap, or as grey sludge floating on the surface of the water reservoir. You also want to see bright-coloured and not brown coolant. Check for any water leaks, too. They are most common from the water-heated inlet manifold, or from corrosion of the metal pipe behind the engine that runs down by the gearbox (replacements are around £30).

There are also the radiator hose connections to consider. The original steel clips for these were cheap and nasty, so feel reassured if you find they've been replaced by something of better quality. You can minimise the chance of future problems by adopting some of the cooling system cures produced for the MGF such as uprated gaskets and the stronger oil rail designed for the Freelander.

Diesels tend to stay together a lot better, but look out for oil leaks from the oil pump area and water leaks from the thermostat housing. Misfires are often blamed on failed head gaskets, but if there are no other symptoms the culprit is almost certainly the inlet manifold O-rings. These can last as little as 25-30,000 miles, but are at least a lot easier to change than a head gasket.

Radiator aside, the 60,000-mile mark is an expensive time, so a lot come up for sale just before then. That's when the cambelt needs to be changed on petrol engines, at which point you should also replace the water pump (£50) and belt tensioner. If you do your own servicing it's not too bad, but if not the costs mount up quite alarmingly, and should at the very least be used for bartering purposes – the vendor's going to know why he's selling at that mileage.

Right: It's a K-series, so head gaskets can go. The 60,000-mile service is expensive, too.

Above: Three doors were always more popular than five on the ZR, especially on the entry-level 105 versions.

Left: Be wary of engine chips and poor air filters; brakes are good with 160's discs best.

MODIFICATIONS

The popularity of ZRs with younger drivers means they are no strangers to being modified, with varying degrees of success. Mods to avoid include those open, cone-shaped air filters that are great for noise but do nothing for performance. It's better and cheaper to fit a performance replacement panel filter in the original housing.

There are also chips advertised, commonly on eBay, that claim to increase power by 20bhp. They may well do this, but not for long, as they damage the engine by over-fuelling it, which is also bad news for your mpg figure. All the chip does is fool the ECU into thinking the engine is cold all the time so it pumps more fuel – it's a bit like running with the choke out on an older car. There's more power to be had by changing the exhaust, but you need at least a 'cat-back' system, not just a big-bore rear silencer. You also want evidence it is good enough to pass the MoT.

The brakes are good, as we've said, but the front discs on the ZR 160 are 20mm bigger diameter and can easily be swapped onto lesser models with the matching calipers. You can improve the already excellent handling by fitting 30mm lower springs – choose a good make like AVO – but be prepared to sacrifice some comfort.

Right: The ZR is a real driver's car and a great way of attracting new owners into the MG fold.

DRIVING

From a driving point of view good things got even better with the ZR's 2004 update. The revised cars might not have shown such a pretty face, but detail improvements had been made where it matters. A repositioned pedal box put the clutch pedal in a more comfortable place, and was combined with improved brake feel and a change to the throttle pedal ratio to make the car feel more responsive. The steering was also sharpened up by changing toe and camber geometry, and fitting a stiffer subframe. Rear suspension bush material was also improved.

It all made a good car better. The ZR always feels lively, gives plenty of feedback and likes corners, which can be taken with precision. Firm without being harsh, its darting nature and wheel-at-each-corner stance are in many ways reminiscent of a Peugeot 205 GTi, if a little less sharp and frenetic. The ZR also shares the 205's high seating position. The brakes are also good, and the gearchange slick.

> 'Vastly greater numbers combined with less desirability make the ZR 105 something of a bargain'

Above: The first ZRs had twin headlamps; single covers replaced them in 2004

COST

Despite good performance and relative modernity, the ZR is a cheap way into MG ownership. Although they were £15,000 cars when new, the most you'll need for a really low-mileage three-year-old ZR 160 or TD is £6750. 2004 models with around 30,000 miles should come in under £5000, and early ('01) 160s are plentiful in the £3000-£3200 range. Reckon on paying £200-£300 less for a ZR 120. Vastly greater numbers combined with less desirability make the ZR 105 something of a bargain. Prices for early ones start at £2200, with lots of 50-70,000-mile cars on the market for

around £2500.

The 105 (and TD) will also cost you noticeably less to run. As well as lower tax and less fuel (a difference that grows markedly from the quoted figures the more you 'enjoy' your ZR), the ZR 105 is rated only as insurance Group 8, with the 120 and TD at Group 10 and the 160 a sobering Group 16. Using the quote we got for a 35-year-old Lincolnshire engineer with six years' no-claims bonus as a guide, that translates into £268 for the ZR 105 with a £220 excess, and £453 for the 160, with a £470 excess. Any lower excess raised the premium considerably. Ⓜ

SPECIFICATIONS

	ZR 105	ZR 120	ZR 160	ZR-TD
Engine	1396cc, 4-cyl	1798cc, 4-cyl	1798cc, 4-cyl	1994cc, 4-cyl
Power	101bhp @ 6000rpm	115bhp @ 5500rpm	158bhp @ 6900rpm	99/111bhp @ 4200rpm
Torque	91lb/ft @ 4500rpm	118lb/ft @ 2750rpm	128lb/ft @ 4500rpm	177/192lb/ft @ 2000rpm
Top speed	111mph	119mph	131mph	114/116mph
0-60mph	10.0secs	8.6secs	7.4secs	9.7/9.1secs
Fuel cons.	41mpg	39mpg	38mpg	54mpg
Gearbox	5-spd man	5-spd man/CVT auto	5-spd man	5-spd man

USEFUL TO KNOW

- www.mg-rover.org
- www.xpower-mg.com
- www.austin-rover.co.uk
- Rimmer Brothers, Lincoln, 01522 563344, www.rimmerbros.co.uk
- MGOC Spares, Cambs, 01954 230928 www.mgspares.co.uk
- Neil Harrod Ltd, Notts, 01623 642461, www.neilharrod.co.uk

HOW TO BUY...

MG ZT

This sporty version of the Rover 75 has become more popular than the car that spawned it, thanks largely to much improved suspension and the Octagon logo. Here's how to get the best you can

Words and photography: Russ Smith

Part of MG-Rover's rapid propagation of MG badges to boost sales, the ZT was launched in January 2001. Despite initial scepticism, both motoring journalists and the public soon warmed to the concept after it became clear that the suspension had been properly tweaked to sportier settings and worked really well. Allegedly there are over 100 differences between the steering and suspension systems in the Rover 75 and MG ZT – and it definitely shows.

ZTs were also set apart visually from their Rover brothers. The MG gained a much more aggressive front panel with a body-coloured grille, chrome was banished from everywhere except the door handles, plus you got a boot spoiler. Inside, wood and leather gave way to sports seats and polished aluminium trim.

The ZT was launched with two versions of the 2.5-litre KV6 engine, putting out 158bhp and 187bhp. Those figures provided the inspiration for the numbers that define the different ZT models – they reflect their horsepower figures, rounded up to the nearest zero for petrol engines or five for the diesels.

Yes, diesels. The rush for oil-burning economy has infected even the most traditionally sporting of marques, and when the ZT's engine range was

Above: Interiors are spacious front and back, comfortable and provide good seating for five.

expanded in July '02 it included a 114bhp version of the BMW diesel four-pot (ZT 115), along with a 1.8-litre turbo version of Rover's K-series to replace the V6 in the ZT 160. Later that year a sportier ZT 135 was added with a 131bhp version of the diesel engine, shaving a second off the 0-60mph time without spoiling the 48mpg fuel consumption.

Summer 2003 saw the almost sheepish arrival of the ZT 120. Raved about by no one then or since, and thankfully quite rare, this contained a 1.8

K-series motor without a turbocharger – and therefore without the guts to pull such a large car along with any degree of enthusiasm. Only its 36mpg is at all attractive.

MG diverted attention from the ZT 120's existence a few short months later by launching the boss of the range – the ZT 260. Yes, that is a big number, brought about by stuffing a 258bhp Ford Mustang engine under the bonnet (in the circumstances we're tempted to call it a hood) and converting the car to rear-wheel drive. That got motoring journalists reaching for *Clarkson's Guide to Superlatives*, and gave the whole range a bit of an image boost.

Sadly, the £30,000 price tag and 20mpg thirst limited buyer appeal for the big ZT and only around 750-800 were sold before MG-Rover coughed its last in 2005. A folly perhaps, but history will get round to remembering it as one of the great British muscle cars, and its future classic status is assured.

The whole range was facelifted in February 2004, with new grille, bumpers, headlamps and some interior trim changes. The late cars also tend to have more goodies as MG chucked what they could in to try and attract more sales. Oh, and all the above were also available as the popular ZT-T estate, or 'Tourer'.

Left: The ZT was part of a very successful plan to boost sales by turning Rover cars into MGs.

INITIAL CHECKS

■ Before you even go near a ZT, make sure that it still has both keys and that they are both in working order. Replacements are not that easy to come by, and as with some other modern cars, there's more to it than just getting a new one cut. If you do have to replace them, you can pay up to £150 each by the time the necessary reprogramming has been done.

■ **Given that these cars are too new to be showing any meaningful signs of corrosion, their history folder has to be considered as the next item of great importance. That's not just stamps in the service book – though these should be looked at in conjunction with past MoTs where possible to confirm mileage and to make sure they match up from geographic and time perspectives. What you really want to see are all the bills the car has racked up for non-service work, and it's a rare ZT that won't have collected a few of these by now – the significance of which will become clearer as we get into the sections on specific areas.**

■ The bottom line is that though generally excellent, ZTs do have weaknesses – and you want as many of them as possible to have been sorted out and paid for by someone else. Apart from the 260s, there are plenty of cars to choose from, so you don't need to rush into a purchase.

■ **The one thing you do need to look out for is cheap repairs to accident damage. The fit and finish of ZTs and Rover 75s was very good, thanks to BMW's input into their construction, so any deviation from that kind of standard should ring alarm bells and at the very least get you bargaining a bit harder.**

■ On metallic painted cars, check the bonnet against the front wings. It might seem like a minor point, but some of the paint finishes – particularly the lighter ones – have proved to be prone to fading from engine heat. It will get worse along with your perception of it, and you'll wind up having to get the panel painted, at the very least before you come to sell the car on, so get some discount for that.

TRIM

ZTs were offered with two trim levels: standard and '+'. In theory the latter signified the addition of a CD player and onboard computer, along with a few other less interesting items. The reality is that many supposedly lesser cars got those anyway, either from buyers ticking boxes or because MG-Rover was racking up the incentives to purchase, so treat each car as a journey of discovery on this point.

On the real plus side, the interiors seem to be wearing pretty well with few particular complaints, so a poor one has obviously not been cared for. Do look out for dampness in the footwells though, which can be caused by blocked drain holes in the double-skinned bulkhead. Apart from anything else, this can lead to ECU failure as the electronic brain sits in the area being drained.

Original radios do seem rather prone to failure, and replacement units are always keenly bid for on eBay, so be pleased rather than surprised to find that someone has fitted an aftermarket stereo.

If there's air-con, check that it's as cool as it should be. One possible reason for failure – the system's fan – we will cover in the engine section; others leave you the choice between large expense or hoping we continue to get poor summers.

Right: Interiors wear well, so a scruffy one suggests a car that has been poorly cared for.

BRAKES/SUSPENSION

Check for a level ride height, especially at the front, as these cars are notorious for broken coil springs. And though the broken end can poke out and cut the tyre, the problem can just as easily remain hidden until MoT time, when you'll need to shell out £200 to have a new pair fitted.

If the car does sit level but you hear any clonks from the front suspension on your test drive, that will be the lower ball joints. They don't have a long life under such a heavy and usually enthusiastically driven car, but as you have to replace the whole lower wishbone at £140 a go, that's not a bill you'll want to shoulder immediately after purchase.

Unless it's been done recently, plan on investing in a full four-wheel alignment check. It will almost certainly need doing anyway, but there has also been a change to the recommended settings that now makes a ZT even nicer to drive.

Left: Radios often fail, so a good quality replacement can be a bonus.

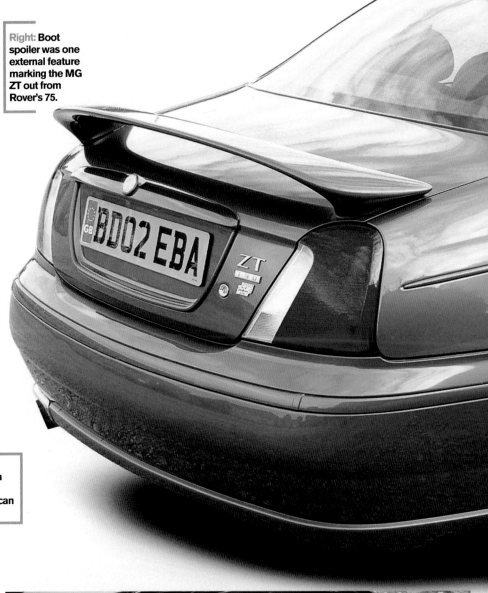

Right: Boot spoiler was one external feature marking the MG ZT out from Rover's 75.

ENGINE

We'll start by checking the cooling fan. This has two jobs, air-con and engine cooling, and should turn at a low speed (or cut in and out) whenever the air-con is turned on. When called upon for engine cooling it runs at high speed. Replacing the fan and its control unit is a £300 DIY job.

As ever with K-series engines, head gaskets are a problem on the 1.8s. You should expect failure between 50,000 and 80,000 miles, so a car that's had a new gasket fitted recently is good news. Otherwise, budget £300-£600 to have the job done. The KV6 is less prone to that problem, but gets expensive at the eight-year or 90,000-mile mark when the three timing belts need changing. This needs seven hours of professional time, plus a proper pulley locking kit that costs £250. Expect the cost to be £400-£500.

The diesel engines are largely trouble-free, but lack of power or rough running are common problems almost always caused by the Mass Air Flow sensor (MAF). Roverron has a £120 permanent cure for this. The V8 engine is tough and unstressed at this output, so no worries there.

Manual transmissions are proving very strong, but clutch replacement is a long-winded job that can cost you £750. And note that the master and slave cylinders must ALWAYS be replaced at the same time. Few ZTs were sold with the JatCo five-speed auto and frankly they are best avoided.

Left: Expect usual head gasket problems on K-series, while timing belt renewal is expensive on the KV6.

'There are over 100 differences between steering and suspension systems in the Rover 75 and MG'

MODIFICATIONS

If you do go down the diesel route, either version can very easily be reprogrammed to produce a completely unfussy 160bhp and, more importantly, around 260lb.ft of torque. It's not a problem for longevity as BMW itself has taken the unit that far, and fuel consumption only drops to 44mpg. We did nearly 50,000 miles in a Rover 75 with that conversion.

Though there is plenty of stuff about for tuning the K-series engine, they have enough problems as it is. It wouldn't be worthwhile unless you spent the money to make it bullet-proof, and then it might be almost as quick as a ZT 190. You get our drift?

The KV6 is worth squeezing a few more horsepower out of, if only by fitting one of the freer-flowing panel filters that are available for £40-£50. You can also go for a cold-air induction kit, as fitted to the car in our photos. Reducing intake air temperature increases power, and you can get a kit such as this for £200. For the more serious, larger throttle bodies are available for similar money to increase airflow.

❯

Left: All but the ZT 115 and 120 have enough power to let the fine chassis entertain you.

DRIVING

For us the ZT 115 and 120 were a mistake. That little power in a 1.5-tonne car means there's not the remotest trace of sporty MG-ness about them. The others are well enough endowed though, and allow you to properly enjoy the chassis's surprising agility. ZTs might appear rather bulbous and tank-like, but find an entertaining A-road and the body seems to shrink around you and encourage spirited driving, with just the right amount of safe understeer to keep you out of trouble.

Even better, the suspension tweaks have achieved all this without ruining the Rover 75's legendary ride qualities.

In fact, all but the most ardent cardigan wearers will probably prefer the ZT's ride/handling compromise. The brakes are impressive, too, with a progressive and well weighted pedal feel.

The ZT 260 is a completely different game, and not just because of its rear-wheel-drive conversion. The suspension is stiffer, road noise from the tyres higher. Combined with the awe-inspiring power, you feel it's an unstoppable force. Its only downside is the awfully heavy gear shift, which really does count as manual labour. Pen-pushing wimps like us will be gritting their teeth at every change.

COST

Predictably, the ZT 260 is way ahead in the price stakes, with the best examples easily topping £9000, though that's not a bad price for what you're getting, and they'll be a lot less affected by depreciation than the other models now. The Tourer version is even more highly coveted, and you'll need an extra £500-£1000 to bag one of those. Even a high-mileage 260 is not going to be found for under £7000 yet.

At the next step down, the 190 and diesel 135 fetch similar prices – between £5000 and £6000 for

really nice stuff, but don't pay that unless you're getting lowish mileage and all the history. Knock £500 off those numbers for a ZT 160 of either persuasion, or a diesel ZT 115. The top price for a ZT 120 is £5000, and that would have to be a glowing example with low mileage and a good story to tell.

Rough or leggy examples of all the FWD ZTs can now be found for under £2000, but do buy with caution and keep your expectations low. Better to pay £3000-£4000 for a nicely kept early car.

Above: The MG ZT's original twin-headlamp front end was replaced by single light covers when the range was facelifted in 2004, only a year before the end

'Find an entertaining A-road and the body seems to shrink around you and encourage spirited driving'

SPECIFICATIONS

	MG ZT 120	MG ZT 190	MG ZT 260	MG ZT 135
Engine	1796cc, 4-cyl, OHC	2497cc, V6, OHC	4601cc, V8, OHV	1951cc, 4-cyl, diesel
Power	118bhp @ 5500rpm	187bhp @ 6500rpm	256bhp @ 5000rpm	129bhp @ 4000rpm
Torque	118lb/ft @ 2750rpm	181lb/ft @ 4000rpm	302lb/ft @ 4000rpm	221lb/ft @ 1900rpm
Top speed	121mph	141mph	155mph	121mph
0-60mph	10.9secs	7.8secs	6.2secs	10.3secs
Fuel cons.	36mpg	29mpg	21mpg	48mpg
Gearbox	Five-speed manual	Five-speed manual	Five-speed manual	Five-speed manual

USEFUL TO KNOW

- Rimmer Bros, www.rimmerbros.co.uk
- Roverron, www.tuning-diesels.com
- www.mg-rover.org
- www.aronline.co.uk
- www.Two-Sixties.com
- Brown&Gammons, www.ukmgparts.com
- SMC Motor Group, www.smc-cars.com
- Thanks to: Alex Ward for providing the car, Peter Simpson for his knowledge of them, and Keith Adams from AR Online.

Every MG ever

14/28
Produced: 1924-27
Value: £30,000-40,000
Based on 14/28 Morris Oxford. Four-cylinder sidevalve 1802cc engine. Single SU carburettor, 1924-25; single Solex, 1926-27. Three-speed gearbox. Rear-wheel brakes, 1924; four-wheel brakes, 1925; bolt-on wire wheels and four-wheel brakes with servo, 1926-27. Three-quarter elliptic springs. 'Bullnose' radiator, 1924-26; flat rad, 1927. Various bodies. Approx 440 built.

Old Number One
Produced: 1925
Value: N/A
Despite name, this was not first MG but was first one built specifically for competition. Based on Morris Cowley chassis and seen here with Cecil Kimber at wheel. Tuned 1548cc engine and three-speed box. Restored by MG in 1930s when changed from grey primer to red. Now a prized exhibit at Gaydon, but still a popular choice with staff for promotional tours. One built.

14/40 Mark IV
Produced: 1927-29
Value: £35,000-40,000
Developed version of flat-radiator 14/28, with similar spec, but half-elliptic springs and wider and heavier chassis. The 40 tag refers optimistically to power, increased to 35bhp at 4000rpm in 1927 to maintain performance despite weight increase. Improved handling and brakes. Contributed to a sales rise leading move to new factory in Edmund Road, Oxford. Approx 700 built.

18/80 Mark I/II
Produced: 1928-32
Value: £40,000-65,000
First known as MG Six and featuring an entirely MG-designed chassis. 2468cc six-cylinder ohc engine. Twin SU carbs. Semi-elliptic springs, centre-lock wire wheels and three-speed box. Mark II introduced in 1929 with stronger chassis, wider track, four-speed box and improved brakes, but sold next to MkI rather than replacing it. Various bodies. Approximately 750 built.

F-type Magna
Produced: 1931-32
Value: £18,000-24,000
Designed to fill the gap between the Midget and the 18/80, the engine was developed from M-type, with two extra cylinders. 1271cc six-cylinder ohc motor (37.2bhp at 4100rpm). Four-speed gearbox. Centre-lock wire wheels. Two-seater (F2) and four-seater tourer and salonette (both F1 and F3). F1, 8in brakes; F2 and F3, 12in. Approximately 1250 built.

J-type Midget
Produced: 1932-34
Value: £10,000-16,000
Further development of M-type. 847cc four-cylinder, ohc. 36bhp at 5500rpm (J1 and J2), 746cc supercharged (J3 and J4). J1 open or closed four-seater; J2 great-value two-seater with sports and racing models. J3 came in 1933, with supercharged racing J4 (72.3bhp at 6000rpm). Four-speed box, centre-lock wire wheels. Approx numbers built: J1/J2, 5500; J3/J4, 30.

K-type Magnette
Produced: 1932-34
Value: £20,000-30,000
Development of F-type. Confusing variety of ohc six-pot options in 1087cc, 1271cc and 1286cc capacities, together with five bodystyles. Early models had three SU carbs, later two. K1s were long-chassis four-seater saloons and tourers, K2s were short-chassis two-seaters. Boxes either four-speed manual or pre-selector units. Centre-lock wire wheels, swept wings. Approx 200 built.

K3 Magnette
Produced: 1933-34
Value: £180,000-240,000
Racing version of K-type (winner of 1933 Ulster TT) brought MG great fame in racing and record breaking. Supercharged 1087cc ohc six-cylinder fitted neatly into Class G (1100cc) category and delivered 120bhp at 6500rpm. Four-speed pre-selector box. Semi-elliptic springs. Centre-lock wire wheels. Two-seater racing body; flat tail with slab tank (1933) or pointed tail (1934). 31 built.

R-type Midget
Produced: 1935
Value: £135,000-160,000
Single-seater racer. Engine similar to Q-type, but chassis entirely new with four-wheel independent suspension – a first for British car. Supercharged 746cc four-cylinder ohc engine (110bhp at 6500rpm). Four-speed pre-selector box. Won 750cc class in 1935 French Grand Prix, but development halted when Leonard Lord closed the racing shop and experimental department. Ten built.

SA-type 2-litre
Produced: 1936-39
Value: £18,000-26,000
Long-wheelbase (10ft 3in) luxury sports-tourer. 2288cc (later 2322cc) pushrod ohv six-cylinder (78.5bhp at 4200rpm). Twin SU carbs, four-speed gearbox, early models non-synchromesh; later, synchromesh on third and top. Semi-elliptic springs, hydraulic brakes, wire wheels. Saloon, four-seater tourer and convertible bodies (as WA and VA). 2745 built.

TA/TB Midget
Produced: 1936-39
Value: £11,000-16,000
Development of PB-type, larger and with 1292cc pushrod ohv four-cylinder engine (50bhp at 4000rpm). Twin SU carbs, four-speed box, hydraulic brakes and semi-elliptic springs. TB arrived May 1939 with 1250cc engine and larger carbs (54bhp at 5200rpm), synchro on upper three ratios. Two-seater sports and Tickford DHC bodies; one fixed-head Airline Coupé. 3003 TAs built, 379 TBs.

VA-type 1.5-litre
Produced: 1937-39
Value: £18,000-26,000
Similar to SA but with 9ft wheelbase and 1548cc four-cylinder ohv engine (55bhp at 4400rpm). Twin SU carbs, four-speed gearbox with synchro on upper three ratios. Conventional chassis unique to VA, but some running gear shared with Morris and Wolseley. Hydraulic brakes. A heavy car capable of over 75mph. Saloon, tourer and convertible bodies. 2400 built.

made

From the first to the latest, this is MG's fine line-up of models, incorporating the great, the good and the slightly dubious of this beloved marque

Values assume a new MoT. The lower price reflects a car that needs work, the higher price is for a car that requires just routine maintenance. Dealer prices would be higher to cover warranties and service. Restoration projects and concours cars fall outside this guide. We recommend an independent assessment before purchase.

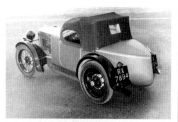

M-type Midget
Produced: 1929-32
Value: £15,000-22,000

First production MG Midget, based on Morris Minor and possibly inspired by sales success of Austin Seven Sports. 847cc ohc four-cylinder engine. Single SU carb (20bhp at 4000rpm). Semi-elliptic springs. Bolt-on wire wheels. Three-speed box (four-speed optional). Open two-seater and closed coupé bodies. Early types panelled in fabric-covered plywood, later in metal. Approx 3200 built.

18/100 MkIII 'Tigress'
Produced: 1930-31
Value: N/A

Racing model, officially called 18/100 MG Six Mark III Road Racing Model, developed from 18/80 Mark II. Similar basic spec, but engine extensively re-worked with dry-sump lubrication and twin-plug head. Close-ratio gearbox, cockpit-adjusted brakes and other minor refinements also added. Four-seater open racing body. MG planned to make 25, but in the end, only five were built.

C-type 'Montlhèry' Midget
Produced: 1931-32
Value: £130,000-150,000

Competition model, developed from M-type. 746cc four-cylinder ohc engine. Single SU carburettor (44bhp at 6400rpm) or supercharged (52.4bhp at 6500rpm). Four-speed gearbox. Semi-elliptic springs. Centre-lock wire wheels. Two-seater racing body with cowled radiator. Humped scuttle became MG trademark. 43 cars built.

D-type Midget
Produced: 1931-32
Value: £22,000-26,000

Built at MG's new factory in Abingdon, this was a touring development of M-type, with four-seater open or 'salonette' body, but no two-seater option. 847cc four-cylinder ohc engine (27bhp at 4500rpm) had a lot of weight to pull. Three-speed gearbox (four-speed option later). Semi-elliptic springs. Centre-lock wire wheels. Approximately 250 built.

L-type Magna
Produced: 1933-34
Value: £30,000-40,000

Development of F-type. 1087cc six-pot ohc engine with new crossflow cylinder head. Combined with two SU carbs, this gave 41bhp at 5500rpm. Four-speed manual box was a Wolseley item as used on the J-type Midgets. Suspension was by semi-elliptic springs. Wire wheels, swept wings. Open two- and four-seaters, also four-seater salonette and two-seater coupé. Approx 575 built.

N-type Magnette
Produced: 1934-36
Value: £26,000-36,000

Development of K and L-types with updated chassis. 1286cc ohc six-cylinder. Twin SU carbs (56bhp at 5500rpm). Four-speed manual. Open two- and four-seater, also Airline Coupé and Allingham-bodied two-/four-seater. NA had rear-hinged doors and plain radiator; NB (1935 on) front-hinged doors and vertical slots; NE racing two-seater. Approx built: NA/NB, 750; NE, seven.

P-type Midget
Produced: 1934-36
Value: £14,000-24,000

Development of J2, which it replaced, with three-bearing crank, sturdier chassis, better brakes. With two or four-seater open bodies and claimed 100 new or improved features, P-type was favourably received. PA (1934), 847cc ohc four-cylinder (36bhp at 5500rpm), twin SU carbs, four-speed box. PB (1935 on), 939cc engine (43bhp at 5500rpm); slatted instead of plain rad. 2500 built.

Q-type Midget
Produced: 1934
Value: N/A

Racing model replaced J4 with longer and wider chassis, stronger blown version of P-type engine and body similar to K3's. Supercharged 746cc ohc four-cylinder evolved to give astonishing 147bhp at 7500rpm. Four-speed pre-selector box. Set 750cc Brooklands track record at 122.4mph, but engine was developed way beyond the chassis capabilities. Eight built.

WA-type 2.6-litre
Produced: 1938-39
Value: £18,000-26,000

Largest car yet from Abingdon. Similar to SA, but wider body and 2561cc six-cylinder ohv engine (100bhp at 4400rpm). Four-speed box, synchro on upper three ratios. Luxurious interior made most of ability to cruise for long periods at high speeds and low revs. Road manners surprisingly good for such a large beast. Saloon, convertible and tourer bodies. Approximately 370 built.

TC-type Midget
Produced: 1945-49
Value: £10,000-16,000

First post-war MG and the one that started USA's love affair with British sports cars. Almost identical to TB, but body four inches wider, different instrumentation and shackles instead of sliding trunnions for front and rear springs. 1250cc four-cylinder ohv engine (54.4bhp at 5200rpm). Twin SU carburettors. Two-seater sports body only. Approximately 10,000 built.

Y-type 1¼-litre
Produced: 1947-53
Value: £3500-6500

Four-seater all-steel saloon with single-carb version of XPAG TC engine (46bhp at 4800rpm), independent front suspension, rack-and-pinion steering, bolt-on disc wheels. Well appointed interior. YT four-seater open tourer (1948-50) had twin carbs (54.4bhp at 5200rpm). YB saloon (1951-53) as YA but with anti-roll bar, uprated brakes, smaller wheels and deeper wings. 8336 built.

TD-type
Produced: 1949-53
Value: £9500-14,000

New two-seater sports design, with rack-and-pinion steering and independent front suspension, as on Y-type. Chassis based on Y-type too, more rigid than TC and capable of taking LHD option. 1250cc four-cylinder, ohv engine (as in TC), 54.4bhp at 5200rpm. Bolt-on-disc wheels. TD MkII available 1950-on with 57bhp at 5500rpm, many got TF wire wheels. Approx 30,000 built.

TF-type Midget
Produced: 1953-55
Value: £12,000-18,000

A stopgap development of the TD MkII with a raked radiator grille, lowered bonnet line and faired headlamps. The TF-type Midget may have received a lukewarm reception when it was new, but it is now very highly prized. It featured a 1250cc four-cylinder ohv engine (producting 57bhp at 5500rpm), along with separate seats and a central instrument panel. TF 1500 (July 1954-on) had XPEG engine of 1466cc (63bhp at 5500rpm). Approximately 9600 built.

ZA/ZB Magnette
Produced: 1953-58
Value: £3500-6000

A chassis-less saloon design which was based on its Wolseley 4/44 stablemate, and boasted independent front suspension, rack-and-pinion steering and a BMC B-series engine – a1489cc four-cylinder ohv powerplant (60bhp at 4600rpm), with twin SU carburettors; the ZB (1956 onwards) had increased power (68.4bhp at 5250rpm). Meanwhile, the Varitone version had a larger rear window. Approximately 36,600 built.

MGA
Produced: 1955-62
Value: £4000-14,000

Two-carburettor B-series, independent front suspension, rack-and-pinion steering. Produced up to May 1959: 1489cc four-cylinder ohv engine, 68bhp (later 72bhp) at 5500rpm. MGA 1600, produced from May 1959 to April 1961: 1588cc and disc front brakes, 80bhp at 5600rpm. MGA 1600 MkII, produced from April 1961-June 1962: 1622cc, 93bhp at 5500rpm. Available in both roadster and coupé bodystyles. Approximately 101,000 built.

MGA Twin Cam
Produced: 1958-60
Value: £10,000-18,000

As with the MGA, yet boasting the 1588cc double-ohc engine (108bhp at 6700rpm) based on the B-series but with many changes. Dunlop disc brakes all round and centre-lock disc wheels. Open roadster and coupé bodies with little to distinguish from the ohv cars. Some later chassis used the 1622cc pushrod engine to clear Twin Cam running gear, known as MGA 1600 MkII De-luxe. Approximately 2000 built.

MGB GT
Produced: 1965-74
Value: £3000-6000

The GT's fastback-style roof could be described as an early influence on the modern hatchback. Raised windscreen height and side windows matched to brand new roof to make this a true all-year, all-weather MG 2+2 – although the rear seats are largely theoretical rather than usable. Carried over all the major mechanical parts from the roadster with five-bearing engine from the start. 98,237 built.

MGC
Produced: 1967-1969
Value: £5000-12,000

Development of MGB, with 2912cc six-cylinder engine (145bhp at 5250rpm); torsion-bar front suspension in place of coil; Girling brakes with servo in place of Lockheed; all-synchromesh four-speed gearbox or Borg-Warner automatic transmission; 15-inch wheels (wire or disc) in place of 14-inchers; Roadster or GT body. Built to replace the Austin-Healey 3000. Not a sales success, but now rehabilitated. 8999 built.

MG 1100/1300
Produced: 1967-71
Value: £1500-3000

The original MG 1100 gained the option of the 1275cc powerplant in 1967, prior to the MkII versions appearing in 1968. The MG 1100 engine gave 55bhp with twin SU carburettors, then the MG 1300 took over, initially with 65bhp, then later 70bhp with a very sporty (for the day) MG 1300 MkII. Discontinued in 1971 and replaced with the Austin 1275GT. Also manufactured in Spain by BMC subsidiary Authi.

MGB GT V8
Produced: 1973-76
Value: £6000-10,000

MG's second try at a big-engined MGB – and it had more success than the first effort because the main ingredient, namely the 3.5-litre Rover V8 powerplant, was simply so right for the car. Weight was very little different to that of the B-series, and since the engine bay was created specially to accept a V-motor, the V8 fitted with few modifications. The 1975 body and bumper modifications were carried over in the V8. 2591 built.

MG Metro Turbo
Produced: 1982-90
Value: £1000-2500

If the MG Metro was a significantly modified version of the base Metro, then the MG Metro Turbo was simply light years apart. Featuring a Garrett T3 turbocharger blowing between four and seven psi (depending on revs), the engine developed a very healthy quoted 93bhp. In reality this was often closer to 100bhp. At the time of its launch this was a seriously quick car, and featured absolutely superb handling and brakes.

MG Maestro
Produced: 1983-91
Value: £600-1500

The early MG Maestro was fitted with a 1600cc engine which was derived from the Austin Maxi. In mid-1984 the original R-series powerplant was replaced by the more familiar S-series motor and incorporated extensive modifications in order to improve the model. Quite why this engine was introduced is a mystery, since just six months later the 2-litre O-series injection unit was introduced in the MG Maestro EFi.

MG Montego
Produced: 1984-91
Value: £600-1500

This model does have some fame in being a pioneer, along with the Maestro, in introducing the famous talking digital dashboard to general sale. In retrospect this and the multiple sensors all over the car were far more advanced than any other vehicle at the time – and for some time to come, in fact. MG version came with front and rear spoilers, alloy wheels and low-profile tyres. Took over as the fastest and most expensive production MG.

MG Metro 6R4
Produced: 1984
Value: £25,000-35,000

The 6R4 used a naturally aspirated 3-litre, four-valve-per-cylinder V6 design based around a shortened Rover V8 block. Producing well in excess of 400bhp in International Specification, the cars remain technically advanced to this day, and extremely fast – with the ability to accelerate to 60mph from a standstill in 2.5 seconds. Clubman version built for homologation with a more modest 250bhp available. 200 built.

MkIII/IV Magnette
Produced: 1959-64
Value: £2500-5000

First MG to be built outside Abingdon for 30 years. Unit-construction saloon designed by Farina, with two-carburettor 1489cc four-cylinder ohv engine (66.5bhp at 5200rpm). Four-speed gearbox, independent front suspension, cam-and-lever steering and drum brakes (MkIII). MkIV introduced October 1961 with 1622cc engine (68bhp at 5000rpm), wider track, longer wheelbase and anti-roll bars front and rear.

Midget MkI-III
Produced: 1961-74
Value: £2000-6000

Developed from Austin-Healey Sprite. 948cc twin-carb four-cylinder ohv engine (46.4bhp at 5500rpm), four-speed gearbox, rack-and-pinion steering, IFS, drum brakes, quarter-elliptic rear springs, bolt-on disc wheels, sliding side-screens. 1098cc and disc brakes from October 1962. MkII of 1964 with more power and winding windows. MkIII of 1966 gets 1275cc engine and better hood. Approximately 152,158 built.

MG 1100 MkI
Produced: 1961-67
Value: £1000-3000

Unit-construction saloon, with transverse-mounted twin-carburettor 1098cc four-cylinder ohv engine (as on later Midgets), 55bhp at 5500rpm. Engine in-unit with four-speed gearbox and final drive to front wheels. Disc front brakes, all-independent suspension with Hydrolastic springing. Four-door, four-seater body, with two-door version for the US market known as the MG Sports Sedan. Approximately 28,000 built.

MGB MkI-III
Produced: 1962-74
Value: £6500-10,000

A unit-construction sports two-seater, featuring a 1798cc twin-carburettor four-cylinder ohv engine (98bhp at 5400rpm). Four-speed gearbox (overdrive available), rack-and-pinion steering, independent front suspension, disc front brakes, bolt-on disc or centre-lock wire wheels. MkII arrived in late 1967, while facelift for 1970 model year became known as MkIII and showed new BL corporate identity. 258,308 built.

Midget 1500
Produced: 1974-79
Value: £2500-4000

The order came down from above that Triumph's 1500cc engine would be easier to make compliant with US emissions regulations than the A-series, and that MG was to make this fit in its Midget. Top speed went up a fraction, but the torque-happy Triumph unit was not a willing rewer and it totally changed the character of the car. Large and heavy black plastic bumpers and raised ride height also had an effect. 73,889 sold.

MGB (rubber bumper)
Produced: 1974-80
Value: £3000-7000

North American regulations requested a raised ride height (1.5-inch) and massive black polyurethane-covered bumpers in order to withstand 5mph impacts with no damage. These changes required numerous major body modifications. Later B-series engines in the same territory were reduced to a single Zenith Stromberg carburettor, emissions equipment and a catalyst, and made barely 60bhp. 128,653 built.

MGB GT (rubber bumper)
Produced: 1974-80
Value: £2000-5000

Mirrored the changes that afflicted the roadster but with extra body weight – so road holding was seriously affected. There was considerable increase in roll and earlier occurrence of rear-end breakaway, though later cars were improved. Makes perhaps the most usable year-round classic MG today, and is far and away the cheapest and easiest way to put a shiny MG sports car on your drive. 27,045 built.

MG Metro
Produced: 1982-90
Value: £1000-2000

The Metro was the car that saved BL. Generous use of red trim and gaudy decals hid the fact that modifications done to the basic Metro to turn it into an MG Metro were considerable, and much greater than for many previous MG saloons. Producing 72bhp it was a sporty vehicle on a par with the best of the Mini Coopers, and the fastest MG saloon ever produced at launch. Proved very popular with the buying public.

MG Montego Turbo
Produced: 1985-91
Value: £1000-2000

When it was introduced, this was the fastest production four-door saloon in the world and boasted a top speed of 126mph. Quite some achievement, and it also pre-dated the ubiquitous Cosworth as a performance turbo saloon. Honda-derived five-speed gearbox, uprated suspension and spoilers both front and rear, power-steering, steel sunroof and electric mirrors were all part of the superb standard package.

MG Maestro Turbo
Produced: 1989-91
Value: £1000-2000

Tickfords completed the final development of this variant, and the company was responsible for the exclusive five-piece bodykit and its fitting to all production cars. Built between January and December 1989, the model transpired to be a slow-seller and some were not shifted until 1991. With a top speed of 130mph and achieving 0-60mph in less than seven seconds, this was at the time the fastest production MG. 505 built.

MG RV8
Produced: 1993-95
Value: £10,000-16,000

In this incarnation of the MGB the rubber bumper-spec body was modified to accept a complete new set of outer panels. The engine was a 3.9-litre Range Rover injection unit producing 185bhp. A five-speed gearbox, derived from the SD1 saloons, was used along with a new Salisbury axle. Very significant modifications were done to the suspension and brakes. The interior was magnolia leather and burr elm. 2000 were made.

MGF
Produced: 1995-02
Value: £2000-5000

The MGF was the first MG to have a mid-transverse-mounted engine, which made the handling superb. There were two engine types available: the 1.8i K-series 1796cc 16v and the 1.8i VVC (Variable Valve Control). The power figures were 120PS and 145PS respectively, which gave a 0-60 time of 8.5 (1.8i) and 7.0 (VVC) seconds. Steptronic CVT box also available with gearchange via paddles on the steering wheel.

❯

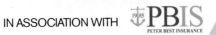

MGF 75th LE
Produced: 1999
Value: £6000-9000

Released in 1999 to mark 75 years of the MG marque. The MGF 75th came in both 1.8i and VVC form. There was a choice of two body colours – Mulberry Red or Black – with contrasting hood shade. Also featured unique bodyside badging and an individually numbered identification plate. 2000 made, 500 for the UK market and the rest (in silver) for export. Air-con, chrome trim and Minilite-style wheels fitted as standard.

MG ZR
Produced: 2001-03
Value: £3000-5000

MG's return to the performance saloon market was led by the MG ZR, which was derived from the Rover 25 but boasted firmer and lower suspension, uprated brakes and steering, increased power outputs and aerodynamic package. K-series petrol powerplants available in ZR 105 with 103PS 1.4 engine, ZR 120 with 117PS 1.8 unit and ZR 160 with 160PS. Diesel and Stepspeed variants were also available.

MG ZS
Produced: 2001-03
Value: £2500-5000

Range-topping MG ZS 180 with the 2.5-litre KV6 engine was a superb driver's car. The MG ZS 120 provided a unique blend of performance and economy, while the 2.0-litre 117PS turbodiesel ZS delivered 50mpg and a 0-60mph time of 9.5 seconds. Stepspeed was available as an option. Marketed as a four-door saloon or five-door hatchback, the ZS was both well specced and powerful at an affordable price.

MG ZT
Produced: 2001-05
Value: £4000-10,000

MG's take on the Rover 75 was heavily tweaked in order to make it a great performer despite its bulk. The ride was compromised slightly, but most buyers were happy with the trade-off. Initial developments centred around the 2.5 V6-engined versions, with power outputs of 160PS and 190PS. The need for economy and fleet sales led to tax-beating 1.8 turbocharged and diesel versions. 2004 saw the introduction of new styling.

MG ZT-T
Produced: 2001-05
Value: £4500-10,500

The development of an estate, or Tourer as it was christened, version of the MG ZT was a first for MG. The resulting ZT-T was an outstanding car that sacrificed nothing in the performance stakes, kept all the comforts and class of the saloon, but added a huge dose of versatility, too. The rear seat folded 60/40. Model variants remained as its saloon stablemate. Facelifted in 2004 in line with the rest of the MG range.

MG TF
Produced: 2002-05
Value: £5000-9000

Successor to MGF saw replacement of Hydragas suspension with coil springs and multi-link rear axle. Steering was sharpened, while the body gained a 20 per cent increase in torsional stiffness. The revised frontal elevation and aerodynamic package included an integrated lip spoiler on the bootlid. Available as TF 115 1.6-litre entry-level model, mainstream TF 135 1.8-litre, TF 120 Stepspeed 1.8-litre and range-topping TF 160 VVC.

MG ZT 260
Produced: 2003-05
Value: £9160-14,500

Powered by the 4.6-litre Ford Mustang V8 mated to a Tremec five-speed gearbox, the MG ZT and ZT-T 260 had a top speed of 155mph and a 0-60mph time of 6.2 seconds. Performance was comparable to BMWs with double the sticker price. Complete re-engineering of the ZT to rear-wheel drive was totally successful. A small number of cars, including the press examples, were completed before the range facelift.

MG SV/SVR
Produced: 2003 on
Value: £32,500-47,055

The handbuilt, carbon-fibre-bodied MG SV and SV-R took MG into supercar territory. After coming to MG Rover via a complicated route through both De Tomaso and Qvale, the aggressively re-styled 175mph SV-R was being delivered to customers at the time of the MG Sport & Racing administration. Prices started at £65,000. Revamped model is now being put back into production, with other models planned.

MG ZR (revised)
Produced: 2004-05
Value: £5000-7300

All MG designs underwent a restyling which was initiated by Peter Stevens. Exterior changes included a new front bumper design with larger integral grille. Other exterior features included twin halogen headlamps with clear lens covers, a new rear bumper and a revised tailgate. Cabin interior was restyled, including a new fascia with four rotary air vents. By February 2005, over 75,000 MG ZRs had been sold.

MG ZS (revised)
Produced: 2004-05
Value: £3900-6500

Undoubtedly the MG ZS benefited greatly from the Peter Stevens facelift, particularly when fitted with the optional bodykit with the vented front wings. As per the ZR, facelifted cars got clear twin lens light units at the front and revised body panels, including a grille that drew inspiration from the SV. The rear numberplate moved to the bumper, and the interior was freshened up with the new corporate dashboard treatment.

MG TF (2005)
Produced: 2005
Value: £7645-9100

Evergreen roadster got a new hood (with glass window), switchgear and finishes. Most fundamental change was a more compliant suspension set-up. At the time of the MG Rover administration in April 2005, 631 cars had been produced to the new specification. Some uncompleted models may have been built up following the NAC acquisition of MGR assets. The TF was the best-selling car in its class in the UK by the time of its demise.

MG TF LE500
Produced: 2008
Value: £16,399

This is the car that restarted MG car production at Longbridge and sales in the UK during 2008. Produced as a limited-run special, with 500 virtually hand-built at Longbridge, the fully equipped LE500 looked like something of a bargain for its launch price of £16,399. Several improvements were incorporated over its MGR predecessor, including standard-fit air-conditioning and a hard-top. K-series was also revised with a stronger head gasket.